WHAT COLOR IS YOUR GOD?

➤ MULTICULTURAL EDUCATION IN THE CHURCH

A BRIDGEPOINT BOOK

BridgePoint,
the academic
imprint of
Victor Books, is
your connection
for the best in
serious reading
that integrates
the passion of
the heart with
the scholarship
of the mind.

WHAT COLOR IS YOUR GOD?

MULTICULTURAL EDUCATION IN THE CHURCH

JAMES & LILLIAN BRECKENRIDGE

A
BRIDGEPOINT
BOOK

Copyediting: Robert N. Hosack
Cover Design: Joe DeLeon

Library of Congress Cataloging-in-Publication Data

Breckenridge, James F.
    What color is your God? : multicultural education in the Church /
    James F. & Lillian J. Breckenridge.
       p.   cm.
    Includes bibliographical references.
    ISBN 1-56476-269-6
    1. Church work with minorities — North America. 2. Christianity and culture.
    3. Ethnicity — Religious aspects — Christianity. 4. Evangelicalism — North
America. I. Breckenridge Lillian J. II. Title.
BV4468.B74   1995
261.8'348'00973 — dc20
                                         94-36907
                                            CIP

BridgePoint is the academic imprint of Victor Books.

© 1995 by Victor Books/SP Publications, Inc.
All rights reserved. Printed in the United States of America.

1 2 3 4 5 6 7 8 9 10 Printing/Year 99 98 97 96 95

➢ CONTENTS

Introduction — 7

ONE
Our Multicultural Challenge — 9

TWO
A Conceptual Framework of Culture — 19

THREE
Communicating a Theology of Cultural Awareness — 40

FOUR
Coming to Terms with Multiculturalism — 55

FIVE
Multiculturalism in the Church Setting — 67

SIX
Parameters of Diversity — 88

SEVEN
Examining Hispanic-American Culture — 100

EIGHT
Examining Native-American Culture — 130

NINE
Examining Asian-American Culture — 157

TEN
Selected Asian Groups — 176

ELEVEN
Examining African-American Culture — 216

TWELVE
Our Multicultural Opportunity — 244

Notes — 257

Index — 285

➤ INTRODUCTION

Perhaps the best place to begin in explaining this attempt to contribute to an understanding of cultural diversity is our search for a textbook dealing with multicultural education in the church. Much to our surprise, none were available. We realized that in spite of myriads of volumes dealing with the subject, most were either concerned with missiology, church planting, or education in general. We could not find a single volume which specifically dealt with multicultural education in the local church.

Our purpose, then, is to present what we hope will be at least a beginning toward achieving this objective. Our audience will hopefully be those students, pastors, and church educators and leaders who seek to enhance the church's ability to understand and communicate with the many diverse groups which comprise North American society.

Our objective is twofold: (1) to provide information about varied peoples and lifestyles, and (2) to enhance a greater sensitivity toward others. Relative to the former, we do not pretend to comprehend each ethnic persona. If anything, our efforts have made us all the more aware of our own prejudices and limitations. We look forward to works which will reflect multiple ethnic viewpoints and authors.

Relative to the latter, our concern is to at least make a beginning toward greater understanding and reconciliation within local churches. We feel our strongest point is that repentance must begin with a change of heart—a genuine commitment toward understanding and appreciation of others. At the same time, what some would see as a threat or problem appears to us as a great opportunity. The diversity of our society has created an opportunity for the true message of Christianity to be heard in a unique and wonderful way. In the midst of failed economic programs and quarrels over political correctness the church has an opportunity to speak peace and equality for all. It is our hope that this volume will be some small contribution toward that goal.

CHAPTER ONE

OUR MULTICULTURAL CHALLENGE

OUR WORLD TODAY

The mission field of the 1990s is North America. The missionaries are church teachers and educators who must not only relate to disparate cultures within the city, but must also cultivate cultural sensitivity outside of it. Both urbanite and suburbanite must face this reality in their Christian witness.

The 1992 Los Angeles riots graphically demonstrated the consequences of ignoring our multicultural world. This city by itself is the home of more than 100 first-generation language groups.[1] High birth rates and expanding immigration has boosted California's population by 26 percent over the last decade. "Asians living in California have doubled since 1980; Latinos have grown by 70 percent. By some estimates, as many as a third of California's inner-city students are in the country illegally."[2] Urban evangelist Ray Bakke notes that the Chicago high school his children attend is now an "entry school for migrants and refugees who study in nearly a dozen different languages and learn English only partially."[3]

Two complicating factors attending our multiethnic groupings are poverty and illiteracy. These provide the catalyst for the explosions we have witnessed. Helen Bernstein, head of the Los Angeles teachers union, relates that

> the majority of children we teach live in poverty. One of every four babies in L.A. is born to a young or unwed mother. More than 20 percent of the city's adults are illiterate. Three quarters of our children enter kindergarten speaking only Spanish. Many graduate from high school without being able to read or write, add or subtract, fill out job applications or understand simple instructions. The Los Angeles public-education system is in intensive care.[4]

All of the above demonstrate a grave inconsistency in American society. Somehow national distinctives of unity, equality, and fairness have not become a reality. Part of the answer may be economic; politics also may be to blame. But the "material cause" for the present state of affairs has to lie in the existence of a deep-seated prejudice within our society.

Journalist Diane Sawyer recently asked Billy Graham what "one earthly problem he would most like to change." Without hesitating Graham replied, "Racism."[5] The accuracy of Graham's convictions is borne out by the frustration experienced by those who have waited for years to see changes. Some feel that racism is so entrenched that no solution is in sight. Pastor Wyatt Walker of Canaan Baptist Church in Harlem feels that neither white or black churches will be willing to accept integration. In the words of Pastor Walker, "Racism is so deep that the effort will fail. The white church is sterile. And I don't want to be absorbed by the dominant society."[6]

The problem is that redemption, restoration, and forgiveness cannot be accomplished through societal structures. Racism and prejudice continue in spite of financial aid and educational innovation. No, the hydra of prejudice and racism can only be conquered through the Spirit of Christ, and the Spirit of Christ speaks to our society through His church.

But how can churches effectively minister to such evils? Can racism and prejudice be most effectively opposed by large donations accompanied by multiple educational and assistance programs? Surely the cries of the powerless and disenfranchised witness against the effectiveness of any materialistic solution. As in the days of Micah, the magnitude of our offerings has not provided a solution for our society. Instead of offering the great society our God instead calls us to "act justly and to love mercy and to walk humbly" (Micah 6:8).

The situation of the American church is much like that of Judaism in the days of John the Baptist. John came preaching a baptism of repentance to the Jewish nation. This theme was necessary because Jewish emphases upon God's promises to His special people, and the expectation of a political messiah, had caused them to forget one simple fact—they were sinners. Somehow the national preoccupation with God's promises had been given priority over confession and repentance before Him. Thus it was time for a recalling to the true spirit of Judaism.

It is the same in North American churches today. We have fascinated ourselves with spiritual promises and become preoccupied with "the blessed hope" of Christ's coming. In the midst of programs, buildings, and prosperity we have forgotten one simple fact—we are sinners. We have failed to repent of our national sin of racism. It is time for a "baptism of repentance" in which we recognize the true spirituality of Christianity.

This can be especially difficult for us to see in that we frequently think of sin in personal and individual terms. We stand forgiven of our personal sins through God's grace, and by Christ's sacrifice our personal guilt is removed. What we may miss, however, is the corporate nature of sin. Where the church has failed to fulfill its mission, or has acted selfishly, we each share in the guilt of that failure. No clearer example exists of such failure than the area of race relations. The presence of prejudice is easily masked by the fact that we tend to associate with people who are like us. Churches naturally assume constituencies which represent their traditions both ethnically and economically. No one is being "kept out," we are simply doing what comes naturally. If prejudice and racism is to be unmasked, however, we must forcefully confront this issue and realize the institutional sinfulness that has contributed to the present state of affairs.

CLARIFYING OUR GOALS

There are at least four goals toward which churches can work to address the problems of racism and bias with intentionality. *First, we must understand the evangelical nature of our task.* Redressing the wrongs of a fallen society is a matter of the Great Commission (Matt. 28:19). Opposing racism and prejudice is most of all a spiritual challenge. Our ability to respond to this challenge is part of God's redemption of this world.

Richard J. Mouw notices that the command to "fill the earth and subdue it" in Genesis 1:28 involves much more than merely having babies. Our mandate is to create a cultural "filling" for society which demonstrates the character and commandments of God.[7]

> We must train ourselves to look at the worlds of commerce, and art and recreation and education and technology, and confess that all of this "filling" belongs to God. And then we must engage in the difficult business of finding patterns of cultural involvement which are consistent with that confession. If in a fundamental and profound sense, God has not given up on human culture, then neither must we.[8]

The point of concern for today's church is that it may be quite evident to see and combat non-Christian worldviews in the areas of the arts and technology. One only has to open a magazine or see a marquee to find such portrayed. When one approaches the issue of human equality, however, the line tends to become blurred.

A second goal, therefore, is for Christians to enhance their own cultural sensitivity. True ministry within a multicultural context must begin with the admission that each of us is prejudiced. This fact demonstrates itself in innumerable ways in our everyday lives. We remember as children the common saying, "That's white of you," stated to one who had settled an issue in a manner that was deemed fair or honest. Hidden cultural assumptions and biases—even latent racism—are present within all of us.

This goal is of special importance for those who labor in the work of teaching or preaching in the church. In addition to lessons, content, and testing, students also spend a considerable amount of time studying their teachers. This means that teachers and pastors must not only become transparent in their own lives, but must also learn to be sensitive to the issues and influences which have shaped students.

For years we have easily spoken of sin and righteousness in terms of "black and white." Scriptural portrayals of righteousness and forgiveness in terms of whiteness or light, and of evil personified in darkness, lend themselves to such common linguistic uses. The problem is that our society has done its own polarizing of the concepts of "black" and "white" in terms which do not speak of redemption or righteousness, but often of its very opposite. Because of this tension we can be needlessly offensive in the presentation of our messages and materials.

> As in the secular educational system, most Christian education materials have been designed primarily to give validity and support to whites, thereby affirming white culture as normative and good, invalidating blacks by denigrating black culture as nonexistent, bad, or evil. This has been most evident in the careless use of color symbolism in church resources—identifying white with good and black with evil or bad. White has been used to symbolize God and Jesus Christ and the good in humanity.[9]

This does not mean that we have to change the text of the Bible or that we should in any way fail to honor the canonical Scriptures as they have been transmitted to us. It does mean, however, that we recognize that every tradition has placed the Gospel in its own cultural container, affecting how it is perceived by those not of that tradition. Every theology reflects its unique social setting. Various forms of church government, for example, show the influences of their contemporary political forms. For example, the Calvinistic doctrine of election can be more clearly seen against the background of a religious tradition which offered little, if any, security to believers.

The danger is to make our theology, or government, or worship an authority equal to that of Scripture itself and thereby violate, albeit unknowingly, a cardinal tenet of the Reformation—*sola Scriptura*. As Dennis P. Hollinger puts it, "There is ultimate truth and final authority against which all human thought can and must be judged. But our theology must not be confused with eternal truth."[10]

The third goal is to heighten the cultural sensitivity of the student. Again, the idea is not simply to create new outreach programs, but rather to enable students to function successfully and empathetically in a multicultural environment. The purpose is to create an attitude, an overall awareness and acceptance of cultural differences, which will enable our students to effectively function in society. Our responsibility is both spiritual *and* social.

Researchers agree that a child's racial awareness has begun by three or four years of age.[11] Further, positive and negative feelings about race seem to appear at about the same age as awareness of race.[12] Studies have shown that children's negative racial attitudes are due in part to their internalization of the positive associations of the word "white" and the negative associations of the word "black" in the English language.[13] Christian educators should therefore be discerning in the cultural "containers" used to convey the truths of sin and forgiveness.

Finally, we want to learn to successfully communicate with and challenge those who approach our religious tradition from another world (or church). How does one influence someone from another race, country, or background?

Because culture is so complex, the Christian educator will have the greatest success by focusing upon that aspect of culture which will be addressed by the Christian message. Richard Niebuhr notes that culture always has at least three characteristics: (1) it is always *social;* (2) it consists of *human achievement,* and (3) it exists in a *world of values.*[14] While all of these have meaningful applications within the church, the latter seems most directly applicable to the goals of Christian education. We may not be able to go to a foreign land, or change our ancestors, or learn another language, but we can affect the values and worldviews of those we teach.

The question is not whether one merely identifies with a culture—the challenge must be to somehow convey Christ to that culture. The challenge for the Christian educator is to identify with varying cultures in a manner that will convey the mind and character of Christ.

OPTIONS FOR THE CHURCH IN CULTURE

Millard Erickson presents two options confronting the church in its relations with society: (1) being a "transformer" or (2) a "translator."[15] The first attempts to adapt Christianity to a world deemed to have undergone a serious transformation since Bible times. This view does not see Christianity as essentially bound to any ancient doctrines or thought patterns. Since human society has radically changed, the Christian message must be "transformed" into terms modern people can understand. This may involve stating Christian doctrines in radically new ways, without regard to biblical or historically based beliefs. An example would be the challenge by Jacquelyn Grant that educators convey biblical teaching in a manner that differentiates between "a first century world view [and] our contemporary world view."[16] In seeking to redress a Christianity viewed as dominated by white male culture, she asserts that doctrinal changes are necessary if the Gospel is to be truly understood in today's society: "As a liberation praxis oriented theology, doctrinal revisions become paramount if we are to understand the true task of theology. The question for us is, how do we reconstruct theological doctrines in order to reflect the liberating focus of the gospel?"[17]

The second option, that of being a "translator," involves conveying the original meaning of a biblical text into terms that can be understood today. This option seems more hospitable to evangelicals in that Scripture is preserved as absolutely authoritative while history retains its important role of shaping and defining Christian doctrine. As Erickson points out, this approach assumes permanent teachings which remain constant across both time and culture.

What we sometimes forget is that the biblical period did not consist of a uniform set of situations. The temporal, geographical, linguistic, and cultural settings found within the canonical Scriptures vary widely. . . . If, then, there is a constancy of biblical teaching across several settings, we may well be in possession of a genuine cultural constant or the essence of the doctrine. Variations may be thought of as part of the form of the doctrine.[18]

Examples would include the doctrines of the sacrificial atonement and the centrality of belief in Jesus Christ. These may be "restated" into numerous cultures, but never "transformed" so that the essential content is changed. In the words of William J. Larkin:

> For this reason evangelical concern should never be to Africanize Christian theology, for example, but rather to biblicize it so that the universal validity of the Christian revelation may be maintained. The Christian interpreter's task should be simply to state "by way of linguistic translation" the biblical message for the contemporary culture.[19]

A primary ingredient in healthy Christian education is recognizing the absolute character of the Christian revelation and value system. We exist to give a message. That message is unchangeable. We cannot afford the critical mistake of giving up the answer in order to find the answer. The Gospel must remain as the total remedy for human ills. Any multicultural approach which in any way compromises the central message of the Cross has no validity for believers who are concerned with the historic doctrines of the Christian faith.

This raises another issue. Those who contend for the existence of foundational Christian doctrines may often be accused of "Eurocentrism." Many minorities feel that North American Christianity has been constructed upon a framework of European values and traditions. It has been Eurocentric in presenting the Christian faith in terms of the dominant culture, overlooking the traditions, history, and literary contributions of other cultures.

Without a doubt, there is much truth in this accusation. It is Eurocentric, for example, to picture Jesus as a Caucasian. Also, it is Eurocentric to assume that democracy was brought to the American continent by our founding fathers when the Iroquois League practiced a well-defined democratic form of government 500 years ago. At the same time, Eurocentrism is a two-edged sword. We are being equally Eurocentric when we fashion theology in a mold of Germanic theology and philosophy. A black liberation theologian, for example, who denies the divinity of Christ and offers instead the "God-conscious man" of Schleiermacher is practicing Eurocentrism at its worst. Likewise, a Latin American liberation theologian who attempts to reformulate human redemption in terms of Marxism is practicing Eurocentrism with a vengeance. In neither case is Scripture being allowed to speak for itself. Instead, it is being judged by the critical concepts of a post-Enlightenment European society.

CONCLUSION

The next question is how, then, we can even speak of a "multicultural" approach. If we have such a transhistorical, unchangeable content in our preaching and teaching, then should we not simply expect the world to adjust as necessary to our message?

Obviously, such an answer would be shortsighted. What we must have is a genuine confrontation with modern culture in which we become determined to reach it on all levels. In the words of Gordon Aeschliman, "The urban challenge is also a call back to the lifestyle of *incarnation*."[20] The challenge facing the local church teacher is more complex than that faced by missionaries in the more remote parts of the world. Rather than dealing with *distinct* races and cultures, contemporary church educators must communicate with *many* races and many cultures, all blended in a homogenous social fabric which defies simple attempts of analysis or reduction. Urban evangelist John E. Kyle notes:

> There are sixty nations represented in my neighborhood in Chicago, sixty nations in the public school where my kids went, and the school teaches in eleven languages. Thirty-five percent of the neighborhood is black, but many black cultures are represented: tobacco culture, cotton culture, coal cultures, Caribbean culture. These are all black cultures, but they are all different. Twenty-eight percent are Asians, but they are all different. There are north, south and east Asians—some of them are refugees and poor, but many are wealthy and elite.[21]

This complexity demands that our teaching be more than (informing) teaching, and our preaching more than (exhorting) preaching. We must know not only our message, but also the lifestyle of those we seek to influence. In other words, we must develop a greater understanding of what "culture" is and how Christianity interacts with it. To this end we turn as we move to the next chapter.

CHAPTER TWO

A CONCEPTUAL FRAMEWORK OF CULTURE

THE ATTEMPT TO FIND A METHOD

One of the first questions which presents itself in any attempt to discuss an abstract concept such as "culture" is the question of exactly how one goes about interpreting this social phenomenon. Robert J. Schreiter notes at least four main approaches.[1] First, the "functionalist" motif attempts an objective analysis of societies through study of its phenomena. The goal is to let each group "speak for itself" without being limited by preconceived theories of development. Second, the "materialist" approach explains culture by appealing to economic or ecological theories which seem to explain social development. Third, "structuralism" seeks to interpret culture psychologically by determining deep-seated conceptual categories which regulate how a society develops. Finally, a "semiotic" study of culture emphasizes the verbal and nonverbal manifestations of these categories as they become evident through speech and cultural phenomena.

While there are many more variations and options,[2] these serve to illustrate that those who wish to define "culture" face a number of challenges. First, there is the problem of interpretation. What standard should be used to "analyze" another culture? Should the standards of Western civilization be used to judge non-Western societies? Any theory which seeks to view culture in an evolutionary sense assumes that the dominant culture of the scientist is the standard for measuring all others. But how can extremely diverse cultures be evaluated by a fixed value system inherited from the West? By what right do we claim to be the standard against which all others must be measured? Social theorists who do this seem to be claiming a universal which cannot be demonstrated.

A second issue is that of relativity. Is it true that a culture cannot be evaluated? And if so, what is the point of categorizing and analyzing? The social analysis of culture apart from values or universals seems self-stultifying.

Then there is a third problem. How is it possible to allow a culture to "speak for itself"? Are we not forever caught in our own cultural "webs" so that any true understanding of other ways is, in fact, impossible? The operative phrase here is "true understanding." Of course we can never completely understand cultures different from our own. All of our knowledge will always be only partial. The point is that even if our attempt to understand is only partial it, nevertheless, can be true. If humanity is truly created in the image of God, we can have foundational understandings of its nature which make cross-cultural communication possible.

Those who would abhor any "unilinear" analysis advocate that each culture must be allowed to stand on its own merits, that each must be viewed "holistically." As in the functionalism of Bronislaw Malinowski, each culture is to be viewed as its own total social expression, much like a scientist would analyze a specimen. But this seems ultimately unsatisfactory in that one is left only with a description. No "precising definition" or value-laden discussion of culture seems possible.

Claude Lévi-Strauss attempts a structuralist analysis of culture in which society is interpreted through the study of "mythemes."[3] The myths of a society are studied by searching for their "internal logic," which in turn reveals foundational binary concepts which govern the values of the community.[4]

Lévi-Strauss believes that we really can know other cultures, but that we must approach them from a context other than that of personal involvement. His goal is to "reconstruct" other cultures by creating a "theoretical model" out of "the particles and fragments of debris" from societies. What we cannot accomplish by entering into another culture can be achieved by theoretical analysis of their language and thought systems.[5]

The problem with this approach is that people per se are not the subjects. Lévi-Strauss is interested in humanity as a universal category, and the final conclusion of his effort seems to be a return to "a technically reconditioned version of Rousseauian moralism."[6] In the words of Clifford Geertz, "What a journey to the heart of darkness could not produce, an immersion in structural linguistics, communication theory, cybernetics, and mathematical logic can."[7]

The semiotic approach of Clifford Geertz approaches culture by studying linguistics. Rather than concentrating upon psychological structures responsible for myths or language, semiotics concentrates upon language and symbolism itself. Prominent figures would be Roman Jakobson, Ferdinand de Saussure, and those involved with the Prague Linguistic Circle. The latter group is responsible for emphasizing the importance of the concept of "texts" in the analysis of culture. While a "text" may include literature, it is understood technically as any "single sign or series of signs" which carry a cultural message.[8] According to Schreiter, "Thus a text can be a set of words, an event, or even a person. Culture then becomes the total sum of these texts shared by a given people."[9]

When one surveys these varied and extensive attempts to arrive at a clearer understanding of "culture," two interesting facts emerge. First, theorists are immediately faced with the question of mechanistic as opposed to spiritually oriented interpretive grids. To appeal to the former would seem to make any analysis other than casual observation a waste of time. To affirm the latter, however, involves questions concerning ultimates and myths which can be very difficult to answer outside of a spiritually oriented framework. Second, there is a continuing emphasis upon the importance of "signs," language, or "texts" in attempting to make sense out of diverse cultures.

Religious studies have been especially affected by the latter approach. Biblical scholars, for example, are well aware of modern attempts to "free" texts from dependence upon authorial intentionality. Scholars such as Paul Ricoeur and Hans-Georg Gadamer feel that each text creates a world of its own as it "tumbles" through history. The goal of theology becomes that of "story" or "narrative" in which the community concentrates upon telling and retelling its own encounter with meaningful texts. Thus the goal is not to recover the original meaning of the author, but rather to tell the "story" of how the text has impacted a particular group.

One obvious point from the foregoing is that scholars have not been able to agree on any one paradigm for interpreting "culture." Modern social sciences seem to lack a satisfactory worldview or conceptual framework within which to adequately define the phenomenon (or the noumenon). As Richard Fenn observes, "sociology lacks a paradigm for knowing what is central as opposed to what is peripheral, what is superficial as opposed to what is latent, and what is material as opposed to matter of appearance alone.[10]

THE ATTEMPT TO FIND A DEFINITION

The same variety demonstrated in research theories is present in definitions. *Webster's Ninth New Collegiate Dictionary* offers six possible meanings for the term as used in our context. Culture could be, for example, the development of intellectual and moral faculties, care and training, enlightenment and excellence, a particular stage of civilization, or the behavior typical of a group or class.

This multiplicity reflects the historical give-and-take of anthropology and sociology as these disciplines have sought to define the concept. A modern "precising definition" of culture has been associated with E.B. Tylor in his portrayal of culture as a complex whole including "knowledge, belief, art, morals, law, custom, and any other capabilities and habits acquired by man as a member of society."[11] Borrowing from the German *kulture,* this view conceived of civilization as consisting of higher classes in which each social unit advanced to higher levels reflective of "universal" concepts of advancement and breeding. The more "culture" a society possessed, the more "cultured" or civilized its members became.[12] In this view societies did not have discrete cultures, but a greater or lesser share in the degree of general culture so far created and developed by humankind as a whole. The goal of cultural anthropology was to attempt to reconstruct the stages that had marked the culture's growth. Societies with the simplest technologies and least elaborate political orders were presumed to represent the lowest stage of growth.[13]

But the question immediately arises whether culture is to be viewed within a context of social evolution. Is it right, for example, to assume that the latest cultures are automatically the most civilized? Hegel, for example, felt that the Germany of his day (1770–1831) was and would remain the highest expression of the historical *Geist,* or world-spirit. Also, was it correct to relate the concept of culture to meanings and values? This was denied by Marx and his followers who applied the philosophical principles of Hegel to economics and sought to base culture on a material base, assuming that "culture" invariably included the material organization of life. Thus meanings and values were harnessed to materialism.

At the end of the nineteenth century Franz Boas began to use "culture" to refer to customs, beliefs, and social institutions characteristic of separate societies. Instead of different societies having different degrees of culture or different stages of cultural development, each society had a culture of its own. This usage became dominant in American anthropology, strongly influenced by Boas.[14]

> Cultural differences were to be understood, therefore, as a result of the accidents of history and the limitations of environment rather than as a reflection of evolutionary stages and a presumed general law of evolutionary growth through which all societies were destined to pass.[15]

Italian Marxist Antonio Gramsci sees culture as the result of "a particular grouping in which is that of all the social elements which share the same mode of thinking and acting."[16] Culture could thus be summarized as

> an order in which a certain way of life and thought is domi-
> nant, in which one concept of reality is diffused throughout
> society in all its institutional and private manifestations, in-
> forming with its spirit all taste, morality, customs, religious
> and political principles, and all social relations, particularly in
> their intellectual and moral connotation.[17]

One common element in any of the above, as well as innumerable other definitions, is that "culture" is somehow expressive of the totality of a society. By whatever standard we measure, culture will be expressive of a holistic social testimony in
which an entire society identifies itself by its political, social,
and religious/philosophical beliefs.

A CHRISTIAN VIEW OF CULTURE

As a social phenomenon, "culture" could be adequately defined
as the self-understanding of a society expressed in its language,
art, music, and social mandates. But what is a "Christian" view
of culture? How can we define a paradigm which comprises the
phenomenon of the church as a social institution?

Viewed from the perspective of modern hermeneutics,[18] the
emphasis upon language and texts is most welcome. As Kevin J.
Vanhoozer puts it, "Augustine and other Christian theologians
would be happy to accept, I think, this textuality of culture. The
dividing of the ways only appears when one asks whether such
and such a text has a determinate meaning."[19]

While subjectivities of tradition and locale are both present
and necessary, the church is, ultimately, a community of people
built upon a text. Scripture becomes the lens through which the
world and our part in it is interpreted and applied. "Culture
that is genuinely evangelical accepts the Gospel as the given
from which it first derived its life and upon which it continues
to draw for its intellectual, imaginative, and practical resources."[20]

Obviously this is not quite as simple as it sounds. As Christians in North America we are faced with the existence of many

subgroups (including our own) interlaced in our broad social fabric. Each of us has experienced Christianity as presented in a cultural container. Each of us also reflects our own cultural "stew." The question then becomes twofold: (1) How do we arrive at our own self-understanding as Christians? and (2) How do we interface with the culture of those who come from different worlds? The conservative Protestant church in North America faces much the same tasks anthropologists and sociologists have confronted in relating to other peoples.

Relative to the first question, we can begin to enhance awareness of our own cultural conditioning. Justo L. González cautions, "There is always the danger, on the part of a dominant culture, not to see the degree to which its understanding of the faith is itself culturally conditioned."[21] R.H.S. Boyd's *India and the Latin Captivity of the Church* exemplifies the confusion produced by introducing Western Trinitarian terminology to another culture without carefully considering the context.[22] It is all too easy to assume that our form of church government or polity is the will of God for all humanity. Likewise it can be very difficult to admit that some church teachings regarding social customs or preferences are, in almost all cases, cultural conditionings of little consequence for the Christian faith.

This does not mean that we should abandon our traditions or lifestyles, but it does mean that we should carefully reconsider before legislating such to other cultures. It can be very difficult for those outside a Christian framework to distinguish between nonessentials and vital doctrines, especially if a church chooses to emphasize the former.

We can address the second issue, that of "hearing," by improving our ability to listen. As Raymond Facélina puts it, we must develop a "listening heart."[23] As evangelicals we have a tendency to address all problems and social situations with proclamation. But, as the Book of James well illustrates, the way we perform during times of great need or crises is a testimony to the validity of our proclamation.

> If a brother or sister is naked and lacks daily food, and one of
> you says to them, "Go in peace, keep warm and eat your fill,"
> and yet you do not supply their bodily needs, what is the good

of that? So faith by itself, if it has no works, is dead (2:15-17, NRSV).

It should also be noticed that listening involves more than social needs. Schreiter states that "the prevailing mode of evangelization and church development should be one of finding Christ in the situation rather than concentrating on bringing Christ into the situation."[24] From an evangelical perspective we should allow other cultures to respond to the Christian message in their own culturally distinctive manners. A "Christian" view of multiculturalism, then, would be "the influence of the living Christ, as perceived through the text of Holy Scripture, upon the language, art, music, and social mandates of the culture which receives Him."

APPLYING OUR PERSPECTIVE

While the challenge of affecting cultures for Christianity appears to be a positive and truly spiritual goal, an important clarification needs to be made. Christians must avoid a cultural Constantianism which would seek to control societies over which we have no authority. The same is true concerning lives of individuals. Christians would never consider taking slaves or oppressing minorities, but it *is* possible to oppress people culturally. We do this by forcing private views upon others or failing to act in a positive and affirming way toward minorities.

We remember a Hispanic-American student named Michael who is now a Harvard Ph.D. Mike assumed a summer internship during his M.Div. program at a large Southwestern seminary. His job was to pastor a church of migrant workers since he spoke fluent Spanish. Everything went well until Mike began to teach the migrants English. At that point the landowners, who belonged to the same denomination which sponsored the seminary, objected. Teaching English would upset the economic conditions and perhaps deprive them of workers.

Paulo Freire speaks of the necessity for equipping and enabling cultures to address their social conditions and redress them in terms of contemporary discourse.

> By predisposing men to reevaluate constantly, to analyze "findings," to adopt scientific methods and processes, and to perceive themselves in dialectical relationship with their social reality, that education could help men to assume an increasingly critical attitude toward the world and so to transform it.[25]

We might never associate ourselves with limitation or deprivation of others, but how many of us are guilty of building cultural castles which serve our purposes while having little or no positive effect upon a needy world? Could it be that the evangelical church is closer to the profile of the rich man than that of Lazarus? One way to avoid such a trap is to develop a spiritually perceptive statement of mission. This means noting biblical patterns, learning about our history, and clearly assessing contemporary cultural needs.

CULTURE IN THE BIBLE

While Scripture does not present a scientific definition of "culture," it does use synonyms which convey clear understandings of how culture should be viewed. The word "world," for example, may be used in a context of warning or disapproval concerning conduct or associations displeasing to God. In the Old Testament the psalmist speaks of "men of the world" who have their destiny in this life and are concerned with only whatthey leave behind them (Ps. 17:14). Isaiah 13:11 makes the world analogous to evil in that God will "punish the world for its evil, and the wicked for their iniquity." A more sociological use is association of the "world" with its peoples in Psalms 24:1; 33:8; 98:7; Isaiah 26:9, 18; Lamentations 4:12; and Nahum 1:5.[26]

In the New Testament the predominant word used for human society is *kosmos*. When discussing human society, the Bible assumes an intuitive understanding of culture on the part of its readers. Christians are warned not to "love the world or anything in the world" (1 John 2:15). Instead, we are to live "soberly, righteously, and godly, in this present world" (Titus 2:12, NKJV). Friendship with the world is described as "enmity with God" (James 4:4, NRSV), and human society is pictured as controlled by "the evil one" (1 John 5:19).

When, however, culture is understood in the sense of ethnic

and social differences among peoples, the Bible seems to assume a neutral attitude. An example would be the attitude of the Israelites toward the Midianites in the story of Moses. Moses, upon fleeing from Egypt, helped the daughters of Jethro, a priest of Midian, and consequently married Zipporah, the priest's daughter (Ex. 3). No mention is made of any cultural hesitancy nor is any disapproval evident. Jethro (also known as Ruel, or "friend of God") demonstrated an attitude of acceptance and belief and was judged accordingly. Later, near the end of Moses' life, Midian joined forces with Moab (Num. 22:4) and then incurred God's punishment (Num. 25:16-18). The basis of their condemnation, however, was spiritual, not racial or ethnic.

The "Cushite wife" of Moses in Numbers 12:1 is another example of the Bible's neutrality toward culture. Scholars are uncertain whether this is the same person as Zipporah, but the attack made against her by Miriam and Aaron was nevertheless based on her racial ancestry.

The attitude of the Old Testament toward association with Canaanites or unbelieving peoples has often been understood as a prohibition against cultural mingling, sometimes in the sense of race. Israel is instructed to separate itself from the people of the land, and from "foreign wives" (Ezra 10:11). Paul urges early Christians to "Come out from them, and be separate, says the Lord. Touch no unclean thing" (2 Cor. 6:17). In all of these instances, however, the separation in mind is from a society which did not honor God. The nations which opposed Israel, notably the Canaanites, were given to a type of nature worship, animism,[27] which led to sexual perversion and oppression. The *King James Version*, for example, mentions "groves," which were places of sexual debauchery and perversion. This is the background of divine prohibitions such as Exodus 34:14-16 and Deuteronomy 7:5-6, as well as later backslidings in Judges and Kings. The term itself is actually a mistranslation of the original *ashera,* a term which referred to the goddess of the Canaanite fertility cult. The "ashera" were actually images of Ashera, to be worshiped in a perverse manner. It is in this sense that Israel sinned later building "high places, and images, and groves."

For they also built them high places, and images, and groves, on every high hill, and under every green tree. And there were also sodomites in the land: and they did according to all the abominations of the nations which the Lord cast out before the children of Israel (1 Kings 14:23-24, KJV).

Since God's separation of Israel was based on religious principles, it would be a grave mistake to conclude that Christianity in any way accommodates racial separatism. Years ago one of us (Jim) played the "devil's advocate" in a debate which challenged Southern integration in the '60s. Even though the purpose was to show the illogical claim of racial separation, the audience, nevertheless, sided with the basic prejudiced arguments that just as Israel was not to intermarry with the Canaanites, so whites were not to intermarry with other races. In point of fact, God's Word nowhere discourages or condemns interracial marriage. God is much more concerned with spiritual compatibility than racial compatibility.

Another interesting Bible question deals with the origin of the races. In past years it was common to hear the account of Ham's sin with Noah cast as the explanation for the black races. In fact, as Old Testament scholars commonly point out, the original sin of Ham was most likely sexual in nature, hence the penchant for sexual perversion characteristic of the Canaanite nations which opposed Israel. No responsible Bible scholar believes that racial differences are in any way due to a curse from God.

The fact that racial differences do exist can be explained by climactic adaptation, each family of the human race developing its own unique characteristics in the part of the world inhabited by them. This perspective need not threaten viewing Scripture as the inerrant Word of God. The critical question for all believers is not how long God took to create the world, but whether we confess, with Genesis 1:26-27, that humanity is especially and directly created in the image of God!

The attitude of Christ toward other cultures provides further guidelines for us. Eugene Nida observes that

nowhere in the Gospels is Christ reported as having specifically dealt with the problem of culture as such. Nevertheless, the fact that all he did and said was related to the immediate context of people's lives makes his orientation toward culture of supreme importance for the Christian.[28]

During His Galilean ministry, following the initial popular period in Judea, Jesus made His headquarters in Capernaum. In the words of William Hendriksen:

> Not mainly to the Jerusalem aristocracy, but especially to the despised, sorely afflicted, and largely ignorant masses of Galilee, a mixed Gentile-Jewish population, did he send his Son. It was in and around Galilee that Jesus spent most of his incarnate life on earth.[29]

It was here that Jesus healed the leper, rewarded the faith of the centurion, and restored the demoniac. His approach to the lowest of cultures was consistently that of love and service.

Paul's ministry to the synagogues following his conversion also demonstrates the humility and sincerity of purpose needed in intracultural relations. He did not cast off his brethren, attempt to rise above them, or castigate them. Instead, he first tried to reach them with the Gospel in their own setting. Christianity was not used to create division or dissension.

Paul also presents what many consider the classical text for equality in Galatians 3:28: "There is neither Jew nor Greek, slave nor free, male nor female, for you are all one in Christ Jesus." Early Christian attitudes toward women and slaves were actually far in advance of that offered by the society of that day.

CULTURE IN THE EARLY CHURCH

The early expansion of the church testifies to the true multicultural attitude which characterizes Christianity. The Day of Pentecost marked a living spiritual experience with all cultures; no identities were lost, no traditions were disvalued. Instead, the Gospel simply permeated each cultural situation as encountered. The early church did not attempt any artificial multiculturalism. Instead, the development of house churches preserved as well as affirmed cultural diversity. As the church grew, larger congregations, such as Antioch, assumed a naturally multicultural character. "Though they preserved the ethnic and cultural character of their individual congregations, the

Antiochene church demonstrated their unity by working together in a larger body that was multi-ethnic."[30]

The Jerusalem Council (Acts 15) was a vibrant example of multiculturalism at its best. When Gentiles were threatened with Jewish legalism, James offered a resolution which compromised neither. The important point of the Gospel, freedom in Christ, was maintained. Judaism was not to regulate outsiders via an appeal to Jewish customs of circumcision. At the same time, Gentiles were not to behave in a manner which would offend Jews. In essentials there was unity, but in nonessentials charity.

One of the earliest expressions of post-Apostolic Christian attitudes toward culture is contained in the *Epistle to Diognetus,* an early second-century tract intended to witness to pagan society. The unknown author observes that believers lived lives that were both exemplary and peaceful.

> For the Christians are distinguished from other men neither by country, nor language, nor the customs which they observe. For they neither inhabit cities of their own, nor employ a peculiar form of speech, nor lead a life which is marked out by any singularity. . . . But, inhabiting Greek as well as barbarian cities, according as the lot of each of them has determined and following the customs of the natives in respect to clothing, food, and the rest of their ordinary conduct, they display to us their wonderful and confessedly striking method of life.[31]

Early Christians seemed to have an attitude of servanthood which accepted others and allowed them to live at peace in the context of non-Christian governments. Clement urges Christians not to leave the "post which His will has assigned us."[32] The Epistle of Ignatius sees society as one unit affected by the Gospel.

> For "in Christ there is neither bond nor free." Let governors be obedient to Caesar; soldiers to those that command them; deacons to the presbyters, as to high-priests; the presbyters and deacons and the rest of the clergy, together with all the people, and the soldiers, and the governors, and Caesar [himself], to the bishop; the bishop to Christ, even as Christ to the Father. And thus unity is preserved throughout.[33]

In the fourth and early fifth centuries Augustine construct-ed a pattern of Christian social relationships which further ad-vanced the optimistic view of Ignatius. In his twenty-two volume work, *The City of God,* Augustine presented a picture of human society consisting of a continuing struggle between two forces or "states," the community of saints as opposed to godless worldly society. In Augustine's view, the state, controlled by Christian laws, was naturally subordinate to the church and fulfilled its highest goal by advancing Christian interests. The earthly was to be subject to the godly; in the depths of its being the state should be truly Christian.

It is important to remember that the "states" treated by Augustine were spiritual in nature. Writing from a period in which Christianity had become the official state religion, he viewed the state as controlled by Christian laws. It would be erroneous to feel he was attempting to state a contemporary theory of church-state relationships. Still, his work had a politi-cal effect in that the concept of a state controlled by Christian laws led to the doctrine of papal supremacy in the Middle Ages.

THE REFORMERS AND CULTURE

The Reformers corrected a number of medieval abuses, but reflected varying attitudes concerning the church's mission to-ward culture. The concept of a Christian state was still very real to them, and their work also has to be viewed within the context of a time when Christianity was integrally associated with the political system. Nevertheless, important lessons can be gleaned from their theories.

There are two primary and yet polar positions to notice in the thought of the Reformers. First is the doctrine of the "two kingdoms" advocated by Luther. Most simply stated, this means that the state never has the right to utilize the functions of the church to accomplish a political purpose, while the church may never use the powers of the state to achieve religious ends. The province of the church and the government are two separate spheres which are not to be intermingled.

Opposite to this is the thought of Calvin, which advocates Christianity as a total life-system which affects every area of human enterprise. Christianity is to affect government, schools, entertainment, the arts, and whatever cultural vehicles are available to a given society. The classical expression of Calvin's thought in modern times has been that of Abraham Kuyper, the founder of the Dutch Free University of Amsterdam, who advocated Christianity as a total life-system with the church permeating every area of human society.

Contemporary Christians face a decision in determining which of these views will characterize their own understanding of the church's relationship to society. Those who follow the tradition of Luther must decide whether their position truly reflects the life-changing purpose of the Gospel. The work of Dietrich Bonhoeffer and his call for a "religionless Christianity" was in response to a Lutheran state church which he felt did not adequately resist the onslaught of Nazism. His accusation of "cheap grace" was directed toward those who were absorbed with Word and Sacrament, yet ignored the public menace of Hitler and his party.

Conversely, those who follow Calvin also have some difficult decisions. What would Jesus have thought about the attempt to kill Hitler? Did Christ or the early church advocate rebellion and lawbreaking in the name of Christianity? Paul certainly did not teach so in Romans 13. Christians who advocate lawbreaking and social disturbance to achieve "Christian" goals must ask themselves whether they truly represent the Gospel.

Perhaps the best response to the issue was provided by Luther's 1520 treatise, "The Freedom of a Christian." The central thesis is that as Christians we are free from sin through faith in God, yet at the same time bound to serve our neighbors in love. We are free from the power of the Law, but not from the power of love. As Luther put it, "A Christian is a perfectly free lord of all, subject to none. A Christian is a perfectly dutiful servant of all, subject to all."[34]

A CONTEMPORARY CHRISTIAN APPROACH

The duty to share Christ within all cultures demands that evangelical Christians have a clear understanding of theological parameters and of the mission of the church.

First, it is critically important to understand that we are not talking about multiple theologies in Scripture, with the consequent relativity such a position implies. It is common to hear such terms as "black theology," "feminist theology," and "liberation theology" used to describe contemporary theological movements. While these groups merit study and are worthwhile additions to the category of contemporary theology, they should not be understood as alternatives to the basic message of the Gospel. Scripture presents one way of salvation. The central truths of the Gospel are the same for all. Missiologist Paul Hiebert, in a helpful essay, presents a critical assessment of the case: "If now we must speak of 'theologies' rather than of 'theology,' have we not reduced Christian faith to subjective human agreements and thereby opened the door for a theological relativism that destroys the meaning of truth?"[35]

This does not mean that Christianity has to ignore cultural context. Quite the opposite, communicating with other cultures represents perhaps the greatest contemporary evangelical challenge. The question is how to relate to other cultures without altering or subtly changing the essential nature of the Christian message.

William A. Dyrness, of Fuller Theological Seminary, believes that such communication can be successful and that Gospel essentials need not be compromised. He proposes, for example, an "interactional model" in which Scripture is allowed to freely interact with the needs of a culture without being limited or prescribed by theological responses from another culture. "Only Scripture, not some particular interpretive schema, is transcultural."[36] In this context, the authority of Scripture is practically applied by the community as it relates the theoretical truth of God's Word to immediate needs and issues. "The truth of Scripture has to be worked down into the fabric of our lived worlds, and this takes place only through struggle and interaction with the actual problems of life."[37]

If Dyrness' analysis is to be anything more than words, it will require that evangelicals master perhaps the most difficult skill for theologians to acquire: the ability to listen. True communication with other cultures demands that we hear what they are saying and realize that Christianity must come to life in the vibrancy of immediate social needs and quests. Robert Schreiter makes an apt observation.

> Ideally, for a genuinely contextual theology, the theological process should begin with the opening of culture, that long and careful listening to a culture to discover its principal values, needs, interests, directions, and symbols. Only in this way can the configurations of a culture become apparent of themselves, without simply responding to other kinds of needs extrinsic to the culture.[38]

Here again the heritage of the Reformation provides a focal point of importance. The question is whether the doctrine of the priesthood of all believers does not naturally result in a pluralistic theology. This tenet, the belief that every Christian had the right to act as a priest to every other Christian (thereby negating the concept of a special order of priests who were above the level of ordinary believers) was a primary component of Luther's reformation. But many feel this principle has also led to numerous interpretations and biased theologies. It should be pointed out, however, that Luther's term was never meant to be used outside the context of the community of faith or as a synonym for theological relativity.

Conversely, while the establishment of a "faith once delivered" was a valid and necessary component of reform, it is also true that the emphasis upon such a faith could lead to its own type of scholasticism. The assumption that theology was somehow normative in itself created an educational system in which Christian truth was equated with adherence to a localized confession. Such a system works well in a monocultural environment, but when the positivistic approach is forced to encounter a multicultural society needless tensions can be created. The evangelical church has depended heavily upon theological education and pure doctrine to fulfill its spiritual mission. Spending too much time in cultural isolation, however, can adversely affect our ability to speak to the present. As Sidney Rooy puts it, "We spend too much time answering questions the world is not asking."[39]

Against this construction, Hiebert would argue for the Anabaptist tradition, in which theology is more highly integrated with experience than confessions. The Anabaptists, he notes, recognized that all truth possessed a subjective element and therefore "it must be understood in terms of the social, cultural and historical contexts in which people live."[40]

The result of this more subjective approach to doctrine led to distinctives which are still characteristic of Anabaptist thought. First, theology became more practical in its application. Rather than becoming absorbed with formulating theorems, Anabaptists focused on the effect of theology upon everyday life. "It was not uncommon for Anabaptists to debate how Jesus would have acted as a businessman in this situation, or as a parent, a teacher, or a farmer in that setting."[41] Second, faith was defined more in terms of "discipleship" than mental assent to dogmatic propositions. "For the Anabaptists, the presence of faith was seen in the transformation of a person's life."[42] The overall result of this view was a greater emphasis upon biblical theology rather than systematic theology.

The result of this more subjective approach was a greater dependence upon the Christian community as a hermeneutical reference point. Limitations of doctrine and interpretation of Scriptures were regulated by the community of believers.[43] While confessional theology will always remain of critical importance for the evangelical believer, Hiebert's position does pose the question of whether it could constitute a different approach for evangelical churches facing a multicultural context.

One way to possibly resolve this apparent tension between theology and *praxis* is to develop a greater emphasis upon axiology in doctrine. Arlin C. Migliazzo distinguishes between two approaches in Christian education. "Message-dominant" institutions stress conservative theology, "fairly precise faith statements," and a considerable number of Bible and theology courses in the curriculum. Contrasted with this is the approach of the "Life-dominant" college which admits non-Christians, is more moderate theologically, and places greater emphasis upon practical application of Christian doctrine.[44] Theological teaching is constantly accompanied by the question of how the truth is practically applied in everyday life.

From a multicultural perspective, a beginning for local churches may be in simply adopting a different attitude or posture toward those who come from different cultures. Churches do not have to do away with the *Book of Concord* or the *Westminster Confession of Faith,* nor do they have to radically alter worship services so that they lose the distinctiveness of their traditional moorings. What they do have to do, however, is to increase their sensitivity to other groups in their midst. The local church "language," teaching methods, and even worship must reflect a charity and genuine openness to those who are strangers to "our" history.

At the same time, theology should be something that is practiced. How does Galatians 3:28, for example, change the way we live our lives? What are the implications for intercultural relations? It is not that we transform our message, that we become existential or relativistic in our message. Rather, the issue is whether we change our hearts and develop our spiritual senses in a manner which will allow our historical message to be communicated in a manner which does not offend or alienate others. We do not have to change our framework, but we do have to change within our framework!

David Lyon notes four options for the church as it confronts social issues: (1) escapism, (2) compartmentalism, (3) acceptance of sociology as a "superior" worldview, and (4) "critical integration."[45] The "escapism" option avoids human relationship issues by retreating to the world of theology. Likewise, "compartmentalism" creates an artificial division between life and practice by labeling social issues as secular, therefore not applicable to church involvement. The third option is just as undesirable, namely, to allow the social sciences to reign over theology so that the Gospel is diminished in its value as a worldview.[46]

The final option of "critical integration," Lyon's recommendation for the church, views social relationships within the context of God's world. This involves meaningful interaction on three levels: "worldview, institution and intellectual practice."[47] It is this type of "critical integration" that the church must seek in dealing with a multicultural society. We must allow our worldview, our institutions, and our practices to become sensitive and open to those from highly different backgrounds and environments.

Perhaps the best model for this approach is supplied by Christ's frequent reference to salt as an agent for permeating society. In Matthew 5:13 He refers to Christians as the "salt of the earth." In Mark 9:50 we are encouraged to "have salt in yourselves" and to be at peace with one another. The model He advances is one in which diverse elements exist in one mixture, being seasoned by one common ingredient, so that each retains its uniqueness while contributing to the unity of the whole.

One of the important sources in addressing Christian cultural relationships is the work of Bartolomé Las Casas (1474–1566). Although Las Casas never visited what we know as the United States, he was the first great figure to speak up for the rights of minorities in the New World.[48] Ministering in a time of Spanish colonialism in which Indian peoples were subjugated and enslaved in the name of Christ, Las Casas contended that the church must see its role primarily as that of a servant rather than as a lord over other cultures.

> Christ did not give the Church power over the pagans to annoy, persecute, afflict and arouse them to riot and sedition, and to hatred of the Christian religion, but [only the power] of gentleness, service, kindness, and the words of the gospel to encourage them to put on the gentle yoke of Christ.[49]

CONCLUSION

One of the reasons the Christian church faces such a problem in multicultural relations is that our transgressions in this area can be purely passive. The issue is similar to Augustine's explanation for sin. Rather than grant it an ontological existence, Augustine simply said that "sin" is the absence of good. When we do not do good sin is present.

The same is true regarding other cultures. A Christian view of multiculturalism requires action. We must forcefully address the spiritual, social, and economic issues that oppress our fellow humans. No one will come knocking at our door asking whether we have done as we ought, but that does not lessen our moral and spiritual obligation. "Truly I tell you, as you did not do it to one of the least of these, you did not do it to me" (Matt. 25:45, NRSV).

A primary factor in facing these challenges is the ability to communicate our faith to other cultural contexts. We must now turn to a crucial question. How do we define our message and communicate our theology in a manner that is faithful to church and Scripture, yet addresses our hearers in a clear and perceptive manner?

➤ CHAPTER THREE

COMMUNICATING A THEOLOGY OF CULTURAL AWARENESS

DEFINING OUR MESSAGE IN ITS SOCIAL CONTEXT

The state of America's multicultural society is a hotly debated topic among social and political theorists. Some feel that we may be heading toward a critical and even dangerous period of division. Arthur M. Schlesinger, Jr., in *The Disuniting of America,* notes that the United States seems in danger of losing its sense of uniqueness as competing ethnic groups each engage in retelling the American story from their own vantage point. "Ethnic and racial conflict," he warns, "will now replace the conflict of ideologies as the explosive issue of our times."[1] Social commentator Dinesh D'Sousa observes that "somehow the intended symphony has become a cacophony."[2]

Opposed to this analysis stands such figures as Ronald Takaki, who bemoans the "Allan Blooms" and "Patrick Buchanans" as representative of a culturally hegemonic Eurocentrism which is the real force behind division. Takaki observes, "America's dilemma has been our resistance to ourselves — our denial of our immensely varied selves. But we have nothing to fear but our fear of our own diversity."[3]

Gerald Graff echoes this sentiment by asking that we "rethink the premise that the eruption of fundamental conflict in education has to mean educational and cultural paralysis. In fact," Graff observes, "there is little reason to think that we Americans are any less divided by class than other nations."[4]

These tensions produce an obvious challenge for the church in today's society. More than ever before we have the opportunity to be peacemakers, to attempt social reconciliation based upon a common Gospel of equality and human worth. But how do we address a splintered society in a manner that reflects openness for all, while at the same time preserving our theological integrity?

The term most commonly used to describe this effort is "contextualization." It comes from a missiological background in which the attempt is made to communicate Christianity within the context of non-Christian cultures. The term itself dates from a 1970 missions statement of the World Council of Churches, which originally expressed a concern for "contextual or experiential" theologizing as opposed to "systematic or dogmatic theologies" of confessional Christians.[5] The concern is to emphasize theology within the context of "praxis," the practice of Christianity in a given environment.[6] By 1972 the missiological arm of the World Council of Churches had introduced the term as a methodology which would replace the customary approach of indigenous missions that had characterized Christian evangelism of the past century. Applied in a broader context, the term conveys the attempt to find meaning within the experience of the community rather than "rationalistic" creeds of previous generations. Examples would be the theology of hope, the theology of liberation, and black theology.[7]

While more conservative Christians may cringe at the mention of liberation theology or black theology, we should question whether much of our theologizing has assumed cultural forms which may not communicate to others. In the words of Charles Kraft:

> The theological questions we raise are those that occur to Euro-Americans (and, often, only the philosophically oriented subculture within Euro-America). And, of course, the answers

we give, couched in the interpretations of the Scriptures that occur to us as applicable, are thoroughly Euro-American.[8]

Ghanian student Michael Ntow recounts how joyfully his people first received the Gospel. Having accepted Christianity they proceeded to worship this new God in the ways common to their culture. They loved drums and kept playing them as lively as always, only that now they were playing for Christ. Then came the day when a large boat anchored in the harbor and the missionaries unloaded a pipe organ. The Ghanians hated the organ—but they were told that this is what they must play! At this point Christianity became integrated with a type of worship which was alien to their way of life. They still accepted Christianity, but had to adapt to a new cultural artifact.[9]

Cultural minorities face many of the same problems as Michael. Ethnic groups may be "Americanized," but this does not mean they are culturally sensitized. Each group has its own tradition and ways of worship. Yet evangelicals rightly feel that certain key beliefs are necessary, and that historic creeds are not open to revision (or restatement). How then can the Gospel be made plain for all?

Perhaps the best solution is to arrive at a methodology of contextualization which will recognize cultural uniqueness while affirming historical Christianity. It is important to note that contextualization may occur on at least three levels. First, it may be *hermeneutical*, dealing with contemporary translations of the Bible. Second, it may be *cultural*, involving the restatement of theology in an up-to-date manner. Finally, it may be *social*, emphasizing liberation of the poor and oppressed. Louis Luzbetak refers to "a translational type, a dialectical type, and a liberational type."[10] "All three types seek to create an inculturation of the Gospel to the extent that the content of the message becomes an expression of the cultural system itself."[11]

While any of the above could demonstrate excesses hostile to evangelical constructs, contemporary theologizing can be successfully practiced if the themes of liberation and contextualization are enunciated in the light of a clear commitment to the authority of Scripture. It is the issue of hermeneutics that forges the mold for how Christianity will be contextualized or how liberation will be experienced. In the words of David J. Hessel-grave, "While adaptation to cultural contexts and existential situations is incumbent upon both theologians and participants in mission, adherence to the Scriptures must be viewed as basic to all authentic theologizing and missionizing."[12]

CONTEXTUAL OPTIONS

Evangelicals do not view this effort in terms of accommodation or of any compromise of the Gospel message.

> Christians need not be walking encyclopedias on matters Christian; nor need they be professional theologians. Their faith, however, must reflect a *creative* imagination and inspi-ration, a constant flowering of a truly contextualized Chris-tianity. Their faith, however simple and imperfect, should nev-ertheless be creative in the sense that it is constantly made relevant to the time and place without compromising the es-sentials of the Gospel or the essentials of the universal tradition. . . .[13]

The best-known modern attempt to accomplish this goal hermeneutically is the "dynamic equivalence" model of Charles Kraft. This approach seeks to convey the original thought of the Bible in terms understandable to contemporary society. Many Bible translations, for example, are what Kraft calls "formal correspondence" models; that is, their aim is to convey the literal meaning of an author's words in contemporary language. Kraft feels such attempts have been unacceptable "because the translators have not carried their task far enough." Examples would be the *Revised Standard Version,* the *New American Stan-dard Bible,* and "largely," the *New International Version.*[14]

Instead, Kraft proposes a "sense-translation" format in which we attempt to convey the author's intent in updated lan-guage. Instead of a "literal" type of translation, one is con-cerned with concepts or ideas, to express the "sense" of what the writer was trying to say. Examples would be Bible para-phrases such as *The Living Bible* and *The Cotton Patch Bible* which "make the events of the Bible seem real."[15] Consider the standard *King James Version* rendition of Genesis 1:1-4.

In the beginning God created the heaven and the earth. And the earth was without form, and void; and darkness was upon the face of the deep. And the Spirit of God moved upon the face of the waters. And God said, Let there be light: and there was light. And God saw the light, that it was good: and God divided the light from the darkness.

Compare the same passage from P.I. McCary's *Black Bible Chronicles: From Genesis to the Promised Land.*

Now when the Almighty was first down with His program, He made the heavens and the earth. The earth was a fashion misfit, being so uncool and dark, but the spirit of the Almighty came down real tough, so that He simply said, "Lighten up!" and that light was right on time.[16]

Whereas the *King James Version* attempts to translate the text into an English equivalent, the *Chronicles* seeks to approximate the meaning using popular terminology which may be more easily apprehended by a youthful audience. Of course attempts to "contextualize" the Gospel are never without risk. In the words of Paul Watney:

Few Christians will disagree that it is important for the biblical message to be communicated in a meaningful way. Evangelicals, on the other hand, have an additional concern: Any reconceptualization of this message may entail a loss of its essential meaning, and this should be resisted at all costs. . . .[17]

William A. Dyrness stresses the importance of remaining consistent with evangelical tenets, but also cautions against being preoccupied with exacting doctrinal definitions. He expresses concern over two errors possible for evangelicals. First, we may be "xenocentric," so tolerant of others that we assume our own thinking is inherently false and in need of correction. Second, we may be fearful of "relativism," fearful that any attempt to define the Gospel outside of our cultural categories will be compromised.[18]

While Dyrness' observations are directed toward missions, his first caution applies especially to Christians in a multicultural environment. We are taught to be "open-minded"; part of being North American is to let each person do "their own thing." We can be especially tolerant regarding the religious

feelings or claims of those who come from outside our environment. Some observers wish to emphasize social reformation in
the Christian quest. The difficulty lies in becoming so tolerant
of others that the Gospel may not be clearly perceived. We
must be very careful to define what truly constitutes deliverance
in the Bible.

As we noted in chapter 1, Erickson discusses the option of
being either a "transformer" or a "translator" of the Gospel.
The former category comprises those who attempt to "update"
the Gospel so that it will fit in modern categories of thought.
Examples would be Bultmann's attempt to "demythologize,"
Bonhoeffer's ideal of "religionless Christianity," and Tillich's
attempt to create a new theological language which would be
understood in a secular world.[19] While the goal of each of these
attempts was laudable, evangelicals question whether Gospel
content is somehow "modified" so that the updated product no
longer contains the essential Christian faith.

Erickson recommends the latter option of "translator," one
whose mission is not to change the fundamental concepts or
language of the Christian faith, but rather attempts to state
eternal Christian truths in a manner which will be understood
by an irreligious world. The goal of the teacher is to convey
meaning rather than terms. The emphasis in this approach is
upon the permanent and unchangeable meaning originally
intended by the author of the biblical text: "What we are doing
instead [of 'dynamic equivalence'] is giving a new concrete expression to the same lasting truth that was concretely conveyed
in biblical times by terms and images which were common
then."[20]

REFINING THE MEANING OF LIBERATION

Gabriel Fackre, in his presidential address to the American
Theological Society on April 12, 1991, presented the results of a
survey of all graduate school systematics teachers and theologians in North America that could be found. One of the main
components characterizing North American theology was diversity.

The dramatic emergence of African-American, feminist, womanist, North American Hispanic, Third World/Two Thirds world, Native American, Asian, Asian-American peoples and points of view is a fact of life in . . . systematics.[21]

Fackre notes that in some cases theology courses have been rewritten to reflect "local theologies" reflective of the students' experiences.

Minority groups have an understandable desire for a theology authentic to their culture. While liberation theology is usually associated with Third-World countries, liberation themes are present whenever Christian mission challenges social repression or mistreatment. Part of social restoration for minorities may be the recasting of Christianity into molds which express their own ethnicity.

Joseph Crockett cautions that Christian education must have "cultural integrity" to be effective in African-American communities.

It is necessary for Christian education to uphold cultural integrity for African-Americans. Christian education for the Black church involves, fundamentally, the process of teaching scripture in light of the experiences and traditions of African-Americans. Christian education involves the processes of teaching the scriptures with respect for the experiences and traditions of particular cultures, so that the person may become transformed and share in God's transforming activity in history.[22]

While this goal is admirably stated, teachers must be careful concerning methodology. Black theology, for example, often views the Exodus as a motif of deliverance from oppression.

Like the captivity and oppression of the Israelites, the African-American experience has been an experience of captivity and oppression. Uprooted from their native soil, Africans were set in shackles to sail on slave ships. The African-American plight in the United States has been an excursion on the freeway of inequality. We have walked on the roadways of racism. We have been made to live on the avenues of injustice. African-Americans have been victims of systematic oppression. But the Exodus narrative gives assurance that right is stronger than might and "that truth crushed to earth will rise again."[23]

The problem with this comparison is that the social-political overtones could present a fundamental conflict with the Christian message. A primary ingredient in the account is the seizure of Egypt's wealth by the Israelites. Viewed in the context of liberation theology, some might feel the Christian message could be distorted into one of "getting back" at the offending majority. There is also the hermeneutical question of whether the Exodus account represents both spiritual and social deliverance. Rosemary Radford Ruether questions whether liberation theologians have not overemphasized the oppressed/oppressor motif.

> Quite simply, what this means is that one cannot dehumanize the oppressor without ultimately dehumanizing oneself, and aborting the possibilities of the liberation movement into an exchange of roles of oppressor and oppressed.[24]

Many blacks justifiably feel that being Christian has often been confused with being "white."[25] Theology which is "culturally relevant" is that which deals with righting this wrong. The Christian concept of salvation may easily assume the context of "relational" theology as opposed to "vertical" theology. The solution to human problems might be viewed as the restoration of right relationships within society rather than the restoration of a right relationship with God. Although God is certainly concerned with both, a problem arises when the question of doctrine becomes secondary to the quest for deliverance from oppression.

> As a liberation praxis oriented theology, doctrinal revisions become paramount if we are to understand the true task of theology. The question for us is, how do we reconstruct theological doctrines in order to reflect the liberating focus of the gospel?[26]

Sometimes the quest to be ethnically "authentic" goes to great lengths. Rev. Herbert Daughtry, a Pentecostal pastor and leader in the movement to Africanize the Bible, observes:

> For centuries everything was European-centered. . . . The biblical interpretations all supported the supremacy of Europeans and Whiteness. What we had to do was Africanize the Bible from an accurate base supported by secular historical sources.[27]

Many, however, might object that "Africanizing" the Bible is just as wrong as any other attempt to insert ethnic meanings not contained or intended by the writer. An example in current classroom theory is the "African-American Baseline Essays" (AABE, also known as the "Portland Baseline Essays), composed under the direction of educational psychologist Asa Hilliard III. First used in 1987 (revised in 1990), these compositions present world history in Afrocentric terms. The AABE is intended as a teacher resource stressing African and African-American contributions to the fields of art, language, mathematics, music, science, and technology.[28] The curriculum is extremely valuable in emphasizing the immense contributions of African-Americans to American society. Some, however, feel that the "Egyptcentric" curriculum creates historical distortions. Critics note that "some of their theories and factual claims often turn out to be 'Africanized' versions of long discredited and discarded European ones."[29] The attempt to "Africanize" Egyptian culture "can only be imposed artificially on Egyptian society."[30]

This public education debate carries important overtones for the educational task of churches. All cultural groups possess "ethnic allegiance." Each of us represents a bond to customs and characteristics centuries removed. Within the context of public education or service we naturally demonstrate loyalty to "who we are." In the church, however, there can be only one allegiance. Each group may represent the traditions of its ancestors, but to rewrite the foundational documents and history of our faith in terms which favor any cultural grouping would be extremely serious revisionism.

AFRICAN CULTURAL CONTRIBUTIONS

While these and other themes may be questionable, African culture also holds some important lessons for European conceptions of Christianity. Monica Wilson notes four ways in which African culture can instruct Westerners.[31] First, African culture can teach us much about the closeness of community. All too often Western worship has deemphasized the value and meaning of human relationships. Many people come to church not because they are seeking a doctrine, but because they are searching for a friend.

Second, Africans have a consciousness of the "reality of evil." Charles Kraft notes the missionary attempts to treat illness medically while at the same time ignoring African perceptions of illness as a theological question. Western society has also been guilty of underemphasizing the reality of spiritual evil.

Third, Africans restrain competition. As Kraft puts it, "Africans know how to be still, how to cooperate, how to get along with each other." While serving in ministry we remember well how one Baptist church sued another because it was placing five $1 bills under one seat in each of its buses. This gave "unfair advantage" in the competition for Sunday School students.

Fourth, Africans emphasize ritual rather than dogma. Wilson notes that this seems to provide a "balance to the intellectual emphasis of the West." Africans have a way of dealing with the passages of life in a heartfelt, emotive manner which seems far distant from emotionally reserved Westerners.

Developing multicultural sensitivity does not mean that the worship customs of any ethnic group should be altered. Each of us brings something unique to the Lord's table, and that uniqueness is enhanced as we learn from each other. What does have to be safeguarded, however, is the content of the worship experience. The crucified Christ can be preached equally effectively in black, Hispanic, and Anglo churches. The forms may vary, but there is no reason the content cannot remain the same.

FEMINIST PERSPECTIVES

The question of liberation is no less intense from feminist theologians who feel the church has been inherently patriarchal and oppressive toward women. Dorothee Söllee, portraying Western society as a "Cain and Abel culture," contends:

> I spent several years of my adult life speaking for Abel and against Cain. For the powerless, whose blood still cries out, and against the gang of unfortunate C-people. For Abel and against the Lord Father who runs the whole show. A theology of pain and rage. The theology of one who is by nature second

class, made out of the rib. But I don't read this story anymore
with Abel's eyes. I am tired of being the blood, the earth and
the scream. I address the storyteller and those who have
passed the tale down, written it down, recited and believed it.
Is that all? I ask the storyteller. Where am I then? Do I have
to be Abel if I don't want to be Cain? Is there no other way?[32]

Feminist theologians occupy a broad spectrum of opinion
ranging from those who seek to reinterpret the role of women
within the church to those who would abandon it altogether.
The first group is represented by such figures as Rosemary
Radford Ruether and Elizabeth Fiorenza. The role of women is
associated with mystical or popular figures who were outside or
independent of the institutional church. Figures such as Theresa
of Avila and Julian of Norwich exemplify a charismatic authority
often neglected by the institutional church. The opposite
pole is exemplified by Mary Daly and Starhawk. This group
contends that women should abandon Christianity and return to
ancient nature religion which offers a female concept of divinity.

MARXIST PERSPECTIVES

Similar tensions come from Marxist thinkers who feel that
Christianity can be allied with revolutionary movements. There
are many examples of devout religious leaders who felt that the
blood of oppressed peoples cried out for social revolution as an
expression of Christianity. Che Guevara, for example, was a
priest before joining Castro's revolution. Camilo Torres was a
Columbian priest turned revolutionary. Upon leaving the priesthood he proclaimed, "When my neighbor has nothing against
me, when I have realized the revolution, I will then say the Holy
Mass again."[33] The common assumption underlying such theology is that Marxism can, if necessary, complement Christian
goals. After all, why should any one form of economics be considered "Christian" as opposed to any other? Conversely, why
should dictators remain in power?

Such problems may seem far removed from the local church.
Yet, given the controversy of the recent "sanctuary movement"
as well as the fact that Hispanics are now the largest growing
cultural minority in the nation, it seems mandatory that

churches learn how to communicate and empathize with Mexi can- and Latin-Americans as well as with all Third-World cultures. The problem Christians have with Marxism is the issue of history. The Christian view of social progress and the meaning of history seems far different than that of Marxism.

A basic problem for all social movements continues to be that of absolutes. Noting the decline of institutions which have championed social and moral values, Joe Klein observes:

> The trouble was, no one could figure out where to draw the line on liberation. It became illiberal to reject any grievance or even to make moral judgments. The motives of criminals had to be understood rather than condemned. And if criminals rated empathy, who could cast judgment on a black teenager in the slums who chose to express herself by having a baby? Lifestyles were neither bad nor good; they were options. Options were terrific.[34]

AFFIRMING THE UNIQUENESS OF OUR FAITH

Evangelicals who communicate to a multicultural society must do three things: (1) define their identity, (2) explain their faith, and (3) apply their theology.

DEFINING IDENTITY

While the attempt to arrive at a precise definition is more difficult than it appears,[35] we can have a basic understanding as to what constitutes an "evangelical" faith. Donald Bloesch reminds us that

> "evangelical" means focusing on the gospel of Christ. It means determining your theological thinking in the light of this gospel. Because this gospel is attested to in Scripture, "evangelical" entails a reverence and respect for Holy Scripture. So an evangelical theology will always be a biblical theology.[36]

Bernard Ramm offers a further amplification.

> In addition to always being "biblical," evangelical thinking will demonstrate a particular attitude toward religious truth, i.e., it will always place the "priority of the Word and act of God over the faith, response, or experiences of men."[37]

Those who have a truly difficult time understanding what evangelicalism is could also try the time-honored method of apophatic theology.[38] While it may appear difficult to inclusively define evangelical beliefs, it is very clear what evangelicals do *not* believe. They do not believe, for example, that the Bible is merely a "human" book. They do not believe that Christ was merely a "human" man. They do not believe that the kingdom of heaven is merely a "human" kingdom. And they do not believe that the Cross was merely a "human" example.

If all the attempted definitions could be distilled into one profile, it would seem that evangelicalism would include the Trinitarian and Christological confessions of the ecumenical church accompanied by the soteriological definitions of the Reformation. Our own experience after a number of years of teaching in pluralistic contexts is that being an "evangelical" almost always involves the Reformation principles of *sola gratia, sola fide,* and *sola Scriptura.* Philip Schaff notes the ingredients of scriptural authority prior to tradition, justification by grace, and the priesthood of believers as opposed to sacerdotalism.[39]

Explaining Faith

The second requisite for a multicultural theology is to explain our faith in terms which truly communicate. A primary accusation levied against evangelicals is that of rationalism. We are thought to have constructed our theology upon a "Grecianized" model. The simple Palestinian story has been brocaded with Greek and scholastic terminology to the point that the "real" background of Christianity has been lost. Catholic scholar Leslie Dewart, for example, proposes a "dehellenization of dogma" in which the church recognizes the influence of Greek metaphysical thought upon the development of doctrine. Deane William Ferm observes:

> The problem prompting the need for dehellenization arose as the secular experience of Christian belief began to depart from that of the hellenistic Christians. Today this departure is virtually complete and new concepts from modern experience must replace such hellenistic elements of faith as the conception of God as Being, and the idea of faith as rational knowledge of certain truths about a strictly supernatural God.[40]

While such challenges may be demanding enough in the rough-and-tumble world of academia, they can be especially troublesome when applied in a context of multicultural ministry. Minority groups may be suspicious that evangelical Christianity is a "white man's" religion. The carefully constructed definitions of a Sunday School class may be viewed as a "Western" approach to religion which does not honor the heritage of Africa, China, or India.

While it is true that Christianity has experienced the effects of Greek and Roman thought, it would be extremely erroneous to suppose that the "essence" of the Christian faith was somehow lost at Nicaca or Chalcedon, and the confessional derivatives represent cultural compromises. The church of the creeds represents not the triumph of Greek philosophy, but rather the "Christianization of Hellenism" in which the clear teachings of Scripture were stated in the language of a particular culture. In other words, the historical beliefs of Christianity have permanent validity in all social situations.

It is the responsibility of the contemporary church to state the same truths in terms which speak with the same content to contemporary culture. Salvation, for example, is always a vertical personal encounter with the limitless grace of God. To deny or modify this concept in terms of a horizontal or relational approach which sees salvation in terms of human relationships would be a most serious misunderstanding. Such efforts result in the production of a horizontal "code language" which sounds religious but has no real content.

Neither should evangelicals hesitate to affirm the cognitive nature of their faith. There is a biblical role for logic and the laws of logic in understanding the Gospel message. The basic laws of logic, as well as a correspondence view of truth, are not just Greek philosophy. These categories of thought existed long before the Greeks. They were present in the first statement of creation (Gen. 1:1), the burning bush (Ex. 3:6), and the pledge of Deuteronomy 29:29. The cognitive nature of faith and the rationality of history may be viewed as an expression of the mind of God. It is not logic that is wrong, it is how we relate it to faith that determines our belief systems.

APPLYING THEOLOGY

The third component, applying our theology, demands that we effectively address the issues of our culture. Christianity must be practically applied to society. This cannot be accomplished without risk. Those who leave the security of a culturally prescribed faith must be willing to admit their own sinfulness and error in that faith. David Hesselgrave notes:

> There is a wrong kind of "cultural relativity" that insists that there are no absolutes and that the distinctions between right and wrong, and good and evil, are no more than the dictates of one's culture. But there is also a right kind of "cultural relativity" that says that although there are divinely dictated absolutes of right and wrong, one's own culturally prescribed assumptions of right and wrong will reflect them imperfectly at best and may not reflect them at all.[41]

Stanley K. Inouye presents a valuable analogy of human society as a "broken mirror," each fragment of which reflects a valid but distorted image of what should have been. A primary factor in preventing our unity, according to Inouye, is "our natural tendency to define belonging as sameness." In addition to listening, we must develop the ability to see — to appreciate the image of God in all humanity.[42]

Communicating a theology of cultural awareness, therefore, means that although Christian beliefs are not compromised, Christianity itself may demonstrate a different social identity. It is not so much that we have to change our own culture as that we must simply accept that of others. To accomplish such openness means that we do not insist on cultural sameness, that we expand our ability to hear, see, and learn from other groups.

Another requisite ingredient in this effort is study — the willingness to learn new terms and concepts which will enhance communication with other cultures. This means not only understanding what terms mean, but being aware of what they do *not* mean. "Multiculturalism," for example, may have a totally different significance to the Political Correctness movement than it would have to a missiologist. In the next chapter we will note some common terms and definitions which are necessary in multicultural dialogue.

CHAPTER FOUR

COMING TO TERMS WITH MULTICULTURALISM

INTRODUCTION

For a theology to be truly comprehensive it must inform and be informed by other scientific fields, both behavioristic and natural. While, from an evangelical standpoint, theology has priority over all other disciplines (just as faith has priority over reason), it is still necessary to study all of the social sciences. In the world of multiculturalism many common sociological terms are used which can enhance one's ability to communicate with those who study human behavior. In this chapter we will define and examine these terms with the goal of gaining greater insight into and understanding of the multicultural world in which we live.

WHAT IS MULTICULTURALISM?

Defining multiculturalism is much like defining Judaism. One can speak of a religion, a diet, a culture, or even a political state. Within our own society it may refer to a complex of issues. Applied to education, it constitutes a call for comprehensiveness and inclusion. Applied to society, it may range from civil rights to an assault upon Western values.

Some prefer a narrow definition of multiculturalism, while others favor a broader concept. Lee and Richardson opt for limiting the term "culture" primarily to the classifications of race and ethnicity, while others espouse a broader approach in which multiculturalism includes "*ethnographic* variables (nationality, ethnicity, language, and religion), *demographic* variables (age, gender, and place of residence), *status variables* (educational and socioeconomic background), and formal and informal *affiliations.*"[1]

James S. Wurzel notes two senses in which "multiculturalism" may be used. First, there is a general sense which simply recognizes that humanity has been "inherently and universally multicultural." Second, multiculturalism can be seen as a "set of principles," or a perspective in which "people act within the context of a multicultural society." But the "key to multiculturalism," Wurzel notes, "is awareness."[2] Those who wish to live in a truly multicultural manner must (1) become aware of their own "ethnocentric conditioning," and (2) "accept the fact that society is indeed multicultural."[3]

The concept of multiculturalism also has its opponents. *Newsday* reporter Lawrence Auster fears that Western traditions are being threatened by the movement. "The defining concept of multiculturalism is that our society is a collection of equal cultures, from which it follows that the United States' dominant Western culture is illegitimate and must be dismantled or drastically weakened."[4]

Diane Ravitch, the former Assistant Secretary and Counsel for the U.S. Department of Education and a principal writer of the California K-12 history-social science curriculum, gives a similar caution. "Those ethnocentrists," she states, "who insist on going to war against the common culture . . . do not understand that the common culture is multicultural."[5] Further,

> we lose no part of our multicultural heritage by appreciating the European ideas that created our democratic institutions and honoring the British men who wrote the Declaration of Independence and the Constitution. Indeed, we are at risk of

losing our democratic heritage if we fail to study and understand the ideas that established our government and institutions.

The common culture is jazz, the blues, the square dance, the waltz, salsa, the polka, rock-and-roll, the foxtrot, and rap. It is "America the Beautiful," "The Star-Spangled Banner," "America," and "Go Down, Moses." It is Shakespeare, Mozart, Bob Dylan, Spike Lee, and Norman Lear.[6]

The quest which awaits anyone pursuing this issue is thus one of candor and accuracy. We must be sure of the nature of our task and have some idea of how to accomplish it.

TERMS AND DEFINITIONS

Before examining multiculturalism from a Christian perspective, it will be helpful to note some common terms. The following list is an attempt to clarify nomenclature by assigning various words to inclusive groups. It is by no means exhaustive, but hopefully is representative of common concepts.

1. CULTURALLY DIVERSE GROUPS

Although one's racial group may also be one's ethnic group, the two are not necessarily the same. The "races" have traditionally been held to represent four groups classified by physical characteristics. Most, however, feel that such categorization is too general. Montagu goes so far as to say that race is "man's most dangerous myth." He feels the concept of race has been a highly destructive factor in the history of humankind.[7]

Currently, most scientists believe that all races are alike in aspects that really make a difference such as the ability to solve problems or to communicate. As a whole, "all racial groups appear to show a wide distribution of every kind of ability." Accordingly, when there are important race differences, they are more directly attributed to environmental factors.[8]

Ethnic, from the Greek, *ethnos,* originally meant a number of people living together, later as a tribe, a people, a nation, or group. The term was widely used in America to identify the early European immigrants, particularly after 1840.[9] *Ethnicity* may be defined as "that part of cultural development which occurs prior to the onset of a child's abstract intellectual powers as a result of his direct, personal contacts with the people around him and with his immediate environment."[10] *Ethnicity* may commonly refer to one's ancestral background,[11] or the nation-state origin from which they have immigrated.[12] *Ethnic group* would then refer to any group demarcated by one or more of the categories of race, religion, and national origin.[13]

According to Dierdre Meintel, the most influential definition of a *minority* was probably that of sociologist Louis Wirth in 1945: "We may define a minority as a group of people who, because of their physical or cultural characteristics, are singled out from the others in the society in which they live for differential and unequal treatment and who therefore regard themselves as objects of collective discrimination."[14] Anthropologists Charles Wagley and Marvin Harris have modified the term to designate status inherited "according to the descent rules of a society," for example, placing anyone having African-American ancestry into the "black" category. "Minority status is thus something one is 'born into,' rather than something acquired later in life."[15]

Especially interesting is the relationship of *minority* to that of culture. Culture provides a given group with a unique identity. A Korean child, for example, who comes to America assumes the role of a minority while retaining the culture of the majority of his origin. "The size of one group (minority) with respect to another (majority) is not an identity; it is only an environmental condition with which a cultural group may find itself."[16] A minority is not necessarily a culture, nor is a culture necessarily a minority.

> Therefore, if we consider the meaning of "minority" used in the United States, it does not refer at all to the cultural experience and identity of a group but to the *power* position of particular groups in the United States. It also connotes the cultural group's experiences of exclusion, exploitation, racism and varying forms of oppression.[17]

2. ACHIEVING CULTURAL STATUS

Viewed from a sociological perspective, multiculturalism would involve *socialization* and/or *enculturation*. The former term was coined by psychologists and sociologists in the 1930s.[18] Social scientists in three disciplines use the term, but each with a slightly different concern. Anthropologists ask how the culture is transmitted from one generation to another. Sociologists are interested in knowing how institutions are continued and changed. Psychologists want to know how people internalize the culture and societal values.[19]

Enculturation was used as an alternative to the term *socialization* by anthropologist Melville Jean Herskovits in 1948.[20] "Enculturation is a natural process of formal and informal, intentional and unintentional means by which children are inducted into a community and acquire its culture."[21] Margaret Mead distinguishes between the two terms by defining enculturation as "the concrete process of learning within a particular culture or subcultural grouping" and socialization as abstract characteristics of learning. Her definitions would liken enculturation to ethnicity.[22]

Three additional terms related to, but distinguished from *enculturation* are *acculturation, assimilation,* and *biculturation.* The definitions of educator John Westerhoff are helpful here. *Acculturation* is "the process by which persons learn to adapt to the general culture while still maintaining their own particular subculture."[23] *Assimilation* is "the process by which adults are inducted into a new culture through conversion, thereby leaving behind the first culture into which they had been enculturated."[24] *Biculturalization* represents "the blending of two cultures, keeping some learned characteristics of each and in time giving birth to a new cultural expression."[25]

3. IDEOLOGICAL TERMS

Viewed within a philosophical or idealistic framework, multiculturalism embraces opposing terms. On one hand, *ethnocentrism* is "the tendency to view the norms and values of one's own culture as absolute and to use them as a standard against which to judge and measure all other cultures."[26] More simply, it is the belief that one's culture is superior to that of other groups.[27]

On the other hand, two terms which express an opposite

view are *cultural relativism* and *pluralism. Cultural relativism* emphasizes the values within other cultures without reference or comparison to those of our own.[28]

Pluralism is synonymous. This view sees all cultures as being equally valid in claims concerning religion, values, and ultimate meaning. Educator Thomas Green notes three understandings of this term. (1) "Structural assimilation" deals with differences by diminishing or even eliminating them. The emphasis here is upon an open society which cuts across all divisions of religion, culture, or race. The problem is that such a goal disvalues and threatens cultural distinctives which are needed and beneficial. The solution to pluralism cannot be to simply create one comprehensive culture. (2) "Insular pluralism" is where cultural groups retreat from society at large to preserve their social unit. The problem is that this approach preserves both differences and divisions. The tensions of pluralism are preserved in both church and society. (3) "Half-way pluralism" is Green's desired option. This approach preserves distinctives related to family and family values, but allows interaction within the broader community of commerce and education.[29]

Intercultural communication attempts a reconciliation between ethnocentrism and pluralism. It denotes the understanding which takes place whenever the sender is a member of one culture and the receiver is a member of another.[30] A new field, the term is also known as *cross-cultural communication, interethnic communication,* and *trans-racial communication.*[31]

A set of additional ideological concepts would be *postmodernism* and *deconstructionism.* These differ from the above in that they are concerned with culture understood as the artistic expression of a society.

Postmodernism is "the precommitment to relativism or pluralism in relation to questions of truth."[32] "To use the language which has become characteristic of the movement, one could say that postmodernism represents a situation in which the signifier (or signifying) has replaced the signified as the focus of orientation and value."[33] In a recent work, Richard J. Mouw and Sander Griffioen note that according to this view the quest for knowledge has been fragmented, "No binding 'meta-narrative' is available to unify these diverse conversations; indeed the unifying visions that guided our lives in the past were instruments used by the powerful classes to impose their wills upon the whole."[34]

A similar term, *deconstructionism,* connotes the postmodern approach to literature which holds that "the identity and intentions of the author of a text are irrelevant to the interpretation of the text, followed by the observation that, in any case, no meaning can be found in it."[35] Applied socially, the term signifies the attempt to effect equality by "deconstructing" Western society and value systems. This view would hold that the best way to create equality is to simply dismantle the institutions of the previous social majority.

4. SOCIAL ATTITUDES

Multiculturalism also involves terms relating to negative social attitudes. *Prejudice* is a set of rigid and unfavorable attitudes toward a particular group or groups.[36] It could also be described as an idea, which, when expressed in words and actions, harms others. The term is seldom used without making reference to the classical work by Gordon Allport, *The Nature of Prejudice* (1954). He defined prejudice as thinking negatively of others without sufficient justification. Prejudice is the process of stereotyping, by which certain characteristics, either positive or negative, are ascribed to all members of a group. Racial prejudice occurs when it is believed that people with different skin color also possess specified differences in behaviors, values, and attitudes.

Discrimination indicates differential behavior directed toward a group.[37] Acts of discrimination occur when persons are treated in an inequal manner because they belong to a certain group. *Racism* constitutes attitudes, beliefs, and policies practiced "when a group has the power to enforce laws, institutions, and norms, based on its beliefs, which oppress and dehumanize another group."[38]

Robert Merton identifies four different types of people when the concepts of prejudice and discrimination are considered, either as a combination or independent of one another.

1. The *unprejudiced nondiscriminator,* in both belief and practice, upholds American ideals of freedom and equality. This person is not prejudiced against other groups and, on principle, will not discriminate against them.

2. The *unprejudiced discriminator* is not personally prejudiced but may sometimes, reluctantly, discriminate against other groups because it seems socially or financially convenient to do so.

3. The *prejudiced nondiscriminator* feels hostile to other groups but recognizes that law and social pressures are opposed to overt discrimination. Reluctantly, this person does not translate prejudice into action.

4. The *prejudiced discriminator* does not believe in the values of freedom and equality and consistently discriminates against other groups in both word and deed.[39]

Contemporary attempts to combat prejudice have taken the form of "prejudice reduction" workshops. However, this approach is viewed negatively by some in that the workshops suggest that prejudice rather than "domination, exploitation, and structural inequality is the core problem."[40]

5. SOCIAL ACTION

Still other concepts convey more constructive attitudes toward social correction. Although often considered hostile to evangelical constructs, they can represent sincere attempts to deal with structural inequalities.

Conscientization comes from the Spanish term *conscientização,* perhaps best translated as "critical consciousness" or "critical cognition."[41]

> Conscientization suggests a coming to an intellectual grasp of the world in such a way as to understand it, appreciate it (sometimes), and change/improve it. Conscientization differs, obviously, from cultural transmission a la socialization/enculturation in that it is "explicitly" concerned about transformation in society.[42]

Simply put, the term signifies "the ongoing struggle on the part of the oppressed to achieve their rightful dignity and status."[43]

Praxis is a basic term in liberation theology. It means "the continuing interaction between practice and theory, doing and thinking." "Theology as praxis is not the search for correct thinking (orthodoxy), but rather the intermingling of thought and action (orthopraxis)."[44] James White notes that this term can be easily misunderstood as "practice," when it really signifies "reflective action," a conscious attempt to integrate theory and practice in a liberating manner.[45]

Liberation is a kindred term which indicates "deliverance from oppression which is sustained by pervasive racism."[46] As demonstrated in films such as *The Mission,* it emphasizes involvement which becomes social and political as well as spiritual. In the film Robert DeNiro and Jeremy Irons portray opposing solutions to the problem of human oppression. DeNiro, a former soldier and slaver who becomes a missionary priest, chooses the option of armed resistance when the Portuguese come to take Indian slaves. His counterpart, the peace-loving figure portrayed by Jeremy Irons, marches resignedly to his death. The issue, of course, is how the church should be identified in its relations with those who experience repression and cruelty.

6. MULTICULTURALISM IN EDUCATION

Perhaps the most common area of application for multiculturalism has been in the field of education. *Multicultural education* in one form or another began to emerge globally as a field of study since the 1950s.[47] Sara Bullard notes that there is disagreement concerning the goals of multicultural education.

> Should it be to promote understanding of and sensitivity to other cultures? To advance academic achievement of minorities? To model a multicultural society where every group shares equal power? To offer a radical critique of Western culture? To provide intensive study of single ethnic groups? To train students in social action skills?[48]

Generally the term suggests a type of education which is concerned with various cultural groups within American society. The major goal is to change the total educational environment to promote a respect for diversity.[49]

Banks and Banks maintain that, "Multicultural education is

at least three things: an idea or concept, an educational reform movement, and a process."[50] They offer the following amplification.

> A multicultural education is an education for life in a free and democratic society. It helps students transcend their cultural boundaries and acquire the knowledge, attitudes, and skills needed to engage in public discourse with people who differ from themselves. Multicultural education also helps students acquire the skills needed to participate in civic action, which is an integral part of a democratic nation.[51]

Sleeter and Grant note at least the five following understandings of multicultural education contained in literature surveyed through 1987:

> 1. Teaching the Culturally Different: used to assimilate students of color into the cultural mainstream via transitional bridges within the existing school program.
> 2. Human Relations: to help students of different backgrounds get along.
> 3. Single Group Studies: fosters cultural pluralism via courses concentrating on ethnic and cultural distinctives.
> 4. Multicultural Education: promotes cultural pluralism and social equality by reforming the school program for all students to make it reflect diversity.
> 5. Education That Is Multicultural and Social Reconstructionist: prepares students to challenge social structural inequality and to promote cultural diversity.[52]

James Banks notes that the concept has become somewhat relative and he espouses instead the concept of *multiethnic education* which "excludes gender, religion, ability, and social class groupings."[53] Verma also cautions against the ambiguity of the term, noting that it does not seem to possess a single clear meaning and that "the term has blind-alley implications which not only take us away from moral and social realities, but direct us towards conceptual confusion."[54]

It is indicative of the complexity of our times that *multicultural education* in itself is difficult to define. Some feel there is no agreed definition of the term with meaning depending "largely upon the standpoints of individuals, whether they take an assimilationist, cultural pluralist or anti-racist approach."[55]

THE CHALLENGE OF MULTICULTURALISM

Multiculturalism can thus be applied across a broad spectrum of social goals, values, and education. We face the task of reducing prejudice, providing equal opportunities, and providing a just balance of power among the many groups that constitute the United States and Canada.

At an earlier time in our history the social theory of a "melting pot" was thought to model the final product of a multicultural society. By 1908 this concept was foundational in sociological thought. A character from a popular play, "The Melting Pot," could make the following statement.

> America is God's Crucible, the Great Melting Pot where all races of Europe are melting and re-forming! Here you stand . . . in your fifty groups, with your fifty languages and histories, and your fifty blood hatred and rivalries. But you won't be long like that, brothers . . . God is making the American . . . the real American has not yet arrived . . . he will be the fusion of all the races, perhaps the coming superman.[56]

Obviously, the above proclamation was far too optimistic. Not only did it contain seeds of supremacist thought, it also neglected the presence of indigenous peoples such as Native Americans and Mexicans.[57]

An additional difficulty with the melting-pot objective is that it could only be counterproductive. By blending our many groups into one, even if such a thing could be done, only the most negative effect would be achieved. The result would be a denial of uniqueness, creativity, and authenticity. Far better is the recognition that we are many and that our very variety is our culture.

A far superior concept would seem to be that of a mosaic.

> Examined too closely, a mosaic presents a discordant picture of poorly, even oddly, juxtaposed individual units strangely cemented together. Yet, on balance, this technique, when viewed from a reasonable distance, presents a complete picture, the total amounting to far more than the sum of the parts.[58]

Viewed from a Christian perspective, the church is just such a mosaic. All patterns of this type, for example, have a frame. Within this frame, however, each distinctive piece is surrounded by its own individually shaped enclosure. The church also has a frame, God's Word as given in Scripture. Each segment of the church, however, has received His Word in its own unique circumstances. The resulting variety is a thing of beauty because although each is different, all exist within the universal boundary of His revealed will. This is the type of unity we must seek. We can see unity in diversity in which one product presents manifold beauty not in spite of, but because of, its many uniquenesses.

Finally, it is important to note that multicultural unity must be more than just a hypothesis. If our "mosaic" is to be anything more than a mere word picture, we must carefully state our philosophical approach and delineate definite goals for enhancing understanding.

CHAPTER FIVE

MULTICULTURALISM IN THE CHURCH SETTING

PHILOSOPHICAL FOUNDATIONS

Multiculturalism has become a powerful force on all levels of society. The increasing cultural diversity of America has produced calls for social readjustment throughout the community spectrum. College and university campuses have been affected by strident challenges from minorities concerning "Eurocentric" or "Anglocentric" curriculums. Historian Arthur M. Schlesinger, Jr. captures the core of the movement: "Salvation lies in breaking the white, Eurocentric, racist grip on the curriculum and providing education that responds to colored races, colored histories, colored ways of learning and behaving."[1]

The tensions produced on college campuses have been significant. An automatic response to the supposed overemphasis upon European heritage has been movements such as Afrocentrism, feminism, gay rights, and any number of reflexive ideologies which attempt to "right the wrong" by offering different interpretations of history as well as different methodologies and curricula for education.

University administrators have attempted to fend off conflicts by initiating "intellectual affirmative action." Minorities may demand that their distinctive perspectives be recognized in class subjects; curricula which was the norm for college studies of the last generation are castigated for conveying a "predominant white, male, European, and heterosexual mentality which, by its very nature, is inescapably racist, indisputably sexist, and manifestly homophobic."[2]

One of the most common titles for this approach to educational and political readjustment is "political correctness," or the "PC" movement. The study of any subject is approached from a "content neutral" perspective. To avoid offending minorities, Western traditions and classical literary frameworks are replaced by exercises in contemporary social expression. In the English Department at Duke University, for example, traditional approaches have been replaced by "politically correct" agendas: "Critical Theory instead emphasizes feminist, gay and lesbian, or Marxist approaches to the text—generally, whatever the reader or theorist wants to glean from it."[3]

The chairperson of the department contends:

> We simply can't teach courses the way they were taught 25 to 30 years ago and be faithful to our discipline. . . . Words on the page are constantly being contextualized and recontextualized as we learn more and more. . . .[4]

One of the problems with such responses is that the perceived correction to injustice often becomes another form of injustice. Colleges and public institutions rush to correct the perceived abuses by granting special privileges and status to minority groups. The result, however, seems to be an increase in racism rather than a reduction. "Reverse discrimination" is a common charge and feelings can run high on every level of the college experience from admissions to the classroom.

Critics such as Dinesh D'Souza note that the "tyranny of the minority" simply leads to a newer type of racism.

> It is impossible to separate the "new racism" on campus from the old racism, because the bigotry which results from preferential treatment strengthens and reinforces the old bigotry which preferential policies were instituted to fight.[5]

Schlesinger fears increasing conflict.

> What happens when people of different ethnic origins, speak-
> ing different languages and professing different religions, set-
> tle in the same geographical locality and live under the same
> political sovereignty? Unless a common purpose binds them
> together, tribal hostilities will drive them apart.[6]

Schlesinger and D'Sousa are not alone in their censure.
Allan Bloom, perhaps the best-known critic of multicultural
methodology, notes that it is opposed to any worldview (*Weltan-
schauung*) which believes that there are universal philosophical
and ethical truths. In the thought of multiculturalism, truth and
meaning vary with each culture.[7]

Evangelicals likewise have difficulty with these movements.
Basically the problem is that of pluralism. Christianity is an
exclusive religion. The Old and New Testaments witness to a
covenant relationship between God and His people which pro-
hibits any other object of worship. Yet when we say that we are
not pluralistic, we must be careful not to give the wrong impression. What is pluralism? Are Christians not supportive of the
rights of all groups in a democratic society? How can we say
that we are not "pluralistic"?

The problem, of course, is how we define the term. Donald A.
Carson, for example, notes at least three different understandings
of pluralism. First, it may refer to the constantly increasing variety
of Western culture. Second, it may refer to "the value of tolera-
tion for diversity." Third, it may refer to a philosophical stance.[8]

> This stance insists that tolerance is mandated on the ground
> that no current in the sea of diversity has the right to take
> precedence over other currents. In the religious sphere, no
> religion has the right to pronounce itself true and the others
> false. The only absolute creed is the creed of pluralism (in this
> third sense) itself.[9]

Christian churches would not hesitate to bear witness to the
first two of these definitions. Philosophically, however, Christianity cannot be committed to pluralism. The church may be
composed of many peoples, but the Christian message is not
pluralistic in content.

A similar ambiguity can attach to the word "multiculturalism." If used as a synonym for pluralism or political correctness, it may become an adversary to Christian thought. Conversely, if used to describe the inclusive nature of God's people, it assumes a foundational importance for Christian thinking.

CULTURE AND CONTEXT

Considering multiculturalism in a church context involves variants which are not relevant to society as a whole. First, churches are not public institutions. They are private, nonprofit entities which operate by their own rules or confessions. Those who decide to join must decide whether they voluntarily accept the terms of a given tradition or confession. Second, churches are not pluralistic institutions. Their purpose is not to provide equal time for all parties. The only "party" that really has a platform is the Christian tradition, and the only "message" is the Gospel. Such a criterion does not mean that the church avoids social obligations, but rather that it seeks to permeate all of society with its principles.

The very term "multiculturalism" challenges us to clarify our understanding of culture. Some contemporary thinkers deny the existence of any "metahistorical" or "metacultural" concept of culture. A staple of the "new hermeneutic," for example, is the assumption that the meaning of a biblical text comes from the reader's interpretation rather than the intentions of the writer. Biblical texts are said to continually create new meanings as they tumble through history and are received by various groups. The assumption of relativity forms the base for both culture and learning. Such an assumption, however, is both unnecessary and untrue.

Theologians such as William J. Larkin contend that there is a "Christian" view of culture which allows for the claims of Christianity across all human groupings. In Larkin's words:

> Culture is that integrated pattern of socially acquired knowledge, particularly ideas, beliefs, and values (ideology) mediated through language, which a people uses to interpret experience and generate patterns of behavior—technological, economic, social, political, religious, and artistic—so that it can survive by adapting to relentlessly changing circumstances.[10]

The point is that culture is more than merely observing behavior. Culture is a matter of worldviews, values, and convictions. If we are created in the image of God, then each cultural worldview is both obligated and responsible for a society which reflects God's character. Cultural pluralism is not our "basic reality."

> If there is such a thing as human nature unified by reason of its creation in God's image, then radical epistemological or moral relativism based on irreconcilable cultural diversity is false. As human beings we have a commonality that enables us to interpret and apply ideas and patterns and forms from other cultures and time periods. This unity provides the framework within which God communicates truth, and this operation, so visible in his dealings with the vast procession of generations and nations, calls into question the foundations of a relativistic approach.[11]

This raises the question of what our response should be to multicultural issues. If we can claim a singular message and if we have a unified view of culture, what response should we make to either pluralism or multiculturalism?

This broaches a critical issue for those who deal in theology and religion. If we can claim a singular message, and if we have a unified view of culture, what response should we make to multiculturalism? It is a complex question in light of the fact that theologians and religious thinkers have failed to develop a theology of culture. David Augsburger points out that we have gone to great lengths to integrate the worlds of theology and psychology, thus prizing both universals and particulars, but in the process have failed to minister to humanity as a cultural being.

> A theology of culture — such as the meaning of being cultural beings and the significance of structures, institutions, and systems — has received much less attention and tends to be overlooked in practice. This excluded middle of human experience is theologically crucial in pastoral care and counseling across cultures.[12]

It is not wrong to be what we are. Any attempt to create culturally neutral worship due to cultural plurality would deny the most positive aspect of multiculturalism—the preservation and recognition of cultural uniqueness. Churches should maintain their distinctives. At the same time, we can effectively improve multicultural tensions by changing the most basic of things—our attitudes. S.D. Gaede puts it clearly.

> If our image of the church is wrong, we also set ourselves up for poor thinking about the issues of multiculturalism. For regardless of what we conclude about the pros and cons of that particular ideology, we ought to feel multicultural in our bones.[13]

Christians can, Gaede insists, arrive at a unified understanding of culture comprised of three basic truths.

> 1. There is one God, Creator of all, and we are all created in his image.
> 2. All of us have sinned and come short of the glory of God.
> 3. Jesus Christ is the Truth, and the Truth calls us to love God and love others as ourselves.[14]

Acceptance of these propositions entails a unified view of truth. In order for Christianity to have any meaning there must be absolute conceptual parameters which allow for the basic statement of the Christian message. At the same time, such limitations need not hinder the true outreach of multiculturalism in a Christian setting. Such an outreach will focus upon the acceptance of persons. James W. Fowler speaks of the "public church" which forsakes a defensive posture in favor of effecting a positive transformation in human relations.

> That God's praxis transforms toward wholeness, justice, and peace finds witness in ecclesial community as congregations practice their principles of equality, partnership, and inclusiveness, as they welcome and extend hospitality to the stranger, and as they give their lives for transformed human community in particular contexts.[15]

CULTURE AND COMMUNITY

The Christian response to multiculturalism calls us to an affirmation of the personal worth of each person in our society.

Such affirmation means entering into a meaningful relationship with all who enter our midst. The attempt to create such community will require churches to address challenges which relate especially to multiculturalism, specifically *stranger anxiety* and *ethnic identity.*

Individuals from a cultural minority who seek identity in a larger group may suffer at least three problems specifically associated with minority status. First, they may experience "persecutory anxiety," a condition that is present when the host environment is perceived as "hostile and persecutory." Second, they may suffer from "depressive anxiety," a troubled attitude that ensues when one becomes preoccupied with losses experienced in migration. Finally, one may experience "disorienting anxiety," the result of the encounter with new concepts of being and living.[16]

Although these terms are intended to describe the psychological condition of immigrating to a new country, they apply equally well to those who may be "immigrating" to our churches. Those who visit or attend face the task of assuming both personal and corporate identities that may have been a lifetime in the making for church constituents. Becoming one with an established tradition is rarely accomplished overnight.

Conversely, feelings of apprehension may be equally present on the part of established congregations. What does one make of "outsiders"? Could they possibly be a threat to church identity and mission? Perhaps there will be new and disturbing expressions of worship.

Morris Inch suggests a practical Christian approach by suggesting that we view culture as a "context in which we may encounter the living God," as a means rather than a goal.[17] Instead of feeling threatened by outsiders, it will help immensely if Christians begin to view other cultures as vehicles through which the Gospel may be expressed.[18] An example of this would be the attitude of the apostles in the conflict of Acts 15. The final answer of the church was a composite of cultural dietary restrictions to avoid Jewish offense and the theological principle of sexual purity. Multicultural sensitivity was also displayed in the makeup of the church leadership. Thom Hopler notes that the deacons chosen to diffuse the situation were multicultural, coming from Hellenistic backgrounds and even including a non-Jew. By sharing the church power structure with a minority the apostles solved the problem of intercultural relations.[19]

Another element of importance in pluralistic relationships is our understanding of ethnicity. Ethnicity applies to all persons, not just to first or second generations of new citizens, nor to people of color. According to Richard Pratte, "Ethnicity, as a concept, suggests a movement of affection and identity, enriched perhaps by the subtle, provocative ways in which one differs from others, and reinforced by a strong attachment to family and relatives."[20]

Michael Novak observes, "The new ethnicity is a form of historical consciousness. Who are you? What history do you come from? And where next? These are its questions."[21] This might be called the "ethnic quest." Novak contends that "the new ethnicity . . . [is] a movement primarily of personal and social identity."[22]

It is our contention that the burden of ethnicity is a reflection of humanity's spiritual quest of a true identity. Scholars such as Novak, Hansen, Glazer, and Moynihan point out that "resurgent ethnicity" is a response to an identity crisis. While this could be an oversimplification, the attempt of cultural minorities to establish a sense of identity is expressive of the universal need to belong. As theologians, we would argue that this need can only be met in the church of Christ, that it is social, racial, ethnic, but most of all, religious in nature.

This means that we must arrive at our own theory of cultural relations. Basically, this means that churches should be concerned with creating culture which is inclusive of all. Ethnic minorities, indeed all minorities, should experience the broader social context of Christianity. The issue becomes one of spiritual acculturation. The goal is to merge our cultures with the Christian faith in a manner which allows our uniquenesses to speak the power of the Gospel. Instead of being defensive, this goal is offensive. It is part of the Great Commission.

Christian multiculturalism must be defined in terms of social interaction and pluralistic relationships. Triandis espouses "*additive multiculturalism* where people learn to be effective and to appreciate others who are different in culture."[23] In his words, "[W]e should develop a pluralism that gives self-respect to all, appreciation of cultural differences and social skills leading to interpersonal relationships with more rewards than costs."[24] Applied to the church, this means that rather than be assimilated, minorities will be appreciated. The Gospel can be received in a manner which gives it new life as it is expressed in ways which enhance self-respect and mutuality within the body of Christ.

Christianity possesses an answer to the dilemma posed by Schlesinger. In Christ we have an answer for the lack of "a common purpose." The splendid multiplicity of the church is based upon one unified faith. At the same time, we have room for differences. Fowler notes that " 'diversity' means racial, ethnic, class, and within confessional bounds, theological differences. In part, the public church's receptiveness to strangers arises from its welcoming of diversity within its community."[25] Because we do have a foundational doctrinal unity, we can look forward to diversity as a central expression of the reality of our faith.

CLARIFYING OUR GOALS

Assuming that a unified field of truth does exist, and that we as God's creation witness that truth, we would like to present the following as a working definition of a Christian perspective on multiculturalism.

> *Christian multiculturalism is the personal application of Christian life and thought to all social groups which seek their spiritual identity in the church.*
>
> *In its broadest sense, a multicultural approach for the church would be viewed as a process that affects the structural organization of the church, pastoral/instructional strategies, and personal values of members of the congregations.*

Careful consideration of both the unitary nature and diverse makeup of Christianity presents the following goals for multiculturalism when applied to the church setting.

STRUCTURAL ORGANIZATION OF THE CHURCH

1. To lead members of the church community to become informed regarding the growing cultural diversity of our society.

In light of present conditions, it is predicted that the traditional majority, Caucasians of Northern European descent, will become an increasingly smaller presence in North American society. The three largest cities in the United States, New York, Los Angeles, and Chicago, already have majorities of minorities.[26]

Significant changes have occurred in North American society since the 1960s so that the result is heterogeneous populations in nearly every social, religious, and educational institution. One church may minister to an influx of Vietnamese families with limited English skills and parents who primarily work out of the home, while another setting may be rural with a large number of its members self-employed or employed in blue-collar occupations. An urban setting may vary in the number of families with one versus two parents or college-educated versus vocationally trained adults.

Just as the increasing cultural diversity of North America challenges public institutions, it also challenges church leaders to understand the values, customs, and traditions of various cultures and to provide responsive multicultural experiences for their membership.

2. To identify those areas in which our own Christian traditions have been affected by culture.

This means that we must ask ourselves what specifically is present in our church education and worship that might be "culture bound" or needlessly additive to the Christian message. Obviously, this is difficult. The attempt to distill Christianity into an objective set of beliefs which are a *sine qua non* for all Christians has a long and frustrated history. We can, however, address the essentials of the Christian message in a manner which expedites understanding.

> As Christian educators we should strive to communicate a biblical world view to our students and one not wrapped in the values and views of our culture. Shirts, ties, short haircuts, and clean-shaven faces have sometimes become synonymous in peoples' minds with the Gospel, for they were imposed

along with its preaching. Again, to forbid dancing to students whose culture is expressed by dance is an imposition not from the Scriptures but from one's own culture. To teach culture along with the Gospel carries the danger that students may be led into unnecessary cultural legalism. Converts are tempted to clean up outwardly and act the part expected while their hearts remain unchanged.[27]

3. To identify and discourage organizational approaches and personal attitudes that are ethnocentric in nature.

Although ethnocentric attitudes may have their origin in loyalty to one's ancestral history, the end result may be negative interethnic relations. We may, for example, be so involved in our own heritage that we fail to understand or appreciate those from other backgrounds. Even worse, we may tend to judge others by the characteristics of our own culture. It is all too easy to suppose that other cultures are somehow inferior to our own, or that the ways in which they differ are negative or culpable. Another error is to assume that all those from another culture are necessarily similar.

When we apply ethnocentric thinking specifically to biblical teaching, we should consider the principles of cross-cultural ministry as given by Reuben H. Brooks.

(1) The Bible shows no ethnically pure "correct" culture.

(2) As in the Bible, so today we should accept people from every culture and ethnic group as our neighbors and treat them with mutual respect and dignity.

(3) The Old Testament Scripture is replete with examples of a transcultural Gospel.

(4) The New Testament does not show one culture to be the correct one and all others wrong.

(5) The true message of Christianity is a person, Jesus Christ.

(6) To cross into other cultures is the expected norm for God's people, not the exception.[28]

The church of the New Testament was a pluralistic group in the best sense of the term. The essential nature of evangelism represented an outpouring to all humanity, regardless of ethnic or cultural backgrounds.

4. To provide a church program that promotes effective and reciprocal relationships with disparate church families.

The same type of discrimination and alienation that members of a family may receive from society may be experienced within church relationships. The church has the opportunity to play a proactive role in providing a social setting that is inclusive of all. Further, it has the potential of operating as an agent of change so that disparate groups are unified and equalized. The church which succeeds in this role will have to act with intentionality in developing every aspect of corporate ministry. Each family has its own unique strengths and gifts. To energize these will require that the church form "a cooperative partnership with families" in which each person is enabled to express individual needs and goals. It must also be emphasized that such ministry reaches into the entire community. This means assisting schools, social enterprises and, yes, other churches.[29]

Pastoral/Instructional Strategies

1. *To model and encourage in others the development and maintenance of positive interethnic relations within the church community.*

An important goal for church leaders is the development and maintenance of positive interethnic relations within the church community. Negative interethnic relationships are either a result of, or results in, attitudes and acts of prejudice and discrimination.

Churches should remember that they also play an additional role in multicultural relations. They may serve as a partial bridge between minorities and the dominant culture. "Christian members of various immigrant groups have traditionally found that the only thing they had in common with the dominant culture was their profession of faith."[30]

2. *To develop cross-cultural skills in teaching so that provision is made for various learning styles.*

With the increasing number of adults in higher education, a great deal of attention has been given to ways in which adult learners differ from the traditional student just out of secondary school. Much of the literature in this area has concentrated on learning styles.

The research on learning styles has included studies on differences in learners from diverse groups. Although no one style has been clearly and consistently documented for specific ethnic groups, it is generally accepted that there are differences. Consequently, there is need for variety in methodology so that information and learning activities are presented to appeal to a multiplicity of learning styles.

3. To assist persons in the process of identity formation as it includes ethnicity.

At this point a critical error can be made in thinking about multiculturalism. If we are truly open and accepting of all, then we naturally expect that all will feel welcome and possibly even come to appreciate the culture we represent. What is easily overlooked is the necessity of assisting others to appreciate their own ethnicity as a part of identity formation. This means hearing from other cultures and positively affirming their contributions to worship and church life. Fowler reminds us, "When the spine of identity is well-established, it is possible to risk relating in depth to those who are different from the self."[31]

4. To help members integrate their ethnic/social culture with that of the church culture.

In order to accomplish this goal, churches must establish an identity that is not ethnocentric in nature. Stanley Hauerwas offers the following challenge: "In short, the challenge to us as Christians is to find a way to witness to the God of Abraham, Isaac, Jacob, and Jesus, without allowing that witness to become an ideology for the powers that would subvert our witness."[32] In order to facilitate a variety of ethnic groups, the identity of the church must be socially inclusive.

5. To empower members of minority groups.

Pastors and educators will amplify their effectiveness by viewing each person within the totality of their existence. "Leadership is 'liberating people to do what is required of them in the most effective and human way possible.' "[33] Such empowering need not be confined to the church or spiritual issues. A large cafeteria chain employs many Hispanics, most of whom do not speak English. These people have a tremendous desire to learn English, but work long hours and have little opportunity.

A good example of empowerment would be to offer mid-afternoon English classes (when most cafeteria workers are off). There does not have to be a "religious" angle. Simply helping people to improve their life situation is an authentic expression of the Gospel.

6. *To teach and preach a Christian commitment to justice.* Again, we refer to Fowler's concept of conditional openness that involves both acceptance and responsibility. Although attitudes purporting acceptance of diversity are an important goal, evidence of such attitudes should be demonstrated in action.

This is possibly the area which harbors the greatest amount of resentment from minorities. Many feel that the evangelical church has not actually "entered into" suffering with them. Churches have offered programs without assuming the burden of disadvantaged minorities. The church which is truly multicultural will accept the risk of suffering, of association, and of participation in the healing of the nations.

Multiculturalism cannot be equated with the development of an awareness of other cultures. Although awareness will certainly be an important goal of multiculturalism, it is imperative that an action phase is included. We must look for indicators that display an awareness of the value of diversity, but we must also look for *intentionality.* Behavior must exist that demonstrates: (1) a promotion of equity in programs and curriculum, (2) an effort to help others become aware of biases, and (3) an organized approach to developing an appreciation for diversity.

Serow distinguishes between symbolic tolerance and functional tolerance as outcomes. Symbolic tolerance is shown when there is a positive attitude toward abstract or hypothetical representation of ethnic diversity. Functional tolerance, however, represents a willingness on the part of members of diverse groups to work together in the pursuit of shared goals. Whereas symbolic tolerance might be considered adequate within a local school setting, it would seem to be inadequate in a religious institution which pursues the goal of presenting and experiencing the Gospel by all people.[34]

7. *To foster social relationships among young children in the church that represent cooperation, openness, an interest in others,*

and a willingness to include others.

Social interaction with peers increases dramatically during the early childhood years. Through this process, the young child learns the importance of peer relationships and social acceptance. These social relationships become an important source of information about the world outside the family. Family and church cooperation is necessary to encourage the development of attitudes which are inclusive of different appearances, behavior, and language.

8. To assist parents in the task of rearing children to appreciate diversity and live together with people of all ethnic backgrounds.

As in all areas, parents will be the strongest influence in the way children react to people of different cultures. Parents with biased attitudes will, in almost all cases, encourage children to develop biased attitudes. The encouraging aspect, however, is that the opposite is also true. Children can grow up rejecting prejudice and hatred of diverse groups as a result of the actions and attitudes that their parents have modeled.

PERSONAL VALUES OF MEMBERS

1. To enable church members to see themselves as part of a larger society and to be able to identify, empathize, and relate with members of diverse groups from this larger society.

This goal is difficult for those influenced by the traditional teaching that there should be a definite separation of the "godly and ungodly" worlds. Setting parameters that separated one from the larger society gave evidence that one was supportive of the "godly" culture. Instead of encouragement to identify and empathize with persons from the "other" cultures, exactly the opposite was advocated.

Healthy Christians do not feel that their perspective is the only "totally correct" view, nor are they defensive or unkind when outsiders are encountered. Church congregations of this type are committed to civility, the idea that we can encounter strangers, even opponents, and respond with civility.[35]

2. To provide educational and social opportunities for church members to learn about different cultures.

Researchers have found that negative attitudes toward ethnic groups often accompany a lack of knowledge regarding and a lack of contact with specific ethnic groups.[36] Thus, the church can assist members to develop more effective interethnic relations by providing both educational and social opportunities to learn about members of groups different from their own.

It is possible for a local church to focus its curricular objectives on either affective or cognitive objectives. Either can be excluded or deemphasized. While attitudes, and consequently emotions, are certainly an integral part of a multicultural approach, the result will be inadequate if substantive content is lacking. In fact, studies have shown that cognitive strategies may be used to achieve affective goals. The results of research by Frech, Knight, and Contreras all found that cognitive-based materials and training were effective in reducing ethnocentrism, stereotyping, and negative attitudes toward ethnic groups.[37]

3. To magnify and celebrate diversity within the church.

Suspicion and fear of "different" groups is often the result when there is a lack of knowledge about the habits, lifestyles, and attitudes of the different group. In the beginning years of social development, individuals should be encouraged to accept a broad range of lifestyles. A major obstacle to this exists for those who were reared in homes in which it was taught that their lifestyle only was "spiritually correct." True Christian nurture will emphasize not only the respect of differences, but in addition will encourage the joy and celebration over their presence in the church!

4. To combat attitudes of prejudice and discrimination.

The Rodney King incident in 1992, in which a black man was beaten by four white police officers, and the aftermath of violence that followed in the Los Angeles area reminded many of the potential feelings of racism that seem to lie just below the surface of the everyday citizen. Although improvement has occurred in some aspects of the struggle, there are other areas which have remained the same or shown little advancement.

Researchers are familiar with the classical studies by the Clarks in the early 1940s when preschool children were asked to choose between white and black dolls on the basis of their identification with the dolls. In that study, 67 percent of the black children selected white dolls. The study has been repeat ed and the results are not a decided improvement. The Hopsons in 1985 found only a 2 percent decrease in the forty-five years of struggle for improvement. In addition to that, they found that "76% of the black children and 82% of the white children said that the black dolls 'looked bad' to them."[38]

Obviously the seeds of prejudice and racism are still flowering, even in our so-called enlightened era.

5. *To help all members develop positive racial, cultural, class, and individual identities and to perceive themselves as members of many different groups.*

It is natural to define oneself on the basis of one's most dominant cultural group. However, a sensitivity can be developed that enables the individual to sense his or her current membership in the context of the larger society which represents greater diversity.

PRINCIPLES FOR APPLICATION

When church leaders are challenged to be more sensitive to cultural pluralism within the local church, they frequently respond as public school teachers do, "Tell us what to do and we will do it." Undoubtedly the demand for multicultural sensitivity in the church and the needs of church leaders who are trying to meet these demands will continue to grow as the degree of cultural differences increases within our culture.

A large suburban church buses children and teenagers from the inner city. While this is very positive, an interesting thing happens when the buses arrive. After being left off at the back door of the church, the youths are divided into their own classes instead of mixing with the local youth of the congregation. They have their own class and programs, while the children of the general church constituency meet with their programs and teachers. Control problems are minimized and children of church members are not exposed to negative examples or influences. A youth worker recently remarked that one inner-city youth has attended the church for three years, all of that time in a separated atmosphere. Is this multicultural ministry?

A more formal church across town offers one adult class each quarter for the specific purpose of becoming more familiar with a particular ethnic group. Their history is studied, related videos watched, and various book reviews are presented. Popular speakers of that ethnic background are invited to visit the class. Is this multicultural ministry?

Another church identifies their missionary education program as a form of multicultural education in the church. This program begins during the early childhood years and has a regular curriculum each year for all ages. The focus is primarily on the particulars of living in countries other than the United States or Canada. Is this multicultural ministry?

What constitutes multiculturalism for a local congregation will vary from church to church and must be a decision made by each parish. No one program can be recommended for universal use. However, that does not mean that there are not some approaches that will be more effective than others. As a church has opportunity to think through its philosophy and objectives related to multiculturalism, it will want to establish a schema which will provide a basis for selecting programs, materials, methodology, and activities.

A church attempting to include multiculturalism in its ministry approach needs to develop a paradigm which accommodates new knowledge and different questions. An approach should not be selected at random, but should be based upon careful consideration of one's theology and philosophy of ministry.

Paradigm is a term commonly used today, especially in the business world, which means a way of seeing things, a lens through which something is viewed. A paradigm, according to Webster, provides an "outstandingly clear or typical example." A paradigm sets rules and regulations that establish boundaries and assist the institution in solving problems within these boundaries. The church needs a paradigmatic approach to multicultural ministry for the same reason Richard K. Fenn maintains that sociology needs a paradigm: "for knowing what is central as opposed to what is peripheral, what is superficial as opposed to what is latent, and what is material as opposed to matter of appearance alone."[39]

APPROACHES TO INTEGRATING MULTICULTURALISM

Several approaches have been used to integrate a multicultural approach in religious and educational settings. Four types are most common.[40]

Among the most frequently used is the *contributions approach*. In this type, content about personalities or ethnic and cultural groups are given on special occasions such as Martin Luther King Day or Women's History Week.

Another approach which is common is the *additive approach*. Various content, concepts, and themes which are cultural in nature are added to the curriculum and to programs, without change in basic structure, purpose, or characteristics. A multicultural Sunday may be scheduled each year or even once a month, or a multicultural course may be scheduled each church year without a change in the overall curriculum.

In the two above approaches, the programs or courses scheduled are often highly representative of the dominant culture, rather than a true reflection of a specific cultural community. The special event is inserted without changing or challenging the basic programs or curriculum of the church. A recent example would be the pastor who for Mother's Day encouraged the congregation to read a book on Susanna Wesley. This was his way of enlightening the audience concerning the role of women. But many contemporary works may have been more challenging to modern listeners. Susanna Wesley reflected the norms and values of the dominant culture and the established institutional role for women of her era.

The *transformational approach* is fundamentally different from the first two mentioned in that individuals are encouraged to view concepts or issues from another's perspective. This will require a change in the basic assumptions of the message communicated or content taught, a paradigm shift, so that one is helped to understand events and people from diverse cultural perspectives. Others are encouraged to analyze the perspective of the preacher or teacher and are given an opportunity to justify their own versions of the concepts presented. The key goal in this approach is to encourage critical thinking and the development of skills to justify conclusions reached.

For example, the teacher might discuss a "missionary endeavor" in which a local church supports missionaries from the U.S. as they begin a church in Korea. What would we call an endeavor of Christians from Korea who begin a church in Fort Worth, Texas? We have a tendency to assume that the term "missionary" refers only to efforts which originate in North America. Banks uses the example of the meaning of "Westward movement" when the Lakota Sioux were already living in the West and considered their homeland the center of the universe.[41] It becomes apparent that "Westward movement" is a Eurocentric term. What do these terms say when we view them from the perspective of the Lakota Sioux or the Korean Christian? Banks suggests that students be encouraged to give a name to the movement that would be more culturally neutral.

A fourth approach is the *decision-making and social-action approach*. This approach is an extension of the transformative approach in that opportunity is given to pursue projects and activities related to ethnic and cultural diversity. Members of a Sunday School class might be given the assignment of identifying the specific roles given to minority characters in television programs during the following week. This could be compared with the roles played by Anglo-Saxons. A popular film might be analyzed by a group, each member representing a different perspective. Listening teams might be assigned for the evening news for one full week to analyze the common perspective of local newscasters.

Of the above approaches, perhaps the most beneficial to the church would be the transformational approach and the decision-making and social-action approach. These two approaches provide for change in the three important categories of goals: the cognitive, the affective, and skills or behavior.

So how does the church begin incorporating a transformational or decision-making and social-action approach? A tempting first step may be to seek multicultural awareness by the compilation of catalogs and books of resources and materials, lists of learning activities, classroom practices and strategies, and accumulated information on the heritage and history of various cultural groups. However, although a simplified beginning, this would suggest the incorrect assumption that effective multiculturalism in the church can be implemented easily with little preparation. The opposite is true in that the development of a multicultural setting in the church is far more complicated and demanding.

A basic principle to keep in mind throughout the implementation process is the *principle of multicultural infusion.* To do so requires certain things of church leadership. First, multiculturalism should not enter into the church program haphazardly or incidentally. Instead, it should be given a deliberate and systematic inclusion. Although there is a great deal of research and literature on conceptual aspects of multiculturalism, specific applications to the classroom and church setting are not as readily available. Thus, emphasis should be given to the problem-solving or decision-making process which requires the church leader to acknowledge and identify specific problems or situations that require a change if it is to fit the need for diverse groups. After awareness has been established, the situation should be analyzed for solutions or decisions. This gives a *contextual decision-making approach* that is superior to the *product approach.* In the latter, leaders are given "how-to" answers which may apply in certain situations and times, but will eventually be insufficient since learning experiences are dynamic and constantly changing.

The ultimate answer to providing a multicultural environment within the church is to empower church leaders to make better decisions for themselves within their own specific contexts. Empowerment in this instance means possessing the content, the will, and the skills to incorporate cultural diversity within their particular sphere.

In this chapter we have examined the importance of having a philosophy of multicultural ministry and supplementing this with practical goals and objectives. To put such principles in practice, however, we must also examine the basic ways in which we perceive diversity. How do various ethnic groups reflect the variety of their identities?

CHAPTER SIX

PARAMETERS OF DIVERSITY

DIFFERENCES OR DIVERSITY?

A local McDonald's for Kids often becomes the source of a fast-food lunch for us between classes. Three or four game computers are popular with the children, and the recorded scripts can be heard repeatedly. One is a story about a bird and an owl that want to claim the same tree as their home. After some disagreement, the owl comes up with a possible compromise. The bird can claim the tree during the day, since the owl only plans to be awake during the night. The owl, in turn, will consider the tree his throughout the night. The little bird exclaims, "You sleep during the day? How strange!" The owl replies, "No, not strange—just different."

Consciously or unconsciously, the perception of being different is often equated with being strange. People from other cultures expose us to customs and values that may be different from our own without being either superior or inferior to ours. Being different does not require a valuative quality. Before the emphasis upon diversity, it was not uncommon for schools to refer to children from ethnic groups or lower socioeconomic levels as "culturally disadvantaged." Currently, of course, it is accepted that a culture different from the mainline culture does not automatically imply a handicap.

One of the goals of a multicultural perspective is to understand individuals from cultures different from our own. By doing so, our own lives are enriched as we learn about the values and customs of various groups. Learning about other cultures also enables us to understand and relate more accurately with people who do not share our own socioeconomic and cultural backgrounds. A society as a whole is enriched as it learns to view events and situations from a different perspective.

In the quest to recognize and to appreciate the diversity of ethnic groups, care must be taken to avoid ethnic labeling and stereotyping. As we study the traditions and lifestyles of various groups, we may allow a few primary characteristics to become the lens by which an entire cultural group is viewed. In actuality, a great deal of heterogeneity exists in each group, regardless of the ethnic background. We must diligently guard against turning the challenge of multiculturalism into a situation of furthered stereotyping and generalizations.

Developing a sensitivity to the characteristics of groups of people is valuable. However, because each group possesses intragroup diversity, one cannot ascribe a general characteristic to all members of a certain group. To do so may result in discriminatory practices or incorrect explanations for attitudes or behavior.

Differences also exist between generations and subgroups within ethnic groups. Assimilation is experienced on different levels so that some tend to abandon certain elements of their traditional culture, while others hold rather tenaciously to their cultural heritage. The degree to which members identify with the group is affected by factors such as skin color, social class, and personal experiences.

An early view of the properties of minority groups included "physical or cultural characteristics that distinguish them from the dominant group."[1] Since the 1960s, groups of color have urged educators and the media to focus on their histories and cultures. More recently, minority and ethnic groups which are not distinctively different in appearance from the dominant group have also asked that attention be given to the history and contributions made by their cultures.

We have selected key concepts related to ethnic groups which we feel are helpful in gaining a better understanding of the diversity and distinctives of such groups in general. One approach to use when considering distinctives of a cultural group is to focus on outward differences or manifestations of a culture, the explicit or surface component. Another approach, the one which we have selected, is to focus on the implicit culture, the less discernable component which is evidenced in values, interaction, and social patterns and behaviors.[2] The concepts which we will include are values and attitudes, relational and family structures, and communication and learning patterns.

Three areas directly related to the above concepts are value orientation, family patterns, and learning patterns. A general definitive background for each of these aspects is needed before the more specific ethnic distinctives are surveyed.

VALUE ORIENTATION

Kluckhohn and Strodtbeck have researched the values of different ethnic minorities along five dimensions: time, activity, social relations, humanity-nature relationship, and the basic nature of humanity.[3] As members of groups experience common social problems within these five areas, they will tend to demonstrate a generalized response.

Although there are many possible solutions to these problems, Kluckhohn and Strodtbeck feel that the selected solutions are primarily limited to three in each area. These selections tend to follow a ranked order. The dominant choice represents first-order value, but may be substituted with a second- or third-order selection.

The dominant Euro-American middle-class perspective will often differ from minority groups in value selection when solving problems. Summarized below are the various ranked values for the above five dimensions as Kluckhohn and Strodtbeck theorize they are preferred by mainline Americans. As various ethnic groups are considered in other chapters, differences will become apparent. It must be remembered, of course, that members of the same minority group will often differ from one another in their responses.

Time for the dominant middle-class takes a Future orientation. What is done today is planned with the future in mind. Tomorrow is valued more than yesterday or today. Second-order would be given to the Present-time orientation, with Past-time receiving third-order placement.

Relative to *Activity,* the dominant middle-class will value Doing. Accomplishment and product are given respect. Upon meeting a new acquaintance, a soon-to-be-asked question will be, "What do you do?" Upon retirement, a sense of loss may be felt because one is left only with Being which has not been consistently valued throughout life.

Preference for the Individual is the primary mainstream North American value for the *Relational* orientation. This first-order choice is expected and rewarded from a young age. Self-interest has become an accepted motivation for action, even if it creates obstacles for others. A second-order choice would be the Collateral orientation, characterized by the democratic nature of America. Supposedly each has an equal opportunity to achieve in our democracy and supposedly power is equally distributed. The lineal or hierarchical framework is given third place value even though government and business sectors often relate to individuals through organizational flow charts in a top down bureaucratic approach.

In the *Humanity-Nature* orientation, mastery over Nature is the first-order choice of dominant society. Almost all, if not all, problems created by Nature will eventually be overcome by Humanity. Second-order choice is Subjugated-to-Nature, necessary when a problem is not overcome and we appeal to the deity. A third choice is Harmony-with-Nature, which assumes that certain problems occur when there is disharmony with nature, a perspective considered somewhat magical or superstitious by mainstream Americans.

The first-order choice for the *Nature of Humanity* during early America was the view that people were born evil. This position has slipped to second-order preference, although it is still maintained by conservative Christianity. This position has been replaced today with a neutral orientation, assuming neither good nor evil but left to the effect of the environment. Third-order preference, based on the views of Rousseau, is the Good-but-Corruptible orientation, a noble savage that can be contaminated by a wicked civilization.

The above views represent the general value orientation of the dominant American public. However, ethnic groups differ in their value orientation in these five areas as they attempt to solve common human problems. As we consider specific ethnic groups, attention will be given to their differing value orientations.

FAMILY STRUCTURE

Family therapists have identified four types of behaviors and patterns that are found in family structure: cultural patterns, dysfunctional patterns of cultural transition, transcultural dysfunctional patterns, and situational stress patterns.[4] It would seem that these four areas are of interest when considering the family structure of specific ethnic groups. Each ethnic group will have a generalized cultural family pattern. The specifics of that family pattern will in turn effect dysfunctional patterns related to cultural differences with other groups. Also inherent in each distinctive group will be stress patterns which occur as the cultural pattern interfaces with society in pragmatic, day-by-day events.

The *cultural family pattern* includes family roles and rules, as well as belief systems and developmental norms, that are culturally determined. *Dysfunctional patterns of cultural transition* are those patterns that were used to assist the family originally in adaptation, but which have since become detrimental to effective family functioning. For example, parents may find it difficult to accept their eldest child's decision to leave home because the family has become dependent upon him or her to relate to a culture different from their own.

Transcultural patterns are those which are more or less universal patterns with families and seem to be characteristic of families regardless of ethnic background. A pattern such as the dependent-independent struggle between parents and children is an expected event across most cultures, despite the fact that the content of the pattern may be described in terms of an ethnic perspective.

Situational stress patterns are events which a family experiences as it interfaces with society. These are often directly affected by factors within the family's culture. For example, the family that does not have finances to buy lunch tickets for their children at school and lacks knowledge of the social service agencies available, due to their inability to speak English, will demonstrate stress patterns that are caused directly by their environment and indirectly by their culture. In such cases, what is needed is assistance from individuals who can serve to negotiate between the family and institutional, state, or federal resources.

Two cautions must be noted when identifying distinctives in cultural family patterns for specific ethnic groups. One is the fact that to make a broad cultural generalization regarding a specific ethnic group does not take into consideration the many variations that will be found in a group due to regional and socioeconomic differences. Marked dissimilarities in the same ethnic group will be found in families that come from rural, semirural, or urban areas. Poor or working-class families will differ from families in professional or middle and upper socioeconomic levels. Generational differences are also important. Thus, the general descriptions need to be given a more specific definement when applied to a specific location or community level.

A second caution is that the cultural norms for a group are those which represent the *public* reality of a group and are characteristic of what a group advocates as relationships and behaviors which "ought" to be true. This is not always consistent with the *private* realities of the group, how things "really" are. What needs to be considered is how both the public and the private will be combined within ethnic families. This fact, of course, is true for both majority and minority families.

LEARNING PATTERNS

The increasing ethnic diversity of the United States and Canada is especially evident in their school systems. It is estimated that by the year 2000, one third of all school children in the U.S. will represent one of the four major ethnic minority groups—African American, Hispanic American, Native American, and Asian American.[5]

An important dimension to consider when discussing diversity in North American education is the differences found in educational achievement and in teaching-learning strategies. It should be noted that it is preferable to focus on cultural differences rather than cultural deficiencies.

An accepted conclusion is that learning differences are demonstrated by the general population of various cultural backgrounds. It must be emphasized, however, that the majority of researchers do not associate cognitive deficiencies and heredity with those differences. It is primarily the "social culture" and not "race" or "social class" that account for the differences found. Styles are learned and not innate. Successful academic performance is possible when the appropriate social culture is provided.

Research has suggested a number of areas in which patterns of mental abilities and motivational systems for ethnic minorities differ from that of the Anglo-American middle-class culture. Stodolsky and Lesser compared four mental abilities among basic ethnic groups in America and concluded that "ethnicity does affect the pattern of mental abilities and, once the pattern specific to the ethnic group emerges, social-class variations within the ethnic group do not alter this basic organization."[6] The seriousness of such conclusions is highlighted when we observe that the educational approach in most learning settings, public or private, religious or secular, are more consistent with the learning patterns and styles of Anglo Americans than with those of ethnic minority groups.

Howard Gardner's 1983 publication, *Frames of Mind,* helped educators realize that there exists "multiple intelligences" and that individuals are capable of several forms of information

processing rather than the one or two types normally emphasized in public education.[7] While not written specifically for a
multicultural application, it certainly has significance for this
area. His research is important because it emphasizes that the
various talents and abilities previously considered inferior or
unexceptional should be considered as part of the many forms
of intelligence. This approach brings to light that it is cultural
values that have often encouraged preconceptions regarding the
inferior status of certain ethnic groups.

Research relative to diversity in education has focused
much of its attention on two areas: learning styles of minority
students and the development of measurement instruments that
give attention to cultural attributes. Objective and comprehensive approaches to assessment are certainly needed so that students are judged equitably. However, for the purposes of this
book, it is believed that the most helpful aspect to stress is
learning patterns or styles, since this is more applicable to
church teaching than measurement instruments.

A definition of "learning style" has been more often debated than universally accepted. The 1983 National Task Force on
Learning Style and Brain Behavior developed a definition that
is commonly accepted. It is used here because of its emphasis
on cultural experiences.

> Learning style is that consistent pattern of behavior and per-
> formance by which an individual approaches educational ex-
> periences. It is the composite of characteristic cognitive, affec-
> tive, and physiological behaviors that serve as relatively stable
> indicators of how a learner perceives, interacts with, and re-
> sponds to the learning environment. It is formed in the deep
> structure of neural organization and personality [that] molds
> and is molded by human development and the cultural experi-
> ences of home, school, and society.[8]

Swisher and Deyhle describe learning styles as the assumption that "people perceive the world in different ways, learn
about the world in different ways, and demonstrate what they
have learned in different ways."[9] Hilliard defines style as the
"consistency in the behavior of a person or a group that tends
to be habitual—the manifestation of a predisposition to ap-

proach things in a characteristic way."[10]

Historically, the interest in learning styles is often traced back to the 1950s when Witkin and associates studied cognitive style in terms of the field-dependent and field-independent dimension. Tests with embedded figures were used to determine how a person's perception of an item was influenced by its surrounding field. Individuals were found to differ in that some saw the items as separate from the surrounding field, designated as *field independent,* while others had difficulty locating the figures. The perception of individuals in the latter category was dominated by the surrounding field, and thus were designated as *field dependent.* Field independent individuals perceived themselves and objects as independent of the surrounding field. Field dependent individuals perceived themselves and objectives in relation to the field and found it more difficult to separate an item from its background.

Other researchers have used different terms to describe the same differences. "Field sensitive" and "field independent" was used by Ramírez and Castañeda,[11] and "analytical" and "relational" by Rosalie Cohen.[12] Cohen distinguished between learners who are "splitters" and those who are "lumpers." "Splitters" are learners who include the total context when giving meaning to a stimulus, whereas "lumpers" perceive a stimulus as having significance in and of itself.[13]

Witkin associated general characteristics with his two designated types of learners.[14] Field-independent learners were thought to be skilled at abstract analytical thought, but considered less sensitive to the emotions of others and having less developed social skills. They were more intrinsically motivated and less influenced by social reinforcement. Field-dependent learners, on the other hand, while less skilled at analytical problem solving, tended to be very much in tune with their social environment and to have highly developed social skills. Consequently, they were more extrinsically motivated and were influenced by their social environment.

Early studies which resulted from Witkin's work in field dependence-independence learning styles identified additional characteristics felt to be representative of the two approaches to learning. The discriminatory factor which received attention was the extent of activity expended in dealing with one's environment. Field-independent individuals, who perceived themselves as independent of the surrounding field, were seen as more active and assertive. Field-dependent individuals, who found it more difficult to separate themselves from the surrounding field, were believed to be more passive in personality. This associated a more negative attitude toward field-dependent individuals. These earlier studies were later revised, based on further research by both Witkin and others, so that the negative association was removed. Witkin and associates presented the field dependence-independence dimension as bipolar rather than unipolar and one of style rather than ability. Consequently, both were viewed as having advantages and disadvantages.

During the past two decades, the research approach used by Witkin has been applied to the relationship between culture and cognitive style. Ramírez and Castañeda are especially to be noted for their extensive research which applies Witkin's theory to ethnic groups. Their studies and those of others have shown that there is a relationship between culture and learning styles and that the socialization practices of a particular culture has a definite role in determining learning behavior preferences in children.[15]

Research on culturally unique learning styles has shown that members of different ethnic groups do exhibit different patterns of learning. Such findings emphasize the fact that each culture focuses on achievement in certain areas and that agents of socialization for that culture employ certain approaches to encourage certain interests and aptitudes.

Schools in our culture have often asked students to reject their established learning approach and to adopt new ones. The sanctioned approaches are those which have been established as superior by educational institutions or majority groups. Schools tend to plan their curriculum goals around learning styles that are more analytical or field independent, creating a potential obstacle for the student whose style tends to be more relational or field dependent.

Researchers do not believe, however, that stylistic differences are the cause of the higher than average number of minority students who score below national averages. Hilliard believes that much of the academic failure in minority groups can be explained by "systematic inequities in the delivery" of the pedagogical approach. It is his belief that preservice training must encourage prospective teachers to develop a variety of pedagogical methods that will accommodate the varied styles represented by the diversity of today's classrooms.[16]

CONCLUSION

A national American culture is common to all Americans. Within Christianity, there are also shared beliefs based on theological truths that are a part of a shared culture. However, in addition, each person has an ethnic heritage which causes one to identify with certain value orientations and behavioral styles that may not be a part of the shared theological or national American culture. The degree to which this exists differs from individual to individual. A multicultural perspective within the church will assist members to develop a sensitivity and awareness of the unique aspects of each group so that effective communication and ministry across different subcultures occurs.

In this chapter we have attempted to give an overview of three general dimensions in which ethnic cultures often differ from the more EuroAmerican perspective. The three areas of diversity emphasized were value orientations, family patterns, and educational patterns. Although there are many specific aspects within, as well as outside of, these three areas are most commonly experienced as a part of day-to-day life.

It is our purpose in the following chapters to provide information which will assist readers in obtaining a general understanding of the distinctives of four primary ethnic groups. Of special interest will be the three dimensions examined in this chapter: value orientation, family patterns, and educational perspectives. This brief synopsis should be viewed only as a starting point in the challenge to understand other cultures.

Two points need to be made about the approach selected. One, the selection of ethnic groups for special attention could mislead the reader since the concern of this book is multicultural and thus is not limited to multiethnic. We would have preferred to include special chapters on other cultural influences as well, but the limitations of time and space do not permit us to do so. Of equal concern would be the factors of poverty, sex, and disabilities.

Second, the four ethnic groups we will discuss were selected because they are most commonly included in research and consequently have the greatest wealth of information available. Again, limitations have required us to survey only four primary groups. It should be noted, however, that the *Harvard Encyclopedia of American Ethnic Groups* describes over 100 different ethnic groups.[17] It is with this awareness of the many groups that are not represented that we proceed to give an overview of four groups.

CHAPTER SEVEN

EXAMINING HISPANIC-AMERICAN CULTURE

BACKGROUND

Linda Chavez, in an article titled "Out of the Barrio," notes that before the "affirmative action age," there were no "Hispanics." Various subgroups were simply referred to by their national appellations, that is, Puerto Ricans, Cubans, Mexicans, and so on. With the 1970s and equal opportunity programs, the term "Hispanic" became a useful term for inclusional reference.[1] In 1975 the Federal Interagency Committee on Education defined *Hispanic* as "a person of Mexican, Puerto Rican, Cuban, Central or South American, or other Spanish culture or origin, regardless of race."[2]

While "Hispanic" more precisely refers to the cultures of Spain, Portugal, and South America, the term is also utilized for those of Mexican ancestry. *Hispanic* will be used in this chapter as a generic reference to all of the diverse communities reflecting this heritage. This would involve such ethnic groupings as Mexican Americans, Chicanos, Spanish Americans, Latin Americans, Mexicans, Puerto Ricans, Cubans, Guatemalans, and Salvadorans.[3]

PROFILE

By far in the United States the largest grouping is that of Mexican heritage. In 1990 the Census Bureau noted a population of 12,565,000 Mexican Americans. They are the most rapidly growing ethnic group.[4] The three other major Hispanic groups are the Puerto Ricans, Cubans, and Central and South Americans. These four groups account for approximately 92 percent of Hispanics in the U.S.[5] These groups together will soon constitute the largest minority in the United States. By the year 2060 it is projected that the total Latino population will number 54.2 million and will surpass the black population (projected to be 53.7 million) as our largest minority group.[6]

The United States is also host to large numbers of Guatemalan and Nicaraguan refugees. It is estimated that there are more than half a million Salvadorans who have fled a ten-year civil war in their country.

With the death of dictator Rafael Trujillo in 1961, large numbers of Dominicans arrived in the United States on immigrant visas. During the early 1960s, Dominican immigration characteristically moved from agricultural regions to urban areas of the Dominican Republic, and then to America. Since then, the pattern is more likely to be a direct movement from rural areas in the Republic to the United States.[7]

Within this chapter, we will attempt to give an overview of the more apparent social and educational distinctives of Hispanic Americans. As information relative to Hispanic-American groups is considered, it is essential to keep in mind that the profile presented is highly generalized. We are not suggesting that there is a *typical* Hispanic American. There is no single description that can be considered typical of a whole culture.

As is true of most ethnic groups, Hispanic Americans are often viewed as a homogeneous group. In reality, they differ with respect to physical characteristics, class, education, and occupation, as well as religious and political beliefs. Further, this perception may include negative stereotypes related to socioeconomic class or educational attainment. Such stereotypes are erroneously applied when the values and lifestyles of Hispanic Americans are not understood.

The diverse backgrounds of Hispanic Americans must be taken into consideration when developing educational programs and procedures specifically for their culture. There is no one characterization that will apply to all. Values will vary in terms of family, community, and ethnic identification. The customs and attitudes of first-generation immigrants will differ greatly from third-generation Hispanic Americans. Even dissimilar geographical locations will result in group differences. The Hispanic American living in the Midwest will have quite different experiences from one living in California or Texas. Salvadorans may vary in many ways from Cubans; even the Spanish language is spoken differently in Mexico, for example, than in Spain.

We must further realize that any culture is dynamic and constantly changing. We can discuss that which has traditionally been true of a cultural group but must understand that the various factors initiating change in all cultures are at work. A new and different culture is always in the process of slowly emerging. Therefore, aspects of the Hispanic-American culture must be considered in terms of its dynamic nature.

This chapter will give a historical overview of the migration of three major subgroups within the Hispanic-American culture: Mexican Americans, Puerto Ricans, and Cubans. This will be followed by social and educational perspectives for Hispanic Americans as a total group, keeping in mind that the various subgroups do not represent racial or cultural unity.

HISTORY

Mexican Americans

Mexican Americans are the largest of all Hispanic groups in America. According to a 1990 census report, they represent 60 percent of all Hispanics in the United States.[8] Their population is also increasing at a faster rate than that of Puerto Ricans and Cubans. As an ethnic group of color, they are second in size only to African Americans. In addition to the census count, there is an undetermined number of undocumented Mexicans living in the United States.[9]

For the sake of uniformity, the term Mexican-Americans

will be used in this section. However, this is done with the understanding that a number of other terms have been used as well for self-identification. Among the terms preferred by some groups are Hispano, Spanish American, Tejano, Latino, Latin American, Mexican, and Mexicano.[10]

A majority of the Mexican-American population reside in Southwestern states, primarily on the land that was acquired from Mexico in 1853. At that time, over 75,000 Mexicans living in the area became United States citizens. This was a relatively small number in relation to the white settlers who were eager to claim the land and who tended to take a superior attitude toward the native Mexicans. By the end of the century, Mexican Americans had lost ownership of much of their land and were a subordinated cultural group.

For the remainder of the eighteenth century, the Mexican-American population experienced a very slow growth. Since the turn of the century, however, the population of Mexican Americans has shown a significant and consistent increase with the exception of the Depression years. As a result of the economic crisis of the Depression, many lost their jobs and returned to Mexico or were deported.

During the later years of World War II, a new wave of Mexican immigration began when farm workers immigrated with temporary work permits. In years following, Mexican immigrants came to America primarily for economic purposes. A majority of this more recent group were either born in Mexico or have parents who were born in Mexico.

Although at one time a primarily rural ethnic group, Hispanic Americans are now very urbanized. Accompanying this is the change from agricultural to urban labor following World War II. However, this move for the Mexican American was approximately a generation later than was true for even recent European immigrants. The pattern of discrimination that Mexican Americans often experienced in employment decreased their opportunity as an ethnic group to experience a general improvement in socioeconomic levels.[11]

Mexican Americans vary greatly in the degree to which they hold to the traditional values of their culture. Some are very *traditional* in that family values will be similar to those of communities in Mexico. A *dualistic* community will be made up of Mexican Americans who hold to values which are a combination of both Anglo-American values and traditional Mexican values. Mexican Americans who represent a *traditional* approach are those in which there is an amalgamation of Anglo- and Mexican-American values.[12] It is believed, however, that even the Mexican-American families who have resided in the United States for a number of years tend to retain many of their traditional characteristics. A large number of Mexican Americans identify Spanish as their native tongue.[13] The tendency is to become acculturated but not assimilated.

During the 1960s, the Chicano Movement gave leadership to the fight for equality in all areas: political, social, economic, and educational. Among the many goals was an increase in the number of Mexican-American leaders in the Catholic Church. The activist members of this movement placed an emphasis on the Mexican-Indian heritage of Mexican Americans as opposed to the Spanish heritage that had traditionally been emphasized.[14] The Chicano Movement was only one of many resistance activities since 1848 in which Mexican Americans have attempted to have more control over their lives and destinies.

Mexican Americans experienced some economic and educational progress in the 1960s. Since that time, an increased number of Mexican Americans in lower-level work positions has nullified economic gains. Likewise, educational attainment has not shown an increase similar to national averages. Approximately 27 percent of Mexican Americans graduate from high school and approximately 6 percent graduate from four years of college. This compares with 39 percent and 20 percent respectively for the total American population.[15] Similar to other ethnic minority groups, the Mexican Americans experience discrimination in nearly every area of life—particularly in housing, education, and employment.

A new middle-class group of Mexican-American professionals developed during the 1980s. This segment of the Mexican-American population is sometimes criticized for having little contact with the overall problems of Mexican Americans as a minority group. They have been more involved in the corporate world than in social causes. Accompanying this movement, however, is an increase in political clout as a number of Mexican Americans have been elected as mayors, governors, and members of Congress.

At the same time, acts of discrimination continue. An example is the English-Only perspective that seeks to have English endorsed as the "official language." However, Mexican-American leaders and communities have responded with creative approaches to such obstacles in the past and can be expected to continue to do so.

Puerto Ricans

The Caribbean island of Puerto Rico is located approximately 1,000 miles southeast of Florida. It is 100 miles long and 35 miles wide. Puerto Rico itself represents a sizable immigrant population. Because of this, it is estimated that if population trends on both the island and the mainland continue, the number of Puerto Ricans on the mainland by the end of this century will either equal or exceed the number of Puerto Ricans living on the island.[16]

The population of Puerto Rico is a mixture of Taino Indians, Africans, and Spaniards. Skin color may vary and include many shades and mixtures.[17] Racially, Puerto Ricans are a mixture of Caucasian, Indian, and black heritages and may often be classified as black in the U.S.[18] There is a higher rate of intermarriage between Puerto Ricans of different color than is true of Americans in general.[19]

Puerto Ricans have their own distinct culture, yet suffer from a lack of knowledge concerning their heritage. This is in part due to the rather obscure and vague manner in which they have been governed by two nations. Until the Spanish-American War, Spain ruled Puerto Rico from across the Atlantic in a rather ambiguous way. In 1898, Puerto Rico was ceded to the United States by the Treaty of Paris, which formally ended the Spanish-American War. Since that time, Puerto Rico has had a somewhat unclear relationship with the United States.

Although Puerto Rico is not considered a state, Puerto-

Ricans have been considered citizens of the United States since 1917. In 1952, Puerto Rico was designated as a commonwealth. Commonwealth status implies a certain amount of dependence on the United States, but without senatorial or congressional representatives. Alternatives which have been suggested for their present status include both total independence and statehood. Others feel that retaining the status quo is best.

In spite of being subject to the military draft, Puerto Ricans may not vote for the President of the United States. At the same time, they do not pay federal taxes. Puerto Ricans who live on the American mainland possess all rights due citizens of the states in which they reside.

Migration of Puerto Ricans to the mainland has been heaviest since World War II. This has been due to a number of reasons. Since Puerto Ricans are American citizens, they were not under quota restriction. Unemployment has continued to be a problem on the island and most have friends and family living in the States so that relocation can be simplified.

As the second largest Hispanic-American group, Puerto Ricans represent about 14 percent of the total number of Hispanics living in the United States.[20] Approximately 42 percent of all Puerto Ricans now reside in the continental United States. About one half of that number were born in the States. The Puerto Rican population on the mainland increased by 32 percent between 1980 and 1990. Current increases are due more to new births than to migration.[21]

A situation which makes Puerto Ricans unique in comparison with other ethnic groups is their ability to travel freely between their homeland and mainland America. At times, the U.S. Census reports have shown almost a balance between the departure rate and the arrival rate. Although it is difficult to separate the number into visitors and permanent residents, it is true that migration back to the island has been heavy.[22]

Because of language and cultural differences, Puerto Ricans arriving in America experience a transition period similar to that of immigrants coming from Europe or Asia. The socioeconomic conditions for second generation Puerto Ricans has improved, but their continuing level of poverty is a problem. Two related facts are the high unemployment rate of Puerto Rican males and the increasing number of female-headed households.[23]

A variety of social organizations have been developed specifically to assist Puerto Ricans. The Puerto Rican Teachers Association represents Puerto Rican teachers and is active in working for Puerto Rican interests within the school system. Of special note is their attempt to increase the number of Puerto Ricans in teaching and administrative positions and their work in the promotion of bilingual education. The Puerto Rican Forum represents social, political, and business interests of Puerto Ricans on both local and national levels. The Puerto Rican Family Institute, established in 1960, has been especially effective in its efforts to preserve the health, well-being, and integrity of Puerto Ricans and other Hispanic families in the United States.[24]

Discrimination in Puerto Rico focuses more on class than on color. As a result, when Puerto Ricans come to the United States, they are not always prepared for the specific designations of "white" or "black" that is more common in America, nor for the discrimination that often accompanies color. On the island, a sensitivity to "whiteness" exists, but this is offset by the prizing of "blackness." "Mi negro," meaning "my black one" represents an endearing phrase.[25]

Puerto Ricans have a higher index of segregation than Mexican Americans or Cuban Americans.[26] The Puerto Rican model may best be identified as one of bicultural adaptation. One reason for this is the close proximity of the island and the resultant flow back and forth from the homeland and the mainland. Another factor is the persistent use of the Spanish language. An estimated 70 to 80 percent of Puerto Ricans consider Spanish as their primary language.[27] In spite of this tendency toward segregation, Puerto Ricans have been able to both retain aspects of their traditional culture and, at the same time, develop creative ways to contribute to the overall American society.

Cuban Americans

Cuba was able to maintain its independence following the Spanish-American War, unlike Puerto Rico which became a colony of the United States. Nevertheless, the United States stayed connected with Cuba economically and politically until the Castro revolution in 1959.

Although Cuban migration occurred as early as the nineteenth century, most of the current population of Cuban Americans is associated with immigration since the 1960s. Three phases of Cuban migration have been identified.[28]

The first phase consists of two waves between the years of 1959 and 1965. The first wave included immigrants who arrived between 1959 and the Bay of Pigs invasion in 1961. When Castro gained power in 1959, a large number of Cuban immigrants came to the United States with the intent of returning when Cuba was more settled politically. These immigrants were characterized as a privileged class, primarily landowners representing professional, managerial, and commercial positions.[29]

The second wave within this first phase consisted of those who arrived during the years following the Bay of Pigs invasion, up to 1965. Travel was limited to more unconventional means such as small boats and rafts. Consequently, the rate of immigration slowed down from the earlier wave in which they arrived primarily on commercial flights. Immigrants in this wave were middle-class professionals, but were more truly representative of refugees since they left without the assumption that they would be returning to Cuba.[30]

Of this early group, approximately 95 percent identified themselves as white in the 1970 census. It is speculated that black Cubans may have been hesitant to immigrate to the United States for fear that they would face racial discrimination.[31]

The second phase, the Cuban Refugee Airlift, occurred between 1965 and 1973. Cubans arriving during the second phase were more likely to be middle and lower-middle class. Their purpose for coming to the United States was often economical.

The population of Cuban Americans as a result of these first two phases was not representative of the people of Cuba as a whole. Immigrants were primarily white and tended more likely to be older adults or women.[32] Cuban Americans represent a higher proportion of business and professional persons than would be true of Cuba. Most of those in the higher socioeconomic levels immigrated during the early 1960s.[33]

A third phase began in 1980 when approximately 129,000 Cubans, called "Marielitos" after the port from which they sailed, came to the U.S. in one year. These more recent immigrants included a greater ratio of the poor and the underprivileged.[34] A portion of this group was made up of prisoners or mental patients allowed to leave by Castro. Hundreds of these later refugees have been imprisoned and in many cases deprived of civil rights.[35]

Although the median income for Cuban Americans is below that of the national level, it is higher than that of Puerto Ricans or Mexican Americans. Cubans arriving with professional training have incurred obstacles in obtaining white-collar employment. Part of the problem has been mastery of the English language. For some, this has resulted in sacrificing one's native language for the sake of " 'decubanized' overassimilation" in order to have some semblance of success. Since the Spanish language is a very important part of the American Cuban's life, this, by inference, means one's ethnic identity.[36]

An additional problem is that degrees earned in Cuba have not been consistently recognized in the United States. In many cases, Cuban Americans have been willing to accept a lesser position with the intent of obtaining their desired status later. As a whole, a slight loss of occupational status has been experienced for Cuban Americans from upper socioeconomic levels in Cuba.[37]

The church is an important source of support for Cubans. Catholicism is a religious preference for many, although studies have shown that interest in the church decreased as the amount of time lived in the United States increased.[38] Folk-healing traditions, combined with various religious practices, are commonly found in Cuban and other Latino communities. Along with the religious perspective is a more philosophical view of life that is existential in nature. "Here and now" experiences may be emphasized with a focus on aspects such as knowledge or consumerism. Action, doing, and the present are all important components of the Cuban value structure.[39]

The Cubans have overcome many obstacles related to their

migration in order to experience "relative success" in their new homeland. They have been credited with restoring and increasing the beauty of urban areas in which they have settled.[40] The present era may be a transitional one for Cuban Americans so that the actual shape and character which their community will take will change as second- and third-generations contribute to their ethnic group and to America.

SOCIAL DISTINCTIVES

Research on the traditional family structure of the Hispanic American is extensive. Although it is not the purpose of this section to provide a thorough coverage of literature in the area, a generalized understanding of family patterns will be helpful.

Studies of Hispanic Americans often do not make sufficient differentiation among the various Spanish-speaking ethnic groups. In our discussion, as well, the generalized approach necessary for our purposes will not make it possible to include the many regional and generational differences of Hispanic-American families, but will limit the discussion to a view of the more dominant influences. This does not discount the fact that there are marked differences in family patterns as they differ across socioeconomical lines.

The family plays a highly valued role in the life of Hispanic Americans. An important characteristic is the strong presence of the extended family. Grandparents, uncles and aunts can easily permeate the boundaries of the nuclear family and share the responsibilities of caretaking and discipline.

The boundaries are also extended by the *compadrazo* system which includes those individuals with whom the parents have established close bonds as a result of relationships of trust. The *compadrazo* custom establishes two relationships: one between godparents and their godchildren and the other between the parents and the godparents or the co-parents. Such persons may be invited to witness the baptism of children in the role of *compadres* for the parents and *padrinos* or godparents to the child.[41] The extension of kinship ties has been called "familism" and is characterized by "personalism," a focus on relationships rather than tasks.[42]

The family structure is normally hierarchical in nature with the father perceived as the authority and the mother subservient in role. Growing girls and boys are exposed to clearly defined sex roles that remain fairly constant considering the many social changes during the last two decades. Age and sex are important determinants of authority, thus the most powerful position belongs to older males. The traditional idea of *machismo* is the strong, more revered male who is protective of the submissive and virtuous woman, the dedicated caregiver of their children. However, the changes in the contemporary role for women during the past decades may have caused these roles to become somewhat less defined.

Close relationships give the parents an important function in the development of identity with their children. The following quote by a Latino adolescent girl demonstrates the mother as a role model of behavior and values.

> As far as I can remember, my mother was strong and independent. She loved us so much that she protected us from the dangers of the barrio. She kept the family together as long as she could, and the traditions were a big part of her life. She is a very pretty woman with strong Mexican Indian features: high cheek-bones and a tired clear face. She is short, heavyset, and has a physically tired body. She always wore a little make-up and red lipstick. . . . "Mi madre" is the pride and joy of my life and she is not only my mother but my closest friend.[43]

Respect is an important value within children-parent relationships. Fathers are respected for their control and mothers for their nurturance, providing a fine balance that remains functional. It is speculated that the meaning of "respect" for Hispanic families differs from its understanding in Anglo-American families. For Anglo-Americans, it reflects a fairly "detached, self-assured egalitarianism." For Hispanics, it implies a relationship involving a "highly emotionalized dependence and dutifulness, within a fairly authoritarian framework."[44]

Households are separate from the extended family, but often located in close proximity. Family size is usually larger than that of the Anglo-American family. Relationships with the family of origin remain strong throughout life, characterized by interdependence and loyalty. The life cycle experiences of the family are occasions for celebration and intergenerational involvement. Respect for parental authority remains intact even after children leave home.

Traditionally, phases in the Hispanic family life cycle have differed from the dominant American pattern. Although not as true today for all subgroups, there has been a longer period of time designated for early and middle childhood, a longer courtship period prior to marriage, and consequently a relatively late departure from home. This has contributed to an extended network of intergenerational connectedness between parents and their children.[45]

This strong sense of family identity and high level of interpersonal involvement is in line with certain characteristics often considered as typical of the Hispanic American. Examples are a desire to achieve for family rather than for self and the preference to function cooperatively with others rather than competitively for self. Hispanics at the age of sixteen may work to earn money to assist their family, placing greater importance on their family's needs than their own personal needs.[46]

Parents are very accepting of their children and do not operate with the same urgency of Anglo Americans to meet developmental milestones. Behaviors for which children will be corrected are disobedience, rudeness or showing a lack of respect, and fighting with siblings.

> Many Puerto Rican parents consider American children — who are taught to be self-reliant, aggressive, competitive, and verbally inquisitive — disrespectful. Ideally, in bringing up Puerto Rican children, independence is curtailed while adherence to parental and family demands is encouraged.[47]

High value is placed on being honest and acting with dignity. Sibling relationships are strong and constitute friendships. The relationship with cousins is often comparable to that of siblings.

Whereas the majority of Hispanic-American homes at one time were two-parent families, this has changed along with national averages. Studies now show that 71 percent of all Hispanic children live in homes in which females are the head of the household.[48] Approximately 6 percent of Hispanic children under the age of eighteen live with their grandparents. This compares with the 3.6 percent of white children who live with their grandparents.[49]

Segregation patterns show a difference when black society is compared to Hispanic society. Historically, efforts in this area have been directed toward black students. The U.S. Supreme Court declared in the Keyes case of 1973 that Hispanics also are entitled to the desegregation remedies. In spite of this, "few attempts to integrate Hispanic and non-Hispanic white students have been made."[50]

> In fact, while the level of black student integration has remained relatively stable since the late 1960s, Hispanic students are more segregated today than they were 20 years ago. Meanwhile, gaps in educational attainment and earnings between Hispanics and non-Hispanics continue to widen, offering strong evidence that segregated schools are not preparing the rapidly growing Hispanic student population to succeed in a predominantly non-Hispanic society.[51]

Part of the reason for this difference is Hispanic attitudes. Castellanos states that since racism "has not been institutionalized in Puerto Rico, Mexico, and Cuba," Hispanics do not see desegregation as a primary issue.[52] There is also a difference in black and Hispanic perspectives concerning equal education opportunities. Hispanics are more concerned with bilingual education while African Americans emphasize desegregation.[53] An additional factor is that the segregation of Hispanics was not as pronounced as that of the blacks.[54]

EDUCATIONAL DISTINCTIVES

Many negative and inaccurate characteristics have been associated with the Hispanics as learners. Texas Christian University currently has a publication on its library shelves in which teachers are urged to assist Hispanic students in personal development by motivating them in the areas of cleanliness, responsibility, and motivation.[55] The work begins with the assumption that Hispanic students will be inferior to other students in these areas.

Researchers are in agreement that the most crucial problem facing Hispanic Americans today is education. They are more likely to drop out of school than members of any other ethnic group. As many as 40 percent leave school before the tenth grade. In specific locations, the percentage is even higher, such as 62 percent in New York State. They continue to be one of the most underrepresented subgroups on the college level.[56]

Studies on Hispanic-American education revealed an Anglo bias when teacher interactions were researched. Hispanic students were described as slow, violent, and prone to erratic behavior. The categories in which teacher bias toward Anglos was determined to be statistically significant were: praising, accepting student ideas, questioning, positive teacher response, noncriticizing teacher talk, and student responses.[57] Students react to the evaluation and labels given by their teachers and respond accordingly. One study even found the same negative attitudes of the dominant society perpetuated by teachers within a Mexican-American community.[58]

Since teachers are considered one of the primary socialization agents that reinforce social-class stratification, their attitudes and student expectations are very important. To whatever degree these earlier conceptions of Hispanics as inferior students are sustained in either public or private sectors, the Hispanic American will be penalized in learning settings.

Various explanations have been given for the negative conception that Hispanics originally faced in the public schools of the United States. This preconception is somewhat due to the earlier belief that the Spanish language interferes with the child's ability to learn English. Another view was that the Hispanic's loyalty to family and ethnic group would interfere with his or her assimilation into the mainstream culture of the United States.

Smith and Caskey note eleven "school generalizations" that continue as challenges to Hispanics in education: segregation, language/cultural exclusion, low academic achievement, academic retention, school financing, unfavorable interactions with teachers, inferior curriculum, lower college enrollment, stress, special education, declining number of Chicano teachers, and a fast-expanding population.[59]

THE MULTIPLE-LINGUISTIC CHALLENGE

Prior to contemporary emphasis upon bilingual education, Hispanics were introduced to American schooling via the "immersion" system. They were placed in English-only classes with the expectation that the most gifted would overcome any problems.

> Emotional scars were deep. Mothers and grandmothers brought six- and seven-year-olds to school for the first time and talked soothingly to them in Spanish while foreign words buzzed around their uncomprehending ears. Then, suddenly, they were torn from loving arms and put into a room full of strange sounds and harsh voices. Pleas for help were ignored and as late as the 1950s children who spoke Spanish in school were made to kneel on upturned bottle caps, forced to hold bricks in outstretched hands in the schoolyard, or told to put their nose in a chalk circle drawn on a blackboard. And this would happen in Texas towns that were 98 percent Spanish-speaking.[60]

It was not until the 1950s that Spanish educational needs were realized as the result of large numbers of Mexican-Americans entering the teaching profession. This was accompanied by thousands of Puerto Rican youth enrolling in the schools of New York City and other Eastern cities. An additional factor was an influx of Cubans into Florida and later to other parts of the East Coast.[61] As late as 1969, over 50 percent of Mexican-American students dropped out of high school in Los Angeles.[62]

While modern emphases upon bilingual education have positively changed this scenario, cultural factors inherent in any language preference constitute a continuing challenge for both teacher and student. Because of this environment a student may experience multiple types of "cultural-linguistic personalities." Jackson and Hernandez note the monolingual English, monolingual Spanish, the bilingual, and also the patois.

> Sometimes within this frame of reference Juanito may no longer be Juanito but Johnny, so that the "transculturative" process is applied in reverse. The concept of the differences between the first and second generations cannot be used as it was with the European. Juanito, moreover, is constantly in a state of transition from one culture to the other.[63]

COGNITIVE STYLE

Information on Hispanic-Americans in relationship to education have been drawn primarily from two types of research. First were descriptive studies based on anthropological and sociological methods. The results of these studies pictured the Hispanic American in a negative way: generally unmotivated, passive, and with a low self-esteem. The second type of research was psychological, primarily emphasizing cognitive style. Most of the research utilized the field dependence-independence dimension of cognitive style. The results of early research in this area also contributed to a negative stereotype of the Hispanic American as a learner. Since that time, studies have reported findings that are inconsistent with these earlier studies or, at the least, inconclusive.

Ramírez and Castañeda published a landmark work on the learning styles of Mexican-American children. They researched cognitive style in four different ethnic cultures (Mexican Americans, European Americans, American Indians, African Americans) and found that the Mexican American showed the strongest tendency toward field dependence of the four groups.[64] Ramírez prefers the term "field *sensitive*" to insure that the style does not have a negative connotation.

As a result of such studies, possible comparisons may be made. According to the characteristics associated with field dependence or sensitivity, Mexican Americans tend to prefer working with others to achieve a common goal. Individuals in this category tend to be more sensitive to the feelings and opinions of others than those from cultures which show a tendency for field independence, such as the Anglo American. It must be remembered, however, that studies have found vast differences among the Hispanic learners, with many either field independent or somewhere between the two poles.[65]

Ramírez believes that the cognitive style of Hispanic Americans is a result of the socialization practices of their culture.[66] The traditional Hispanic community encourages the individual to view oneself always within the scope of the family. The Hispanic child is encouraged to be independent and assertive, but

only within the perspective of family needs. Such action is encouraged for the purpose of protecting the family or achieving
for the family. With importance placed on interpersonal relationships, sensitivity to social cues is encouraged. This differs
from the typical middle-class Anglo who is encouraged to establish an identity independent of the family community.

Some studies have found Chicano youth to be more externally controlled than internally controlled. In comparison, Anglos tend to be more internally than externally controlled.[67] Internally controlled individuals have a feeling of control over
their own success or failure. In contrast, externally controlled
individuals tend to feel that they can do little to shape their
destiny but that it will be more controlled by others external to
them. Interestingly, the methodology generally used by teachers
in the American classroom is more effective in motivating those
who are internally controlled than those who are externally
controlled.

Recognizing that different cultures may possess a favored
learning style should encourage church teachers of diverse
classrooms to provide a variety of activities that will utilize different styles. At the same time, giving attention to a group's
preferred style should not stereotype the group with prescribed
methodology. For example, teachers may stress the "cooperative" attribute of the field-dependent learning style and approach Hispanic children primarily in groups, seldom granting
opportunity for single performances or independent choices and
expect more sharing of classroom materials. What may be a
discriminatory practice could be rationalized or justified as a
pedagogical decision.

APPLICATION WITHIN THE CHURCH

The cultural and linguistic factors for any of the groups mentioned in this book may appear so complex that Christian leaders could well question their ability to really make a difference.
It is important to keep in mind that the primary purpose of the
church is not to function in the areas of sociology, anthropology,
or linguistics. Rather, it is the church's purpose to exemplify the

person and teachings of Christ in a manner that can be clearly perceived across all cultures.

Two areas will be noted for application in this section. Although they will be applied especially to the Hispanic-American culture, they are applicable to other minority groups as well. Thus, they are generalized principles for application rather than specialized guidelines.

One area is the family and opportunities for ministry that it provides through pastoral care and counseling. As a whole, minority groups have emphasized family roles and relationships to a greater degree than have Americans with a European background. This has been demonstrated in both the nuclear family unit and in the extended family structure.

The second area we will discuss is the Christian education curriculum. Education through the church provides the setting for change. Communication on a personal level is possible because of small group settings. An exchange of ideas is permitted in the teaching-learning process that is not encouraged through large group meetings. The goal is a multicultural classroom climate in which the atmosphere reflects and respects racial, cultural, gender, ability, and age diversity. This can be accomplished through careful attention to classroom design and conscientious selection and use of curriculum. Of more importance, is the relationship between teacher and student, which, if Christlike, will be that of multicultural personal interaction.

MINISTRY WITH HISPANIC-AMERICAN FAMILIES

The family is an important entry level for the church with any cultural group. It is especially so for the Hispanic population due to the extensive family network included. The values of family loyalty, cohesiveness, and respect for parental authority are all areas in which education and counseling ministries will be appreciated.

Special attention should be given to areas of potential culture conflict. The influences of the dominant society will influence Hispanic youth and young adults in a manner that is inconsistent with the traditional views of the instrumental role for the father and the expressive role for the mother. If a young bride lives with her husband's family, she may find it less tolerable to accept the traditional obligations expected in relationship to her mother-in-law. While most will be able to balance this inconsistency, others may wish for opportunities to discuss conflict that is experienced.

Assistance through both counseling and education is more effectively directed at parent-child relationships than marital relationships. The existence of children validates the marriage more than intimacy issues between spouses in Hispanic-American families.[68]

Most of the Mexican-American population are immigrants and consequently are in the process of cultural transition. Migration requires adaptation by both individual family members and the family unit itself. Church leaders must keep this in the forefront as they plan programs and services for this ethnic group. There will be a great deal of variation as to their position in the process of moving from cultural alienation to cultural integration. Regardless of the position, however, there will be a sense of constant change that needs to be kept in mind when structuring ministry approaches.

Two or three specific situations which will have impact on the family as a result of migration should be noted. As a Hispanic-American family becomes more acculturated, there may be strains on the traditionally accepted rules regarding family roles. Many families will experience separations and reunions of family members which require reorganization of the family unit. The family as a unit may also experience sociocultural isolation. The separation from family members will often motivate the solicitation of new support systems or groups to compensate for lost relationships. The church setting can provide a comfortable environment for members of an ethnic family during this transitional time.

The presence of the extended family will be a source of strength in situations requiring adaptation to poverty, change, or sociocultural isolation. Whereas Anglo-Americans tend to move away from this relational network, Mexican-Americans have been found to move toward the family network.[69] However, migration often involves separation from the extended family. If the family is living in a situation in which the usual family network is not available, greater strain may be experienced by all members of the family unit. The relationship between parents and adolescents may become strained as the developing child seeks influences outside the family and parents become fearful as they sense the lack of supervisory influences that would have been present in the extended family. Consequently, they may react by becoming overly restrictive. Church ministries should focus on both the strengths available when the extended family is present and the potential problems when the influence of the extended family is absent.

Additional problems occur as values of the past must coexist with the generalized values of contemporary America. This problem is especially acute when members of different generations have experienced different degrees of acculturation. Falicov has done extensive study on the process of family reorganization among Mexican-Americans as a result of immigration and acculturation.[70] Three levels of acculturation were identified as common within an extended Mexican-American family. The children will often exist at the most advanced level; the mother and grandparents at the least advanced level. The father usually exists at the intermediate level.

The differences in these acculturation levels can give rise to other intergenerational problems. Adolescent girls who have grown up in North America may demand more autonomy than is traditionally expected of the female. Parents and grandparents may resist the demands for dating at an earlier than expected age. In recent years, an increasing number of Mexican-American females are leaving home to further their education and, in many cases, causing stress in families that hold to more traditional sex roles.[71] There may also be discord when parents in the younger generation adopt a child-rearing pattern that is more complementary to the dominant pattern in society. Grandparents may resist the change, while expecting to have an active role in this task as would have been true traditionally.

Family therapists have noted that it is not uncommon for Hispanic-American couples to experience a sense of emotional separation in mid-life as children begin to leave home. It is projected that this may be more likely when couples have placed greater value on parenting than on relating as a married couple. At the same time, members of the younger generation may not show the same loyalty to this value orientation and create intergenerational stress as a result.

The potential family problems or situations mentioned above are ones which church leaders can use as ministry opportunities through educational and counseling programs. At the same time, it should be noted that the focus should be enhancement of the strengths of the present family organization as opposed to a problem-centered approach. Despite the problems experienced from the effects of immigration, the Hispanic-American family continues to maintain positive intergenerational relationships and to establish healthy family units which reflect their value orientation.

DESIGNING A CHRISTIAN EDUCATION PROGRAM

One of the earliest attempts to identify religious education resources for Hispanic Americans occurred in the late 1970s. A group of Hispanic religious educators met in California with the specific purpose of identifying materials "produced by Hispanics for Hispanics."[72]

This was a refreshing shift from earlier practices. Religious education materials had commonly been the result of simply translating English-language materials produced by the major publishing companies into the Spanish language. Missing in such attempts, of course, was the value orientation and personal perspective of the Hispanic-American heritage.

This same group of Hispanic educators also considered the development of appropriate methodology for preparing Hispanic Americans as religious educators. In some cases, leadership has come from majority groups rather than minority groups because minority members were untrained. In other instances, Hispanic Americans have served as leaders but without specific ministry training. Manuel Ortiz emphasizes the need for leadership training of Hispanic Americans in *The Hispanic Challenge*. He calls attention to the fact that Hispanic Americans represent only a small percentage of the enrollment in Christian College

Coalition schools and Association of Theological Schools institutions.[73]

Listed below are guidelines for the development of a Christian education curriculum for use in Hispanic-American contexts. Although applied to Hispanic Americans in this chapter, the same guidelines are applicable to other minority groups that will be discussed in future chapters.

1. The curriculum should include the basic concerns of the Hispanic-American culture.

As a minority group, Hispanic Americans face many of the same problems incurred by other ethnic groups. Common are the problems of insufficient education, inadequate housing, poverty, and unemployment. Added to this is the development of a cultural identity and the areas of social injustice which they often face, such as unfair judicial practices and racism.

2. The curriculum should acknowledge that the Hispanic-American community has been the recipient of unjust and non-Christian practices and behaviors. Further, that some of this injustice has come either directly or indirectly from members of the body of Christ.

A study commissioned by the World Council of Churches concluded that white racism has affected nearly every aspect of civilization. Further, that all Western institutions, including the church, have inherited this racism in a way that continues today in both manifest and latent forms.[74] A Christian education curriculum which is sensitive to diversity will provide opportunity to both "forgive and be forgiven." The need to forgive or to be forgiven, however, will only occur when there is acknowledgment of past and present injustices. When able to show Christ's love to others, Christians reach out to one another with unconditional acceptance, regardless of past actions and hurts.

3. The Christian education curriculum for Hispanic Americans must include more than just programs, materials, and methodology. The focus must be upon education as a living experience.

The "lived experience" includes attitudes, values, and relationships. Paulo Freire refers to this as "practice" and feels that education can be a liberating process when viewed in this way. Freire's concept of education as liberation is especially meaningful when applied to minority issues.[75]

The emphasis upon education as a "living experience" encourages us to view each culture as in-process. Rather than studying a culture only in terms of its traditions, customs, and practices, the emphasis is upon the dynamic nature of the culture. An attempt is made to understand the culture of an ethnic group as it is "in creation." Culture in-process builds upon the past as it moves toward a future.

4. Group interaction and reflection should be an intentional part of the curriculum.

"Monologism" is a form of teaching that involves unidirectional communication. Someone who knows, *tells* the truth to someone who does not know, but does not *listen* to the other.

This approach to teaching has been identified as a problem found in Latin American evangelical churches and also affects Hispanic theological education in America.[76] Needless to say, it is a problem found in the majority of U.S. churches and schools as well.

The tendency toward monologism can be counteracted by programming small group opportunities and developing cell groups in which authentic sharing can occur. Learning that racism must be eradicated will not change lives until the truth becomes personalized. Opportunities must be given to acknowledge and accept responsibility both to forgive and be forgiven. This can be possible as provision is made for informal interaction and candid reflection on the issues of racism.

5. The Christian education curriculum materials should reflect the diversity of American people in the visual environment of the physical facilities.

If the church is predominantly Hispanic American, more than half of the images and materials in the environment should reflect their background. If the church is predominately white, at least one-half of the images and materials should reflect other cultures in order to emphasize the diversity of America and to offset the "white as dominant culture" perspective.

Diversity in images and materials includes more than ethnic diversity. Diversity in materials should include differently abled children, the working-class life, single-parent families as well as men and women in nontraditional role positions.

Purchasing new materials to show this diversity is not always necessary. Begin by developing a file of accurate, nonstereotypic pictures of people with impairments, people of color, and men and women in nontraditional roles. Magazines such as *Young Children, Ebony,* and *Life* are good sources. Calendars produced by special interest groups provide excellent pictures. Taking your own photographs or obtaining pictures from families in the congregation is another source. Children can make small books for their classrooms entitled, "All Kinds of Families" or "All Kinds of People," in which they have included their own script and pictures.

At the same time, a portion of the budget should be set aside to add resources. Dolls representing the various cultures are a good addition for both boys and girls in children's class-rooms. Books representing the Hispanic-American culture are a must. Since there is presently a limited number of titles written from a Christian perspective, general books should be added even though they will need teacher-led discussion to apply Christian truths.

Other cautions are to be considered. Current images may need to be eliminated from our facilities if they are inaccurate or stereotypic. Curriculum materials should picture biblical characters accurately according to their ethnic background. To-ken diversity of a particular group within the dominant group should be avoided. Images of Hispanic Americans in the past should not be substituted for current images. Images of people in other countries, such as the common missions approach, should not be used as a substitute for Americans of that culture. An example would be using pictures and books about Mexico to teach about Hispanic Americans.

6. *The Christian education curriculum for a church whose constituents are primarily Hispanic American should be planned and designed by members of the Hispanic-American ethnic group.*

Major publishing companies have taken the beginning steps in offering curriculum materials developed by ethnic writers. These are steps in the right direction but sufficient progress has not been made. However, Hispanic Americans must be active rather than passive in bringing this goal into existence. As mentioned in the introduction, some groups are active in identifying materials developed by Hispanic Americans for Hispanic Americans. This is to be desired over the passive approach of waiting for non-Hispanics to develop material through the process of adaptation. The goal is more than token representation.

7. Christian education within the Hispanic-American context should include mentoring.

The message of mentoring is "you can do it and it will be worth the effort." Although primarily applied to children and youth, the concept is of importance to all. The church must assume the responsibility to provide mentors during the formative years of childhood and adolescence. Older youth and young adults can actively seek out a mentor from their ethnic group. Hispanic-American adults must assume the responsibility of being a mentor and intentionally reach out to those of younger generations.

Mentoring is a vital element in the task of training Hispanic Americans for leadership. Manuel Ortiz applied mentoring specifically to the area of leadership training for Hispanic Americans when he defined mentoring as "a personal undertaking by the pastor, elder, servant-leader or well-equipped layperson who will train others for effective ministry."[77]

Church workers must be aware that their influence upon the development of self-identity and self-perception of minority children and adolescents is similar to that of public school teachers. Studies have suggested that school failure is often the result of the devaluation students experience in the academic setting.[78] Church ministers and teachers must examine themselves to determine if they have differential expectations for or interact differently with children of color.

8. The Christian education program should provide the opportunity for leaders and laypersons to become sensitized to and develop an appreciation for both the differences and similarities that exist between cultures.

Learning about the differences and similarities of other cultures is certainly a goal of multiculturalism. Therefore, the Christian education program should assist individuals to learn about the values, attitudes, and behaviors of Hispanic Americans, as well as people from other cultures. At the same time, certain cautions must be heeded. First, this should be accomplished in such a way that the information is integrated throughout all aspects of the religious education program. This is preferred to separated, isolated presentations. Second, care must be taken that the tourist curriculum does not occur. This approach tends to emphasize aspects of a culture such as specific celebrations, artifacts of the culture, special events, food and music, and holidays. It is interesting to note that the Anglo-European culture is not studied in this way. The tourist approach tends to present the culture being studied as the "other" culture.

Guidelines to avoid the "tourism" error were given by an Anti-Bias Curriculum task force working in conjunction with the National Association for the Education of Young Children.[79] Although developed for younger children, the guidelines would seem to apply across all age levels.

1. Connect cultural activities to individual children and their families.

2. Remember that while cultural patterns are real and affect all members of an ethnic group, families live their culture in their own individual ways.

3. Connect cultural activities to concrete, daily life.

4. Explore cultural diversity within the principle that everyone has a culture.

5. Have cultural diversity permeate the daily life of the classroom, through frequent, concrete, hands-on experiences related to young children's interests.

6. Avoid the editorial "we" when talking with children.

7. Explore the similarities among people through their differences.

8. Begin with the cultural diversity among the children and staff in your classroom.

9. *The Christian education curriculum should provide empowerment opportunities for members of the Hispanic-American culture.*

Empowerment may be the most important goal for a multicultural curriculum. This objective should be present both in the church that is primarily Hispanic American as well as the church that is primarily white with only a few minority individuals present.

Jack and Judith Balswick, authors of *The Family,* give a description of empowerment for family roles that seems to be very applicable for members of the "church family."

> Empowering is the active, intentional process of enabling another person to acquire power. The person who is empowered has gained power because of the encouraging behavior of the other.
>
> Empowering is the process of helping another recognize strengths and potential within, as well as encouraging and guiding the development of these qualities. It is the affirmation of another's ability to learn and grow and become all that he or she can be. It may require that the empowerer be willing to step back and allow the empowered to learn by doing and not by depending. The empowered must respect the uniqueness of those being empowered and see strength in their individual ways to be competent. Empowering does not involve controlling or enforcing a certain way of doing and being. It is, rather, a reciprocal process in which empowering takes place between people in mutually enhancing ways.[80]

Empowerment will assist Hispanic Americans, as well as members of other minority groups, to possess the intellectual and emotional ability to confront oppression. Christians from all cultures must work together to create a more just society. Further, denominations and religious organizations must devote themselves to the development of church ministries which will result in empowerment and self-determination for minority group members. Individuals are entitled to a church environment in which they are accepted for who they are and a church educational curriculum that fosters their autonomy and development of alternative modes of interaction and Christian service.

BEYOND MONOCULTURALISM

In considering the church's ministry to Hispanic Americans, we have discussed three aspects. First, the Hispanic-American emphasis upon the family unit makes it a logical beginning point for ministry direction. Many pastoral care and counseling opportunities will be available in prevention, enhancement, and intervention settings. Second, the Christian education curriculum which includes programs, activities, and materials, as well as "living experience," is an excellent opportunity for initiating multiculturalism within the local church. A number of guidelines were presented to give direction to curricular design for multiracial Christian education. Through the Christian education program, a greater sensitivity toward other cultures can result. Communication and understanding are enhanced when inclusion of cultural diversity is the norm as opposed to a monocultural perspective. All are enriched as the lives and customs of various groups present new alternatives for our own lives.

Beyond this enrichment, however, there is need for a third approach. We cannot be satisfied to simply accentuate the strengths and celebrate the uniqueness of all groups. Nor will it be sufficient to provide opportunities for increased interaction with the various cultural groups. The third consideration involves an active stance on the part of the church. In the educational setting this has often been referred to as an antibias curriculum. Such activity is required to counteract the prejudice and discrimination that less powerful groups suffer at the expense of the groups which hold the power.

Current research is still in agreement with Mary Ellen Goodman's classic work, *Race Awareness in Young Children,*[81] which pointed out that direct contact is not enough to overcome prejudice and racial bias. Researchers have concluded that active intervention by others is necessary in order to develop positive attitudes about people of color.[82]

The church curriculum must provide instruction which involves direct confrontation regarding prejudice and discrimination. Without this, there will only be temporary changes in the patterns of social interaction and acceptance between diversified groups.

A number of suggestions have been given in this chapter for counteracting the lack of diversity often found in local churches. Although some have been applied specifically to the Hispanic

American culture, most concepts will apply equally to all minority groups which are subjected to prejudice and discriminatory treatment. Ministry leaders have a serious responsibility to find ways to prevent non-Christian attitudes and treatment of minority groups. Although the steps in this section can only be considered a beginning approach, it is a beginning.

In sum, if Christians are to develop the attitudes and actions necessary for living as authentic Christians in a complex, diverse world, our church programs must actively challenge the impact of inequality in the lives of fellow Christians and provide ministry opportunities for changing lives.

CHAPTER EIGHT

EXAMINING NATIVE-AMERICAN CULTURE

BACKGROUND

One of the interesting aspects about studying Native Americans is the origin of the term "Indian." In 1851 William Apes observed that

> I have often been led to inquire where the whites received this word, which they so often threw as an opprobrious epithet at the sons of the forest. I could not find it in the Bible, and therefore concluded, that it was a word imported for the special purpose of degrading us. At other times I thought it was derived from the term in-gen-uity. But the proper term which ought to be applied to our nation to distinguish it from the rest of the human family is that of "Natives" — and I humbly conceive that the natives of this country are the only people under heaven who have a just title to the name, inasmuch as we are the only people who retain the original complexion of our father Adam.[1]

"Original Americans," "Native People," "American Indians," "Amerindians," and "Native Americans" are all names applied to the original inhabitants of our continent.[2] While the term "Indian" may have originated in a mistaken association with the "Indians" of India, its ambiguity illustrates the complexities behind any generalizations regarding this people group.

This book will use the term "Native American" as the primary term for describing the first inhabitants of North America. While "American Indian" is often used in newspapers and is well-known generally, we feel that the former more accurately recognizes the antiquity and geographical priority of our first inhabitants.

The original Native Americans were not wandering nomads, but rather farmers and fishermen living in semipermanent enclaves.[3] When horses were acquired from the Spaniards, many tribes began a plains existence. Sioux, Cheyennes, and Arapahos came from the East; Comanches and Kiowas from the West. Some abandoned farming to follow the buffalo herds. As one Cheyenne put it, "We lost the corn."[4]

In the 1970s, 173 Native-American groups could be counted. These could variously be called tribes, nations, bands, peoples, and ethnic groups. The largest were the Navajos of Arizona and New Mexico (approximately 160,000), the smallest the Chumash of California or the Modocs of Oklahoma, numbering fewer than a hundred. "Nearly as many Indian tribes exist in the 20th century as when Europeans first encountered them in the 1600s."[5] Estimates of Native-American groupings have varied between approximately 300 to 500 tribes.[6]

The practice of making "treaties" with the Native Americans began with the British, especially following English victory in the French and Indian War (1754–1763). Following the American Revolution, the United States also utilized the treaty system and signed its first treaty with the Delawares in 1778.[7] The most important early treaties were those of Fort Stanwix (1768 and 1784), dealing with the Iroquois League, and the Treaty of Greenville (1795) which surrendered part of the Northwest Territory to the United States. By 1815 most of the territory north of the Ohio River had been subdued and Native Americans were forced to settle west of the Mississippi River. Treaties eventually gave way to force and coercion, prompting the Indian Wars of the nineteenth century.[8] In 1871, the process of making treaties was terminated by Congress, with Native-American affairs being governed by legislation or executive agreements. On August 13, 1946, Congress created the Indian Claims Commission (I.C.C.) to consider land claims. The I.C.C. existed until 1978 after which claims were heard by the Court of Claims and, after 1982, the U.S. Claims Court. By 1989 nearly $1.4 billion in claims had been awarded.[9]

One of the most negative factors in the treatment of Native Americans has been the absence of any significant middle class. Federal attempts at subsidies and reservation life have created a culture which is "probably the least prepared to participate [in society] of all the disadvantaged groups."[10] A further complication is the considerable number of Indian tribes, "all culturally different in varying degrees from one another."[11]

Some have suggested that this be addressed by moving Native Americans out of reservations into the mainstream of society, a modern-day "trail of tears," only in reverse. The problem, however, as Kenneth Johnson points out, is that *the value system of American Indian culture is opposed to the highly competitive, specialized American value system. In short, Indians simply can't survive with their value system in direct competition with the dominant culture."[12] This creates a "catch-22" situation in that one of the greatest needs for Native Americans is contact with the dominant culture in order to develop patterns for survival within that culture.[13] At the same time, their contact with such culture often has negative consequences.

Perhaps more than any other group, Native Americans have been affected by revisionism. Portrayals of the original Native Americans as bloodthirsty savages have been reinforced by hundreds of Western movies and pulp novels. Yet an accurate survey of original events most often proves just the opposite.

Contemporary representations may be equally misleading. Native Americans are quite often presented as they *were* rather than as they *are*. Children may be pictured wearing feathers; reservation life may be portrayed as it was a hundred years ago. Instead of affirmation, a distorted picture is presented which only increases misunderstanding of this culture.

Another example of revisionism is the assumption that original Native-American culture was primitive and inferior. Only in the 1960s did North America recognize that the Native Americans had a religion.[14] In reality, their civilization shows examples of advanced development. The Iroquois League practiced many of the tenets of a democratic republic, yet flourished over 500 years ago. It is very possible that one of the architects of the American Republic, John Rutledge, used the Iroquois League of Nations as a pattern for the Constitution of the United States.[15]

HISTORY OF NATIVE-AMERICAN EDUCATION

The early North American perspective on Native Americans is most evident in their attempts to both educate and convert them. These two processes were so closely connected that they cannot be separated.

Since Native Americans could not read or write when the Europeans reached America, they were viewed as uneducated. This was true in spite of the fact that nearly 1 million Native Americans at that time represented several hundred language groups.[16] In 1792, Brigadier General Rufus Putman was instructed by Secretary of War Henry Knox to inform the Indians of the government's willingness to teach them to "read and write, to plough, and to sow, in order to raise their own bread and meat, with certainty, as the white people do."[17]

The preceding statement revealed a dominant early American attitude that the traditional Native-American educational process involving the tribe and family was not of importance. In addition to this, American educators also ascribed to the belief that humanity was a special creation of God. Since all human beings were created in the image of God, Native Americans could and should imitate the social framework received from European culture. This was, of course, accompanied by the assumption that Native-American culture was inferior to white culture.[18]

From as early as 1600 to about 1850, educational opportunities for the Native Americans came primarily from missionary agencies. Reading and writing were taught, but more importance was placed on learning a way of life consistent with Christianity. The educational efforts of missionaries were the means of accomplishing a dual purpose: conversion and civilization. It was believed that these two aspects were mutually reinforcing and that both could be obtained through education. In educational endeavors in which there were few converts, the work would often be discontinued. Students' ultimate success was determined by whether they became Christians and accepted the American way of life. The success of the school itself was determined by these two factors.[19]

Mission schools were plagued with problems of poor attendance, and the children's home environment was often considered the cause. For this reason, a majority of the missionaries felt that the assimilation of the Native American through education could most effectively be accomplished through Indian removal. This was the stimulus for the development of the Indian boarding schools.

The non-reservation school was the creation of Chaplain R.H. Pratt, an army officer, who developed a plan of providing education in centers away from reservation life. His philosophy of education was: "To civilize the Indian, put him in the midst of civilization. To keep him civilized, keep him there."[20] Pratt established the famous Carlisle Indian School in 1879. The program was especially popular with those who felt that Native-American children needed to live continuously within the white culture to become civilized.[21]

The decades of the 1930s and 1940s brought a change in governmental dealing with Native Americans. The Indian Reorganizational Act of 1934 authorized Native Americans to organize for self-government. Under this act, tribes could revive their native religion and develop handicraft industries. Many traditional Christian organizations opposed the act on the basis that tribalism meant paganism, and it was their belief that Native Americans wanted to be assimilated into the larger society.

It was not until the late 1960s, however, that Indian tribes were given authority to direct the formal education of their children.[22] At the end of World War II, there was a movement to "set the American Indian free."[23] Thus, the "Termination Period" of 1944–1969 resulted, which led to "self-determination," the key concept of reform in every aspect of the life of the Native American.

SOCIAL DISTINCTIVES

Ella, a Native-American seminary student, shared the following anecdote in a human development course.

> My mother would take the family to church. Each week, we as a family would practice "democracy." While stopped at the stop sign at the end of the street, we would vote to either go to the "white church" or to the "Indian church." My mother and I enjoyed going to the "Indian church," but my brothers (three older) liked the "white church." The three younger siblings could be influenced in their vote. If we became too loud or could not agree, then Mom would choose.

The variations in the "white church" and the "Indian church" which Ella attended could have taken many forms. Beyond the differences in music, language, and structure, however, the greatest contrast experienced is value orientation.

No culture exists without values. In the same way that an ideology shapes an individual, the value system gives shape to a culture. One cannot study the Native-American culture without being acutely aware of how much their value system has influenced their lives. That awareness is perhaps due to two factors: (1) the Native-American culture has one of the most concise and thoroughly articulated value systems of all cultural groups, and (2) the Native-American value system possesses a great deal of dissonance with the majority value orientation.

Choices made by Ella and her family in our illustration above is an obvious decision experience. Less obvious choices throughout the life of the Native American occur on a daily basis. Indian students have experienced cultural confusion as their school experiences focus on values different from their own. If they are influenced by the Anglo-American culture, they may question allegiance to their cultural identification. This creates a problem for the developing child or adolescent who wishes to both succeed in the larger dominant culture and at the same time hold true to his or her rich cultural heritage.

THE NATIVE-AMERICAN VALUE ORIENTATION

The values and beliefs that Native Americans consider important differ markedly from those identified for mainstream Americans earlier. The Native American faces the task of selecting a culture as the basis for an identity: the Native-American culture, the Anglo-American culture, or some cultural combination. The combination would seem a likely choice, but this requires gaining proficiency in two cultures, as well as maintaining harmony with family and nature while ascribing to the Anglo-American worldview.

As is true with all ethnic cultures, attention must be given to the diversity within Indian groups themselves. To equally apply one value orientation to a general group which represents a wide diversity of tribes is not reasonable. Even beyond this, we have the differences that are present due to residence, reservations, rural nonreservation communities, small town communities, and large metropolitan communities.

Bryde identified four value objects in Native-American culture that have maintained importance over the years: God, self, others, and world.[24] From these values a lifestyle has developed that includes beliefs, behaviors, traditions, and customs.

We will discuss the above four values from the Native-American perspective in terms of Clyde Kluckhohn's basic value orientations. In all of these areas, dissonance exists between the North American culture and the middle-class mainline culture of America. However, this does not mean that the traditional value system of the Native American represents an incongruence with a Christian value system. To the contrary, the following views contain theological overtones which can be put to good use by all churches.

Harmony with Nature vs. Control over Nature
One of the most important value distinctions of the Native-American culture is the relationship between individuals and the natural world. Their worldview is that of working for harmony with natural forces versus conquest over nature. Nature is indivisible, and the individual is only a part of it. They accept the world and do not try to change it. Submission to natural

events that cannot be controlled is considered acceptable. Nature is their school, and they learn to endure all natural happenings.

Historically, the Native American has understood nature as the essence of God. Therefore, the existence of God has not been an issue. If there was no God there could be no nature. God is viewed as the inner spiritual power and the great power above all else. God, humanity, and self are all connected. Having the right relationship with nature gives the right relationship with God, which gives the right relationship with the self.

Following this first-order preference of harmony with nature, second-order preference would follow with being subject to nature. Control over nature would be chosen only when no other choice is available.

In contrast with the above, the dominant North-American approach is aimed at controlling nature, including other people. Mastery of the physical world is valued. Only when there is no other choice is it understandable to simply work with nature.

From a Christian perspective, humanity lives in an active relationship with nature. Rather than existing passively, the Christian mandate is to "subdue" the earth and rule over it (Gen. 1:28). The Native-American acceptance of the "goodness" of the earth is an important complement to this mission. All too often the needs of ecology and preservation of natural resources are neglected while Christians attend to more strident social issues. Questions of nuclear power and warfare are serious matters that concern the commission given humanity from the beginning.

Consensual Collateral vs. Individual Decisions

The value orientation for relationship with others gives first-order selection to the consensual collateral form of social organization and decision-making. In the Native-American culture, value is placed on cooperation and conformity instead of competition. The group takes precedence over individual decisions and preferences, first-order selections for dominant North American society. Mainline North Americans value competition as necessary for progress. In like manner, a lack of competition will be considered synonymous with a lack of progress.

After the first-order preference for the group or collateral, the Native American gives preference to the individual, with the lineal as a third-order preference.[25] However, the individual as a second-order preference differs from the dominant society view of individualism. In the majority society, individual needs and rights often have precedence over the group and involve doing what one wants to do within the confines of the law. Individual freedom for the Native American accepts the confines of maintaining harmony with nature.[26] This second-order preference of the individual is also embedded within collateral relationships. There is respect for the development of the individual, especially as one is empowered to take charge and contribute rather than to be a threat to the group.

Another value difference in the area of social relationships is the position of respect given to age. Native Americans respect age as opposed to the general American focus and fascination with youth. Respect for age is due to its association with wisdom and knowledge for the world within which they live. The elderly are believed to possess the wisdom of life, and it is their responsibility to transmit the traditions, legends, and myths of their culture to the younger generation. It is also a reasoned respect in that "in the days of their strength they also contributed to the common weal."[27]

Generosity vs. Accumulated Wealth

Of significance to the Native American is the value of generosity and sharing. This value was evident in the traditional Native-American life in two areas: food and shelter and praise and shame.[28]

Generosity is more respected than personal acquisitions and material achievement. Rather than respect for individual wealth, the one who gives the most is the most respected. For the Anglo American, the one who accumulates the most is the most respected. The concept of sharing is said to be more revered among Native Americans than the Anglo-American ethic of saving. A Sioux youth during the 1870s is quoted as describing the non-Indian in the following words: "The greatest object of their lives seems to be to acquire possessions—to be rich. They desire to possess the whole world."[29] It is interesting how little that description has changed for the dominant culture in over 100 years.

Being-in-Becoming vs. Doing

The preferred mode of activity is "being-in-becoming." The second-order preference is both doing and being, equally valued and differing only according to the situation.

The concept of being-in-becoming to the Native American represents a balanced life of achieving and growing. This may include competition both individually and between groups, but not at the expense of competitors. Doing, however, does not involve activity for the sake of keeping busy, and activity for the sake of the group is valued more than doing as an act of self-expression.

In educational and career settings, the Native American is sometimes viewed in a negative way as a result of this value. The lack of aggressive competition, along with an attitude of cooperation or patience, may be misunderstood in urban business settings as laziness or inactivity and a lack of initiative.

This concept of being includes the principle of Indian mores that is currently labeled "noninterference." It is based on the belief that each individual has the innate potential to develop so that respect for the autonomous personality is granted through noninterference. Ideally, the individual needs only to be made aware of the consequences of behavior and then left to the direction of this innate force. The need to control behavior is not considered the responsibility of others, but of the individual. Direct confrontation is required only to provide information and in life-threatening situations. In child rearing, therefore, the focus will not be on discipline and control but on encouraging and empowering the development of this innate potential. This idealization has in some cases resulted in negative results. For example, there may be a lack of any social assertion and control in situations needing some form of action.

Present vs. Future Time Orientation

The Native-American preference for time orientation is the present with a second- and third-order preference for past and future respectively.[30] The reflected past is utilized for the present, and both the past and the present will be visualized for the future. While the Anglo American is planning and looking forward to tomorrow, the Native American is enjoying and living for today. The future does not serve as a motivating factor unless it has a direct affect on today's satisfaction. Focus is placed on the present stage of life without undue thought or concern for the next stage since it is accepted as inevitable.[31]

Although more of an exception, there have been some examples in the last two or three decades in which the more traditional version of Indian life of the past is idealized and utilized for present or future action. Wounded Knee might be an example of this when in 1973 the American Indian Movement took control of the village of Wounded Knee, South Dakota, the site of the last Indian resistance in 1890. Another example might be the Pan-Indian movement, with its roots in the seventeenth century, which attempts to establish an American Indian ethnic identity instead of just a tribal identity.

A related value is the difference in time consciousness. Although some identify this difference as having or not having time consciousness,[32] it would be more accurate to say that it is a difference rather than a lack of time consciousness. For the Native American, time consciousness is measured in terms of natural phenomena such as days, nights, moons, and seasons. Time is cyclical rather than linear, months and years as opposed to this minute or this hour. The annual seasonal cycle is important and gives significance to varying activities. And in the final analysis, *what* happened is more important than *when* it happened.[33]

Native Americans feel that there will be time to accomplish the necessary tasks, even if not today. Anglo Americans feel that promptness is a necessity in and of itself; a lack of promptness is regarded in a negative manner. Regardless of diversity in this value, the average work environment has insisted on conformity to an orientation of time consciousness. Successful career movement in urban settings usually requires an adherence to this more mechanistic, technical value of time orientation.

Internal vs. External Controls

The Native-American culture views humanity as generally good. There is the possibility of evil in humanity, but it is believed to exist because individuals did not develop to their fullest.

One type of evil is the misuse of power. This temptation is so respected that some are cautious in accepting positions of leadership for fear that they will submit to evil. This, along with similar attitudes, may act as inhibiting influences which curtail career development.

It is believed that social relationships will include both the good and the bad in people and in things. However, it is good people who will triumph in the end. Lewis and Ho share the Native-American folk tale of Iktomi the spider, who takes advantage of good people. However, Iktomi loses in the end, emphasizing the belief that good people will eventually triumph and that the evil person loses.[34]

An important distinction between the dominant religious society and the Native American is the role of guilt in their lives. Many Americans feel that productive moral living is important in their relationship with God. This is true in spite of the strong emphasis on a "grace relationship," subscribed to as a result of the theology of the Reformation. When this type of living is not maintained, individuals are subject to self-guilt, and for some, the expectation of punishment from God.

Instead of feeling guilt, the Native American feels that he or she must assume a sense of responsibility for the result of the offense. Sin is not represented by offending God, but in effecting an imbalance in nature. Such imbalance will result in the individual's own destruction. Living in ignorance of one's relationship to nature is more likely to cause destruction than will moral sin.[35]

Neither does the Native American utilize guilt as a means of controlling others. Whereas the traditional American culture, and especially conservative Christianity, has been able to motivate and control constituents, the Native-American view of non-interference would simply allow each to be responsible for the results of their decisions. This also removes the need for self-guilt when those that we feel responsible for are not responsive to our guidance. Americans are almost crippled at times by self-guilt when their children are not successful or make poor choices in marriage or schooling. The Native-American parents are free from this because they feel that no matter how much they might disagree, their children have the right to make decisions which are developmentally appropriate for their respective age-levels.

In the Native-American perspective, God requires humanity to relate with respect to both nature and itself. Self-destruction is more likely to come as a result of causing an imbalance in nature than is offending God through moral sin.[36] If one is in disharmony with nature, there will be an imbalance in the self and there will be dysfunctional human relationships. Having the right relationship with nature gives the right relationship with God, which gives the right relationship with the self.

Although norms for behavior exist, others will not be judged specifically by whether or not they adhere to the norms. Consideration will first be given to the reason for their behavior.[37]

FAMILY ORGANIZATION AND RELATIONSHIPS

Value orientations are transmitted to each generation by the family. In families of the majority culture, the nuclear family is the most important unit for this task. The extended family is important but in a more indirect way. Within the Native-American culture, this function is not limited to just parents but is shared by several adults. A high priority is placed on both the immediate and the extended family. As many as three generations may be involved in an active way with multiple parental delegations.

Grandparents are given an official role of leadership within the family community. They maintain close proximity to the grandchildren and actively monitor their behavior. Parents will seldom contradict the child-rearing and discipline methods provided by the grandparents. If grandparents are absent, symbolic leadership might be given to elders unrelated to the family.[38] In addition to this, uncles and aunts will have disciplinary responsibilities in certain situations. There may be a naming ceremony in which the supportive network of aunts, uncles, and cousins is confirmed. This pattern of family organization provides a variety of role models and a generally secure environment with bonding to several parental figures.

Different family lifestyle patterns have been identified for Native Americans as they relate to assimilation in contemporary American society.[39] One is the traditional pattern which adheres to defined styles of living according to the traditional Native-American culture. Another is the nontraditional lifestyle representing a bicultural approach in which many aspects of non-Indian styles of living have been adopted. Third is a group that is in a conscious struggle to redefine the American Indian lifestyle, often one that represents a previous cultural style such as Pan-Indianism.

Behaviors in the area of language, religion, and social engagement were found to differ according to which of the three lifestyle patterns a group characterized. For example, in the area of social engagement, the traditional family lifestyle focused on cultural activities such as feasts, religion, and pow wows. In the bicultural family lifestyle pattern, the activities of the dominant society prevailed. The pan-traditional pattern represented an open rejection of the activities of the dominant society with a focus on traditional cultural activities.[40]

Differences similar to the example above were found for language and religion. However, one aspect remained the same for all three family lifestyle patterns, that of the extended network as the pattern of family relationships. This is an illustration of the fact that regardless of the lifestyle pattern, studies have shown that American Indian core values are retained and that the changing of these family patterns do not represent eroding cultural values, nor can they be utilized to measure "Indian-ness." The three groups will probably vary in language, religion, and in their acceptance of the dominant society's activities, but in each case, the family relational field will be the extended network.[41]

In the traditional Native-American culture, sex roles were clearly defined and the contributions of each gender appreciated. The same-sex parent was responsible to teach the necessary skills and restrictions. Economic pressures have caused some changes in this pattern, especially for the lower socioeconomic classes.

There is an increase in the number of female-headed households and in the number of urban families that are more removed from the extended family. In general, women have been able to adapt more successfully in employment opportunities because their skills have been used in domestic service roles. However, many mothers report problems in attempting to raise boys without the assistance and example of male figures and a supportive environment. Another problem is that some lack good parenting models in their own lives because they were a part of the boarding school experiences of the 1950s. As a result, they lost out on many years of direct parent-child guidance and may be following the unrealistic patterns presented to them in the government schools or reading texts. Along with this, many of their parents spent years in TB sanitariums and were not in the home for the normal child-rearing years.

Although the group receives first-order preference in the Native-American culture, developing a strong sense of individual responsibility is included in child rearing. The early development of autonomy is stressed so that the child becomes a contributing member of the group and assumes his or her share of responsibility for the family.

However, the belief that each is innately an individual means that parents see their responsibility as fostering rather than forcing independence. It is assumed that growing up will be a result of self-discovery and will occur according to a pattern of developmental readiness. This will be accomplished through natural opportunities for decision-making and assuming family responsibilities.

The primary purpose for direct confrontation is limited to making children aware of the consequences of behavior. Although limitations are set, the children will be relatively free to make decisions unless their behaviors are life-threatening to themselves or others. Instead of control methods, parents may use the more indirect methods of persuasion and distraction or rely on the effects of shame or ridicule. If necessary, the logical consequences of a behavior may be used to teach self-control.

This approach to child rearing is often evaluated by non-Indians as lacking discipline. However, the approach is very intentional and corresponds to the principle of "noninterference" referred to earlier.

DEVELOPMENT OF A SELF-IDENTITY

Ella, the Native-American seminary student referred to earlier, wrote the following in an assignment.

> During my first year in elementary school I discovered two things. First, that my skin was darker than the other children, and, second, that I was a Seminole Indian. This happened after school one day early in the year when a group of boys from the upper grades began yelling at me and throwing rocks. I looked and my brothers were nowhere in sight. I was frightened and began pedaling my little bike as fast as it would go. Just then the chain jumped off the track. I stopped to repair the chain and as I looked up, the boy had almost caught up with me. The thought came to me: "You are my friends, I would die for you, why are you throwing rocks at me?"
>
> When I arrived home I spoke with my mother about the experience. That was the day I was labeled an Indian. All Mom said was, "You are Indian, be proud of who you are."

The development of a "self" for the Native American has a definite relationship with other values. There is an integral relationship with nature. It is believed that one learns about his or her own nature from nature itself. Some personality traits which are valued are honesty and strength, respect for others, self-respect and individual worth, controlled emotions, and the endurance of suffering with silence.[42]

Native-American youth face the same task of identity development as do all adolescents. This developmental task is especially complex for them, however, because they often face the conflicting values of two groups—those of their own ethnic groups and those of the larger non-Indian society. The ideal is to sort through these two sets of values and arrive at a coherent identity. This, however, is difficult. Those whose identity strongly represents the larger society face the possibility of rejection or disapproval of tribal members. As a result, many vacillate between an identity with the larger majority and an identity with their minority group.

The social phenomenon of "marginality" was coined by Robert E. Park in the 1920s. The concept refers to those, often minority-group members, who find themselves caught between identifying with the values of their own cultural group and the necessity to behave in certain ways to be accepted by the dominant group. The marginal person is neither completely at ease in his or her own group nor fully a part of the reference group (the group they refer to for evaluative purposes). Although sociologists have differed in their interpretation of the exact effects of marginality over the years, most are in general agreement that a conflict of values and loyalties will cause anxiety among both adults and children. This is not to say, however, that individuals with a marginal status cannot live within either their minority culture or the dominant society without encountering stress to a destructive degree.

EDUCATIONAL DISTINCTIVES OF THE NATIVE AMERICAN

ACADEMIC ACHIEVEMENT

Literature on the Native-American student commonly focuses on the high dropout rate at the high school level and the tendency of students to score below average academically. What is not given attention is the fact that Native-American children function at the average-to-superior range until the fourth grade and that the decline only begins at that point. This gradual decline continues until the typical Native-American adolescent is found to score below the national average by grade ten. The question that needs to be asked, of course, is why the Native American does not continue to score at the average-to-superior range or why they have one of the highest dropout rates at the high school level of any ethnic group. A factor which may increase the likelihood of academic failure is the cultural conflict which many young Native Americans experience.[43]

The meaning of achievement in the Anglo-American school

system may be one example of cultural conflict for the Native American. Research has shown that while Anglo-American teachers emphasize competition, aggressiveness, and personal goals, the Native-American culture emphasizes cooperation, sharing, consideration of group needs, and giving others the opportunity to proceed first.[44]

The Anglo-American concept of achievement does not easily accommodate the Native-American values of "not setting yourself apart from others" or "the importance of being humble."[45] Academic competence may be hidden in order to avoid violating the value of being humble. Brown concluded that the Cherokee value which emphasized cooperation over competition was a factor that seemed to produce lower achievement scores for the Cherokee children.[46]

As a future goal, the accumulation of material possessions serves as a motivation for achievement in the Anglo-American culture. However, the Native American does not determine an individual's worth by private property or savings but, instead, feels that worth comes from the ability and willingness to share.[47]

This clash of culture may cause the Native American to experience a general lack of self-confidence and a sense of helplessness. The Anglo-American teacher may easily interpret this as a lack of motivation or an attitude of unconcern. Alienation occurs as the vicious cycle leading to failure begins. The teacher indirectly communicates an attitude toward the Native American that shows an expectation of failure. The result is steady decline in achievement and the development of a low academic self-concept.

One of us (Lillian) recalls an experience as an elementary teacher working with Native-American parents during parent-teacher conferences. As a zealous first-year teacher in North Dakota, I tried to explain to the parents how their children needed to improve their study habits. All the time I was talking, the parents (especially mothers) would simply smile and look at the floor or away from eye contact with me. My interpretation, of course, was that they were unconcerned with their child's academic achievement. I was making the mistake that educators often make, perceiving the Native American's lack of eye contact as a sign of withdrawal or disinterest.

COGNITIVE STYLE

Most accept the fact that individuals have different ways in which they perceive things, learn about their world, and demonstrate what they have learned. Further, it is generally accepted that these differences have been influenced by early socialization experiences.

To determine a characteristic learning style for the American Indian is difficult when one considers the large number of existing tribal groups and the many differences they represent. Researchers Swisher and Deyhle have presented a thorough review of literature regarding Native-American learning styles. The conclusion of their review was that similarities exist but that there are differences as well.[48] In their own assessment of Jicarilla Apache learning styles to test the commonly assumed association with field dependence, Swisher and Deyhle concluded that further research was needed in order to identify a learning style. Within-group differences prohibited them from identifying a general tendency toward one specific learning style.[49]

Some studies (Ramírez and Castañeda as one example) have concluded that Native-American students tend to be more field sensitive than field independent. If true, this would mean that they are likely to learn best in a highly social context, when guided by a teacher and when working cooperatively with other learners. A characteristic true of field sensitive learners, which has been found to be true of Native Americans as well, is a global/analytic approach to processing information. This means that learning will focus on the whole rather than a part.

METHODOLOGY AND INSTRUCTION IN THE CLASSROOM

Instructional methods in traditional classroom settings are often inconsistent with child-rearing patterns and value orientations of the traditional Native-American culture. Teachers and leaders in the church educational setting should search for instructional methods that take into consideration the ways in which children have "learned to learn" in their individual cultures.

Methods of instruction and communication should be selected *both* for what we want to accomplish, as well as the fact that they reflect the developmental stage and cultural background of the recipient.

Traditionally, Native-American learners have not been encouraged to be aggressive or competitive in academics. This conflicts with having been taught to value cooperation and harmony. In comparison with the majority population, they tend to remain relatively passive and quiet in their learning approach.

A major difference in the cognitive style of Native Americans is the area of student participation. Teachers and group leaders often rely extensively on verbal participation, an approach valued by Anglo, African, and Hispanic Americans. However, this method is not given the same value by Native Americans. Related methods which are designed to increase positive self-talk can be compared in the same way. Group activities in which children are encouraged to talk about "something I do well" or "ways our family helps the church" may work well with Anglo or African Americans and yet not be effective with Native-American children.

Sanders noted a number of ways in which the communication style of the Native-American culture may differ from the style normally used by Anglo-American teachers. The Anglo-American teacher speaks louder and faster than Native Americans, addressing the listener directly, possibly by name. The Native American speaks more softly and at a slower rate, often avoiding direct contact with the speaker or listener. The Anglo-American teacher will value verbal skills and will supply an immediate response or feel free to interrupt at times. In the Native-American culture, nonverbal communication is respected, few interjections are made, and the response to an auditory message may be delayed.[50]

The Native-American child learns from his or her family members by watching an activity repeatedly before attempting to perform the act. The activity will be reviewed in their heads first. When they feel that they can perform, they attempt the activity. However, Anglo Americans do not feel that competence must precede performance. In public school settings, teachers will urge children to perform an activity as soon as possible, staying nearby to help and correct. One teacher compared her Anglo and Indian students in this area: "My Anglo students are quick to jump into the task. The Indian students seem to need time to think about things before they take action on their assignment. It is almost like they have to make sure they can do it before they try."[51]

In a study of the Navajos, the difference was noted in the following way. The philosophy of the Native Americans seems to be, "If at first you don't think, and think again, don't bother trying." The contrasting white culture would state it as, "If at first you don't succeed, try, try, again."[52]

Many Native Americans prefer a visual approach to learning rather than a verbal approach. One Native-American student described his study method in the following way. "When I am ready to study for a test, I read over my class notes until I can see them in my mind. When I am taking the test, I can see my notes in my mind." This method, of course, is consistent with learning the correct way to perform by watching while someone else does it repeatedly.

Teachers of religion have more recently utilized a more visual approach to teaching, but it has been common in the past to depend almost entirely upon the verbal mode. In situations when the verbal seems to be required, the teacher needs to supplement with visuals, as well as assist their visual-oriented students to improve skills in verbal learning. Studies have found that many Native-American learners have met this challenge by utilizing mental images to understand concepts rather than associating words.[53]

Non-Indian teachers tend to use induced guilt as a means of social control and motivation. They do not appreciate the autonomous efforts of children and will show an impatience with silence or individual efforts. In the Native-American culture, of course, there is a lack of induced guilt and, in its place, the encouragement of autonomy. As a reaction to this difference, the Native-American child may simply withdraw or resort to silence in the traditional public school setting. In the earlier years of schooling this behavior gives the appearance of well-behaved children. The same behaviors in upper grades may be interpreted as stubbornness or as a lack of motivation. An added problem in this area is the tendency of Native-American children to look the other way rather than have direct eye contact. The non-Indian teacher may interpret this as an additional sign of a lack of cooperation or withdrawal.

Research indicates that Native-American children will be more likely to participate verbally and/or actively in group projects, in small groups as opposed to large groups, and in situations in which there is volunteer participation. They are less likely to respond when the teacher "puts them on the spot" with a question which requires public response in a group. This method of answering questions or reciting when called upon by the teacher is especially incompatible with younger children.[54]

APPLICATION TO THE CHURCH SETTING

RESPONSES TO MINISTRY

The differing family lifestyle patterns that will be found among the Native Americans serve as an important guideline for ministry approach. Each pattern should be taken into consideration as a context for ministry. Different family responses to ministry can be expected. For example, traditional families may hesitate to respond to mainline church approaches and hold to their own traditional religious culture instead. The same may be true of pan-traditional families. These will tend to demand or mainstream approaches in their attempt to recapture cultural methodologies. Bicultural families may be more ready to respond with minor adaptations. Traditional families and pan-traditional families will generally be courteous to ministers and politely listen but will be slow to respond if the ministry is only in terms of mainstream North America.

A well-developed ministry to the family is needed in each local church in order to capitalize on the strengths of Indian families. This is true, of course, in the family network of most ethnic minorities.

In a study of Native-American families in the San Francisco

Bay area, it was found that most urban families were surviving quite well. Two characteristics were found to be true of those families which were coping best. One was an openness to learning and using tools of other cultures. Second was the ability to keep tribal language and culture a viable part of life. If this study can be verified for other settings, these two aspects could be used as a guideline for a church ministry to ethnic families.[55] Mainline religious institutions would do well to combine the values of individual cultures with their ministry approaches. Without a sensitivity to traditional cultural values, church programs may simply serve as a hindrance, rather than as a strengthening factor for the Native-American family.

A distinct, closed Native-American community has developed as a result of the extended family pattern and reservation living. Outsiders will not have immediate access, and this may include church leaders. In a survey by health-care professionals of American Indian clients in Minnesota, 90 percent indicated that they would prefer receiving health and welfare services from American Indian workers.[56] Lewis developed a schema which showed the sequential path that urban Indians follow in seeking help. Self was first, followed by the family network, and then the social network. The religious leader was fourth, followed by the tribal community as a fifth source. Only after these five avenues were exhausted would the Native American turn to the mainstream health care system.[57] Although the religious leader was fourth, this selection was made with the assumption that the religious leader was a member of the tribal community. A non-Indian religious leader would probably rank with other mainstream systems as a viable selection only to be considered when all cultural contacts are exhausted. This underlines the importance of having Native Americans on the church staff in ministerial and teaching positions.

As the local church presents its religious belief system, it must be remembered that, in almost all cases, the Native American already possesses such a belief system. This means that integration may present conflict for the Native American. A therapist related how an urbanized Indian patient was traumatized by the feeling that she had lost her earlier values system in accepting Christianity. Some process of reaffirmation is needed in these cases and should be possible without compromise of the essentials of Christianity.

RELIGIOUS INSTRUCTION

Educational leaders in the church should be aware of the diversity represented by the Native-American culture and accommodate goals and practices accordingly. Religious education for Native Americans should empower them to function effectively as Christians within the Native-American community and within their country.

McConnell suggests that religious education informed by the wisdom of the Native-American tradition would possibly include certain aspects. The following is an adapted list:

> 1. respect for every person
> 2. respect for the wisdom of children and of the elderly
> 3. respect for the land
> 4. respect for the right of all animals to exist cooperatively with humanity
> 5. awareness of our dependence upon one another
> 6. harmony between individual and group needs
> 7. appreciation for continuing life which comes as a result of the death of plants and animals
> 8. gratitude to God for the harmony of all elements that we might have life.[58]

Studies on the academic progress of Native-Americans often note their tendency toward a poor academic self-concept. Although the school setting has a strong influence on the development of the self-concept, the church setting can also play an influential role in this area. Studies have shown that a teacher's negative attitude toward a student contributes to both the development of a poor academic self-concept and lack of academic progress. However, the theory of self-fulfillment prophecy also has positive results when support and encouragement from significant others is provided.

Motivational approaches to learning will be especially needed in church educational settings. Studies have documented poor study habits and attitudes for Native-American students, especially during the junior high school years and among boys in public school.[59] Negativism from school experiences will be easily associated with religious educational settings in the church.

Non-Indian church leaders should be aware that at times their style of communication is incompatible with the Native-American style of interaction. This incompatibility needs to be addressed in training sessions so that teachers and leaders accommodate their style to maximize understanding.

Church teachers and leaders must take time to obtain accurate information regarding the role of the Native American within American history, making an honest attempt to perceive it from their historical point of view. Education both in public schools and on reservations has been characterized by an insensitivity and non-receptivity to Native-American culture and history. An example is given of Chippewa children at a reservation school in the Northwest who were given the assignment to write a composition on "Why we are happy the Pilgrims landed."[60]

Complementary to this, ministry leaders should read about the Native-American culture and talk to Native Americans to learn more about their historical heritage. Special organizations exist in most communities to promote the Native American welfare and determination for equality. These can be contacted for printed information or special speakers. An objective cultural portrait should be developed which is based upon factual information about Native-American religions, language, family system, and general worldview.

In summary, the following general guidelines are given for religious education settings that include Native Americans:

- Evaluate the discussion style that is utilized in classrooms and small groups.
- Keep in mind that there will be some participants that do not prefer to be "put on the spot" in group settings.
- Allow each participant to choose the time when they are comfortable to perform, at the same time communicating that it is acceptable to make mistakes.
- Organize small group meetings and classrooms so that different types of interaction are encouraged.

● Provide social and learning activities that promote the development of both independence and cooperation.

CONCLUDING PERSPECTIVES FOR MINISTRY

For the Native American, worship of God is not focused primarily in the formal gathering on a weekly basis. Worship is a part of daily life and an integral part of the total culture.

Possibly one of the most important distinctions in the religious experiences of Native Americans is their ability to allow for an ecumenical relationship with other religious views. Syncretistic elements may also be present. Both traditional and new religious symbols may be found side by side in a church. At a church in Pine Ridge, South Dakota, images of the peace pipe, the buffalo, and Jesus Christ were all located on an altar.[61] We remember attending a Native-American wake in which a Catholic crucifix and feather totem were placed side-by-side above the deceased.

Native Americans seem to function and think in terms of a "collective unity." Organizations which stress denominational distinctives or separatism are speaking in terms alien to the Native-American way of life. Church workers who wish to make a maximum impact will stress Christian essentials rather than denominational distinctives. The latter have a place, but not in the prologue of the Christian walk.

The Euro-American emphasis on denominations has resulted in strict boundaries around religious groups. Membership lists suggest that the individual will be loyal and supportive of one group only. Native Americans do not operate with this same inclusivity in relationship to different groups. Their emphasis on cooperation and sharing makes it reasonable that they will be open to worship with many groups rather than inclusively with one.

From the Euro-American perspective, this may represent a lack of commitment, almost a sense of irresponsibility. In essence, this perspective is very complementary with a view of a God that exists in harmony with nature that is experienced by all, and with a belief in a God that is equally shared by all. Factor into this religious perspective a concept of sharing and cooperation and it is apparent that the approach is quite consistent with the values of the Native American.[62]

Cross-cultural ministry and understanding can be facilitated if church leaders will recognize the significance of identifying and comprehending the role of values in the life of the Native American. Although value and belief differences exist among all major ethnic groups, it is especially evident in this culture which had its origin in North America before that of others.

Careful consideration of the traditional Indian value system will certainly give us a good example for "being-in-becoming" the Christlike personality. Although we do not equate personality with salvation, we must be careful not to insist that such characteristics fit a traditional mold that has its origin in an ethnocentric system. The critical objective is to provide a church identity for Native Americans which fulfills their own unique essence with Christian distinctives of Christlikeness and humility.

CHAPTER NINE

EXAMINING ASIAN-AMERICAN CULTURE

BACKGROUND

Sam Sue, a Chinese-American lawyer, wrote in *Asian Americans* about being raised in Mississippi during the '60s.

> There is this shot in the opening scene of the movie, *Mississippi Burning,* where you see two water fountains. One is broken, and chipped, and water is dripping from it. The other is modern, and shining. A white guy goes up to the nice one, and the black kid goes up to the old one. I remember saying to myself, "If I was in the scene, where would I drink?"
>
> I guess I was always considered marginal with whites and blacks, though I think I got along better with blacks. I really didn't have any childhood friends. I just felt I had nothing in common with them. And I guess I felt there was this invisible barrier. I stayed mostly with my family.[1]

In May 1992, Americans were captivated by media reports of the racial unrest in Los Angeles. Imprinted in most of our minds is the image of Korean shop owners standing with guns in front of their stores, trying to protect their businesses from looters while the police were absent from the scene. Who can forget the touching scene in which a Korean woman begs the looters rushing into her store to "please be careful" as they surge past to scavenger her stock?

The increasing number of Asians who have arrived in the United States to pursue their American dream has set into place an economic war in various parts of the country. Other minorities who are economically threatened frequently express their own fight for survival with anti-Asian sentiments. Such discrimination and persecution is not new to Asian Americans, who have faced similar feelings and experiences as early as the late 1800s when the Chinese first came to the United States as part of the California gold rush.

Because stereotypes can involve emotions of hate or fear, they are difficult to change, even with evidence that they are inaccurate. Consequently, whether or not the business environment could have expanded to include the Korean shop owners in Los Angeles, when the opportunity arose, emotional truth determined behavior. One more example of racism became apparent in our contemporary race-conscious society.

By the early twentieth century almost a million Asians from China, Japan, Korea, the Philippines, and India had settled in the United States. This number contrasts with almost 35 million European immigrants coming to America between 1850 and 1930.[2] From 1965 to 1990, however, over 80 percent of all immigrants have been non-Europeans. The American-Asian population had a 141 percent increase from 1970 to 1980.[3] The cities with the greatest population of Asian Americans are Chicago, Honolulu, Los Angeles, New York, and San Francisco. In the San Diego school district, the total enrollment of Asians doubled in the four years between 1982 and 1986.[4] More than half of all Asian Americans live in the above five metropolitan areas, and more than 90 percent are found in urban centers.

Who are the Asians? A universal definition is difficult to find, and sources seem to differ as to the groups that are included. According to the *Harvard Encyclopedia of American Ethnic Groups,* the term Asian "refers to people of East Asian ancestry, most often to the Chinese, Filipinos, Koreans, and Japanese, as well as to Southeast Asians—Burmese, Indochinese,

Indonesians, and Thai."[5] The Indochinese refugees in the United States have included primarily Vietnamese, with a smaller percentage of Cambodians and Laotians.

The groups included in the 1990 U.S. Census as Asian Americans are Chinese, Filipinos, Japanese, Asian Indians, Koreans, Vietnamese, Laotians, Cambodians, Thais, Hmong, and approximately 300,000 persons from "other parts of Asia." Another category in the census report is the Pacific Islander label which includes Polynesians, Micronesians, and Melanesians. Donald Ng uses the term Asian-Pacific Americans to describe those whose heritage comes from an "Asian continent bordering on the Pacific Ocean or in the Pacific islands."[6]

Asian Americans are the fastest-growing minority in America. In 1940, they were calculated as less than four-tenths of 1 percent of the American people. In 1980 that percentage had increased to 1.5 percent and by 1990 it had doubled to approximately 3 percent of the population. The 1990 U.S. Census shows that 4.6 million Asian Americans are foreign-born and 2.7 million are American-born.[7]

In 1980, Chinese was the largest Asian-American group, followed in population size by Filipino, Japanese, Asian Indian, Korean, and Vietnamese. By 1988, this listing had changed so that Filipinos represented the largest group, followed in order by the Chinese, Korean, Vietnamese, and Asian Indians.[8]

If Asians are looked at in terms of one group, data shows them to be younger than the average American. They have smaller families. They are less likely to be unemployed or to be in jail.[9] As a group, they have excelled educationally, financially, and professionally.[10] They are more likely to get higher education than the average American and have a higher than average representation at elite universities. They have received scholarships from prestigious universities and music conservatories as a result of their achievement.[11] It is from such demographics that they are often called the "model minority."

Sucheng Chan notes that five groups of Asian immigrants came to America under three sets of circumstances. First, the Chinese left unfavorable conditions for the gold discoveries in California, the Pacific Northwest, and British Columbia. Also attractive were numerous jobs which opened as the American West developed. Second, the Japanese, Korean, and Filipinos were attracted by Hawaiian sugar plantations. Third were Asian Indians who came seeking work through Canada and the Pacific Coast.[12] Added to the above immigration from the past is the more recent influx of Southeast Asians (Vietnamese, Cambodians, and Laotians). Since 1975 approximately 800,000 Southeast Asians have immigrated to the United States with half of these being under eighteen years of age.[13]

What is it like for the newly arrived Asian in America? One Korean American compared his arrival at an airport in California as a teenager with that of landing on Mars. He found the Caucasians with their different colored hair and eyes and oversized noses and feet as being especially frightening. The Caucasians looked like giants to him and his family and they actually feared that they might be run over by one.

Asians arriving in the States have experienced varying degrees of discomfort over the vast differences between Asian and American cultures. For some, there has been an overwhelming desire to blend into mainstream America, and this has caused the Asian immigrant to minimize the obstacles. In turn, mainline Americans tend to assume this willingness to overcome obstacles means that the differences are insignificant. The Asian-American culture represents an interesting contrast to the dominant non-Asian culture. Becoming aware of the differences is an important means by which the non-Asian church community can relate to Asian Americans both within and without the church walls.

Aspects discussed in this chapter will be applied to Asian Americans as a group; the following chapter will more specifically focus on selected people groups. Of certainty is the fact that subgroups included within the Asian American culture represent a great deal of diversity. There are twenty-nine distinct subgroups that differ in language, religion, and customs. In addition, diversity exists within the subgroups.[14] The use of generalizations with Asians as a group must be read with the recognition of between-group differences, as well as within-group differences that are equal to, if not greater than, between-group differences.

CULTURAL CHARACTERISTICS

RELIGIOUS TRADITIONS

The various Asian ethnic groups in the United States have remained discrete, certainly an example of the misleading symbol
of the melting pot that dominated views of American immigration during the earlier years. With the exception of one or two
groups, they also have been unaffected by the "triple melting
pot." This term was used by some to refer to the diffusion of
ethnic differences as a result of the larger ethnocultural religious differences—Catholicism, Protestantism, and Judaism.

Asian Americans have increased religious pluralism in
America. The various groups include Buddhists, Taoists, Roman Catholics, and Protestants. Although the exact percentage
is unknown, a good number of the Chinese and Japanese Americans are Buddhists. One study noted that five of the fifty plus
divisions within Japanese Buddhism were represented in the
United States.[15] Laotians, Cambodians, and Vietnamese are also
primarily Buddhists. A small number of Asian Indians represent
the Muslim and Hindu religions. The majority of the Indian
subcontinent are believers of Hinduism, but very few of them
emigrated. Many Asian Indian Christians reside in the state of
Kerala in India. A large percentage of the early Asian Indian
immigrants were Sikhs, a nontheistic faith based on the doctrinal teaching of its first ten gurus. The first Sikh temple in the
states was built in Stockton, California and served as a spiritual
center for Asian Indians on the Pacific Coast.[16]

Protestant denominations began proselytizing efforts among
Asian Americans as early as 1851 in competition with the Chinese and Japanese religious institutions. One of the first efforts
was Bible classes offered by the Presbyterians for Chinese in
California.[17] Wesley Woo did a thorough study of the mission
movement with Chinese in California and notes that in addition
to the Presbyterians, Baptists, Methodists, and Congregationalists were also active among the immigrants.[18] One of the first
missionaries, William Speer, opened a mission in 1852. As a
former missionary to China, he was especially liked by the Chinese because he could speak their language, but still had made

few converts by the time the mission was closed in 1857.

Denominations in the states tended to utilize the Chinese and Japanese immigrants only as assistants in church leadership positions, but in Hawaii they were more likely to serve as pastors for the new churches. The Baptists, Methodists, and Congregationalists headed mission efforts in addition to the Presbyterians. Despite the consistent effort expended, there was not a significant number of Chinese and Japanese converted.

The Koreans were different in that many had converted to Christianity before arriving in Hawaii and mainland America. In Hawaii, they organized the Korean Evangelical Society in less than a year after their arrival. Methodist and Episcopal churches dominated the Christian membership in Hawaii, and Methodists and Presbyterians were predominant on the mainland. Currently, an estimated 65 percent of the Korean-American population are members of Protestant churches, but only 25 percent are identified as Christian.[19]

Some Asian-American groups are highly influenced by the Roman Catholic church. An example is the Filipino-American community which is estimated to be 90 percent Roman Catholic, whereas Korean Americans are estimated at 10 percent Roman Catholic.[20] Many Asians embrace aspects of Confucianism although in more of a philosophical way than in a religious way.[21]

FAMILY TRADITIONS

The true sense of the extended family was associated with rural China and Japan in the early 1900s. That same situation in which different generations live under the same roof is rare among Asians living in America today. Studies have found that Asian-American families today show a preference for living alone rather than with married children. Further, by 1970 their family structure and size showed a diversity common to all American families.[22]

In spite of the diversity, there are ways in which there is an adherence to the more traditional family approach of the Asian culture. The Asian-American family will represent a close-knit unit and a community of kin and friends. There is usually a stronger emotional attachment to members of the family even though not living under the same roof. Young people are expected to show deference to their elders. A sense of pride and responsibility for the family persists.

The family structure is still influenced by the traditional male-dominated household in which family members had well-defined roles and obligations. Authority rested in the father and was passed to sons in his absence. Historically, sons have been more welcome than daughters since women have held an inferior position. A daughter may be viewed as a liability because once she marries, she will transfer her loyalties to the new family.

Although greater variety in family patterns is now practiced among Asian-American families, cultural tensions in this area still exist. Asian seminary students in reflection groups have shared the agony of Asian-American wives who have not been able to give birth to a son. Female college students of Asian descent stated, in interviews, that their parents wanted them to be successful in their professions, but at the same time tended to instruct them as to the age by which they should be married and expected them to pursue a career that would permit ample time for being a wife and mother.

Some Asian-American females feel that their brothers still receive preferential treatment in the family. Dr. Audrey Yamagata-Noji, of Rancho Santiago College, has observed that due to being a woman "a young Vietnamese immigrant woman would be put last in order in terms of financing her education; that is, she could be expected to quit school if her younger brother came of college age."[23]

The specific culture and the length of time in America influences the rigidness to which the traditional Asian family structure is adhered. Cultural tensions for women are most strongly felt in the first- and second-generation Asian-American families. The longer a family has been in the United States and the rise of their family income level seem to be major change factors. For example, a Chinese-American family that had been in the United States for some time would not be likely to distinguish between educating a daughter or a son as long as they have sufficient funds.

Traditional values are strongly ingrained and operate as motivators of decisions and behavior. Shame and dishonor are to be avoided. One's ancestors are respected. Achievement and good performance will bring honor to one's family.[24]

SOCIAL INTERACTION

Differences in the patterns of group interaction between Asian Americans and Caucasian Westerners are usually the result of differing cultural values. Westerners tend to feel that a responsible person will talk so that something can be accomplished and that silence is negative. The Asian American, on the other hand, feels that it is better to be quiet unless one has carefully thought out what should be said. The talkative person may be simply seeking attention or may not be able to think well if they talk too much.

The Westerner is quick to give emotional expressions and may judge those who are nonemotional as uncaring. The Asian American sees emotional expressions as a sign of immaturity. Striving for emotional restraint is an example of adult behavior.

The Asian American values subordination of oneself in conflict situations. Individuals who insist on having their way, even if they are justified, are often viewed with disapproval. This means that even though the Asian American feels their position is correct, they may disengage from the discussion in order to avoid conflict.

The traditional greeting of East Asians involves some variation of a bow, although Japanese bow more frequently than Chinese. The standard form will be a gesture with hands joined together and raised with a slight bowing of the head. Asian men are more likely to shake hands than are Asian females. An Asian man will seldom shake hands with a woman unless she offers her hand first. Traditionally, members of the opposite sex have avoided touching one another in the presence of others.

Some Asian Americans view time differently in that it does not have the same importance that it does for most mainline

Americans. This is more true of Southeast Asians than for persons from industrialized countries such as Japan and Taiwan. Southeast Asians may have a more elastic perspective of time and may not put a great deal of emphasis on punctuality as is expected by non-Asians.[25]

Accuracy in communication with Asian Americans will require paying careful attention to nonverbal communication as well as verbal interactions. Although less obvious in mainline American culture, nonverbal communication conveys emotional responses in all cultures. Asian Americans make greater use of nonverbal communication than do non-Asian Americans, so misunderstanding can occur if this is overlooked.

The Asian American's use of the eyes or hands, or the positioning of the body, can give additional meaning to the conversation but gets little attention from the Anglo American. For example, backward leaning of the body indicates withdrawal, while a forward lean says that the listener is concerned and involved. In a study of Japanese-Americans, females were found to express anxiety through increased speaking and males express anxiety through silence.[26]

Nonverbal communication may also be given different interpretations by various cultures. For example, Westerners often use an index finger to motion for someone to approach. This would be considered a sign of contempt for some Asian cultures.

Mainline Americans make frequent use of slang without the realization that interpretation of its use can be very difficult for those using English as a second language. Karen Chia-Yu Liu shared several interesting examples in a seminar.

> A word being translated into a particular Asian language, may have a totally different meaning from its use in the United States. For example, "potluck" dinner means bring a dish to pass around. Potluck, translated in Chinese, means come to my house and join us for supper. It has no indication that the guests have to bring something with them when they come.
>
> To communicate with Americans, most newcomers will translate English literally, word for word, into their own language. If the meaning of the word is used differently from the way it has been translated, it could create some misunderstanding and confusion. For example, "bring a dish" means

bring a cooked dish to share. One Asian family brought empty dishes to a party; they were very embarrassed.[27]

Various Asian groups will follow different patterns for their names. The names of most Asians will begin with the family name and the given name will be last. If a middle name is used, it is placed between the family name and given name. The middle name often distinguishes between a male and a female.

Vietnamese usually include a middle name but Chinese, Japanese, Koreans, Cambodians, and Laotians may not. In such cases, they will use the given name to distinguish female and male names.

A typical Vietnamese name will follow the order of family, middle, and given name. The order used for writing their name in English is the reverse of that used in Vietnam. The name that is used in address is the given name rather than the family name. However, Vietnamese do not normally use a family or given name on a daily basis. Instead they use a polite term plus a personal pronoun which does not actually have a good American parallel. A rough comparison might be "distinguished teacher." In conversations, the use of actual names is considered impolite in Vietnamese.[28]

The Asian students in our seminary student body are quick to give us an easy version of their names when they sense that teachers and students are having difficulty pronouncing their name. Ng becomes Eng, Dong becomes Don, and Jung becomes John. However, it is important to learn to pronounce their names clearly and correctly and to show respect for the names given to them by their family rather than using a convenient substitute.

The educational achievement of Asian Americans is to be appreciated even more when consideration is given to the difficulty with language that many experience. In many instances, the students must study far longer and more diligently than their classmates. Many children and adolescents live in homes where the native language is the primary language. This represents the cultural conflict that a younger generation may feel when their loyalties are demanded by two different cultural groups.

STEREOTYPING AND DISCRIMINATION

Asian Americans have been subjected to racial discrimination in America as early as the 1850s. The discrimination has come in the forms of rejection, deportation, relocation, and even murder. As a response, many Asians developed tightly knit enclaves such as Chinatowns and Little Tokyos. Asian immigration was halted in 1924 and remained so until the McCarran-Walters Bill in 1952.

Prejudice during the earliest days of Asian immigration centered in California. As the Asian groups entered the United States, they were viewed as a threat to homogeneity and the view of America as a "white man's country." In addition to this, America was unexpectedly facing a national crisis of unemployment.

The *New York Tribune* in 1869 published an article addressing the problem of Asians as immigrants "without the slightest attachment to the country." The article went on to describe Chinese as "utter heathens, treacherous, sensual, cowardly, and cruel."[29] Second- and third-generation Americans were sufficiently threatened to refer to the Chinese as "yellow peril." Within a few decades, newspapers were addressing the "Japanese problem," which included the Koreans.

At the turn of the century, Asian children were forced into segregated schooling in Chinatown when the San Francisco school board ordered all "Chinese, Japanese, and Korean children to the Oriental School." Even Washington took part as President Wilson stated during the 1912 presidential campaign that "we cannot make a homogeneous population of a people who do not blend with the Caucasian race."

Experts in Asian-American studies feel that racial discrimination often isolates Asian Americans to a greater extent than many other ethnic groups. Dr. Shirley Hune, Associate Dean at the University of California, states that no matter how hard they try, Asian Americans simply cannot blend in as someone could from the Euro-American heritage. She further states that it is not unusual for Asian Americans who represent the third or fourth generation in America to still be asked questions such as

"Were you born here?" or "Do you speak English?"[30]

In sharp contrast to the "yellow peril" image of early Asian immigrants, bright and highly motivated young Asian Americans have increasingly populated university campuses since the 1970s. Media and research has focused on their academic achievement, especially that of the Koreans, Japanese, and Chinese, giving them the image of the "model minority." This is understandable when one realizes that they score better on college entrance exams than any other group of students. The average scores in reading, language, and math for Koreans, Chinese, and Japanese students who were fluent in English was in the 90th percentile for California students. They maintain high academic levels regardless of the parents' education, family income, or social status.[31]

Stereotyping, whether positive or negative, can be distasteful to those who are recipients. In America, representing the Asian American primarily as a model minority is a form of positive stereotyping, but still has disadvantages in that the total image of the Asian American is not considered. Even though many studies appear on the surface to suggest that Asian Americans are a model minority, it is imperative that this stereotype be avoided.

The model minority concept had its origin in a 1966 *New York Times* article.[32] Attention was given to the academic achievement, income level, and rate of unemployment of Asian Americans. The concept has been a controversial one in that there is considerable disagreement regarding the current socioeconomic status and educational level when all Asian Americans are considered. Those who disagree with the concept feel that there are a large number of Asian Americans who are still suffering from discrimination in the labor market and who are not having a share in the improved educational and economic standing. For example, studies of Vietnamese refugees have presented a rosy picture at the same time that a large percentage remain on public assistance.[33]

One might question the insistence on presenting Asian Americans as a model minority. It has been suggested that the author who introduced the term was actually attempting to divert attention from racism. Ideologically, the concept may serve to justify continued inequality on the part of minorities in America as a whole. It gives an example of a minority group that does succeed in spite of obstacles. The suggestion is that any minority group can "make it" if they really want to. Thus, the assumed American promise of equal opportunity for all is reinforced.

VALUE ORIENTATION

Value systems are in transition today in all countries. Therefore it is impossible to attribute specific values and behaviors to Asian Americans with any degree of certainty. However, an attempt will be made to describe some general values which are characteristics of the more traditional Asian cultures. At the same time, we are acknowledging that a great deal of variety in behavior and adherence to these values will exist within as well as between the different Asian groups.

THE ENRYO SYNDROME

The Asian "situational orientation" places an emphasis upon the total situation rather than the individual, which is more common to mainline America. The behavior or action for a situation will be determined according to what is best for all in the situation, even if it is not to the individual's benefit. The situational orientation requires a collection of behaviors called the *enryo syndrome* that will show restraint and reserve in social interactions. Originally the enryo syndrome behaviors were for situations that involved levels of power and authority. However, they have been more generally applied to embarrassing or anxiety-producing situations.

Asians believe that the expression of negative feelings can damage relationships among people who will need to continue to interact. Rather than have this occur, it is better to seek a "situational solution" in which the situation changes so that confrontation no longer exists. Asian Americans would do all that is within their power to avoid bringing shame into a social relationship. To cause shame for another is to suggest that the other is responsible or that they did not fulfill their responsibility. To suggest this is a serious breach of social interaction for the Asian American. To save face does not involve simply saving face for the self, but involves saving face of the other.

Western Americans who tend to utilize confrontation may cause the Asian American to withdraw and remain silent. This will especially be true if the situation involves a person of position who is deserving of respect. The Asian American will attempt to communicate his or her preference for a lack of confrontation by a general attitude of nonresponsiveness.

Harmony is valued more than direct confrontation in which one party may lose face. If necessary, the more traditional Asian will accept blame for a situation even though the mistake is on the part of the other. In such cases, the expected response of the other is to deny that this is true. However, Asian Americans have often been used as a scapegoat by mainline Americans who have taken advantage of the Asian situational orientation.

Duane Elmer in *Cross-Cultural Conflict* notes that Westerners, who value directness, tend to misinterpret the indirect method of handling conflict. He gives four possible assumptions that the Westerner might make: (1) the person lacks courage to confront, (2) the person is unwilling to deal with the issue, (3) the person is not sufficiently committed to solve the problem, or (4) the person simply refuses to take responsibility for his or her actions. As Elmer further notes, utilizing the indirect method of handling conflict in actuality requires both courage and commitment. The lack of appreciation for this method is the result of not understanding the value orientation of a culture different from our own.[34]

Another behavior that is part of the enryo syndrome is the Asian response to praise. Humility and modesty is valued, and it is not acceptable to act proud of oneself or one's family. Therefore, the accepted response to praise is to deny the praise with a statement such as "I did not do well." The one giving the praise would ignore the denial. Such reactions should be viewed as good manners and not due to a poor self-image.

The use of the English word "yes" is also associated with

the enryo syndrome and has caused a certain amount of confusion in communication. Asian Americans may say "yes" to communicate that they are listening, rather than that they understand or are in agreement with what has been said. It may be the polite response if the interchange is with someone who has authority. For example, it would be impolite to tell a minister or teacher that the message was not understood since this may imply that the message was not a clear or well-communicated message.

Confusion can be avoided by asking for more than a "no" or "yes" answer. The use of negative questions should also be avoided. The question, "Aren't you going with us?" may be answered with a "yes" that means, "Yes, I am not going with you." It is important to remember this difference in the use of "yes" to avoid misunderstanding.

FILIAL PIETY

In the traditional Asian culture, it is the duty of the child, especially the son, to care for parents when they are elderly. This duty was part of the teachings of Confucius, who regarded it as the root of all virtue. In Eastern ancestor worship, this relationship between son and parents is important in that the son will continue to revere them after they are dead, ensuring family continuity. For example, September 25 is a Korean holiday known as Moon Harvest Day in which both the bountiful harvest and one's ancestors are honored.

Filial piety is the basis for the patriarchal family in which the father is the authority, the wife is subservient to the husband, and the son expresses relational reverance toward the father. Idealistically, the elderly in the Asian-American family will be cared for by their children. However, studies have found that realistically there is a decrease in the extent to which this practice is being carried out even in the Asian countries today. Various situations and differences within subgroups are affecting whether or not the care of parents is highly valued. It is believed that second generation Japanese Americans continue to feel a sense of responsibility and care for their elderly parents who were immigrants to America. It is less likely to be true of young adult Asian couples in general.[35]

Along with the concept of filial piety is the characteristic of "place" which gives importance to whether one is the firstborn son or the third born daughter. There is also the "place" of the daughter-in-law in relationship to her mother-in-law. A future awaits the woman who bears a son because after her years of serving another, she knows that she will someday have the role as the mother-in-law. Leslie describes the tradition of the Chinese New Year in which it is the practice for children to visit their parents, beginning with the husband's parents. He writes that a son who visited his mother-in-law first would be considered an unfilial son even by the mother-in-law.[36]

Changes have occurred in the degree to which the patriarchal family pattern is consistently followed in Asian Americans today. However, even if the strength of this structure is somewhat eroding, its psychological impact will continue to be felt. A bright Asian-American female completing her Ph.D. shares that she still feels the effect of her parents' disappointment as they express their concern about her single status at thirty-five years of age. Even with her professional competence, they tell her that they feel that she will not be cared for unless she marries. Further, at her age, the unlikelihood that she will bear children makes her a poor marriage candidate. Thus, a very capable Asian woman has to deal with the psychological threat of inadequacy because she may not carry out her traditional "place" as wife and mother.

COLLECTIVE FAMILY

The concept of "saving face" actually has its association with a value for the *collective family.* This is in direct contrast with the Western value placed on the independent, autonomous functioning of the individual. This basic difference between Asians and Westerners is especially evident in those with a Chinese ethnic background. The primary idea of saving face is not to save face for oneself but to save face for the family. The interdependence of family members means that all actions are viewed in terms of family honor. For many of the Asian groups, the family name comes first, which implies the primary significance of the family unit.

Traditionally, Asian identity cannot be simply an individual matter. It will take place within the family context. This makes it easier to understand why the female Ph.D. referred to above will find it difficult to be unaffected by her parents' perception of her unmarried status. Any achievement as well as any failure is a family achievement or failure. Saving face for the sake of the family is a stronger motivation than saving face for the individual.

Saving face for the family will have implications for some counseling situations within the church. It may be very difficult for the Asian American to share a family problem which shows weakness or indiscretion because the family will lose face. Although there is less resistance on the part of some to seek help outside of the family, decision-making is still very much a family affair.

Leslie notes that an aspect of face-saving that is distinctively Chinese is the feeling of shame as opposed to feeling of guilt. Shame involves perceptions of others, while guilt is internal.[37] However, researchers Sue and Sue feel that both guilt and shame are used as means of social control in the more traditional Asian families. Guilt would result when the expectations of the family system are not met. Shame is related to the family, community, and ethnic group.[38]

The practice of saving face is for the sake of all parties involved in communication or negotiating. Thus, the collective orientation goes beyond just the family and includes all who are involved. It is apparent that face-saving is an important factor in interpersonal relating for Asian Americans.

MODERATION IN EXPRESSION

Asian children are taught to value *moderation* in their expressions. Emotional outbursts are discouraged; girls are taught to be submissive and to suppress their feelings. It is not common for anger to be expressed. Such behavior has its source in a value for moderation. The patriarchal family with its understanding of "place" is conducive to this control. An exception might be seen in certain circumstances. Men might be expected to express themselves more than women, and men in higher echelon occupations with higher socioeconomic status more than those from lower echelon occupations and lower socioeconomic levels.

Chang, in writing about health care, notes that Asian-American patients will often deny pain. She writes about a nursing supervisor who instructed the nursing staff that "one-half the dose is sufficient" for Asian-American patients. However, Chang was well aware from interviews that the expressions of the patients were due to not wanting to bother the staff and/or not wanting to admit feeling pain.[39]

The concept of balance is complementary to the characteristic of inconspicuousness that is often associated with Asians. In the early years of discrimination, Asian Americans reasoned that if they were not noticed by the majority population, they would be less likely to be persecuted or even killed.

This value for balance and moderation may cause the Asian American to internalize problems rather than to express them in a healthy way. It is possible that guilt and hostility will be turned inward by the individual, rather than seeking help from others.

CONCLUSION

Asian Americans view their heritage as a source of strength. Their modesty, determination, self-sacrifice, and hard work to achieve goals fit well with the traditional American value of self-reliance. However, they must also be helped to see that the church community can be a part of an extended family network for support and encouragement. As Asian Americans seek ways to communicate their needs to the church community, members of the church community can search for ways to embrace them into a caring and giving atmosphere of Christian love.

For the most part, Asians view themselves as belonging to a specific ethnic group and possibly to a subgroup. Non-Asian Americans often view people of Asian descent as a homogeneous group with the assumption that they share the same characteristics. Although there are certain similarities among the groups, definite differences exist as well. Even within groups, distinction can be made according to the differences of sub-groups, such as the number of generations in the United States for the Japanese, and for Chinese and Japanese living in Hawaii as opposed to those living in the states.

As is true for all ethnic groups, individuals generally dislike being mistaken for a member of another group. A consideration of selected Asian cultures will amplify the fact that distinctive similarities and differences are both present and important.

The next chapter will include a historical overview of selected Asian people groups to assist in understanding their historical context. We will also describe the major cultural values and concepts of that group. The limitations of time and space prohibit full coverage of any or all Asian-American groups, but the general group characteristics gleaned will provide sufficent implications for ministry in the church and classroom.

CHAPTER TEN

SELECTED ASIAN GROUPS

BACKGROUND

Harper's Encyclopedia of Religious Education categorizes the majority of Asian Americans into three categories—East Asians, Southeast Asians, and Southern Asians—with the recognition that there are other Asian groups in the United States as well. The respective three categories with their primary groups are: East Asians (Japanese, Koreans, Chinese); Southeast Asians (Filipinos, Vietnamese, Indonesians); and Southern Asians (Indians, Pakistanis).[1] Other Asian groups include those from Burma, Cambodia, Laos, Malaysia, Singapore, Sri Lanka, and Thailand. Immigrants considered Pacific Islanders include primarily Samoans, Tongans, and Guamanians, as well as smaller numbers from Tahiti and the Fijis.

Only a few of the Asian-American groups have been selected for more specific consideration in this chapter. We will present the experiences of the Chinese, Japanese, Koreans, and Vietnamese in greater detail. The Chinese and Japanese Americans, along with Filipino Americans, were among the earliest Asian immigrants. Research has focused primarily on the Chinese and Japanese. This may be due to the fact that Filipinos represent greater diversity and have not developed communities with the same degree of cohesiveness that is characteristic of Chinese and Japanese Americans. Some researchers have referred to the Filipinos as the "hidden minority."[2]

Because of the vast mission work that has occurred in Korea, a larger percentage of Koreans are Christian when arriving in America than is true of other Asian Americans. This gives their group more importance in a practical sense. Because there is a greater possibility of contact, there is a need for understanding the similarities and differences between Korean Americans and other groups, both majority and minorities.

Vietnamese Americans are among the more recent immigrants. They differ drastically from other Asian groups in that the majority did not come to America voluntarily, but because they had no choice but to leave their country. Vietnamese, along with Laotians and Cambodians, are considered Indochinese. About 90 percent of Indochinese immigration to America has been Vietnamese.

CHINESE AMERICANS

The Chinese were the first Asian immigrant group to settle in the United States in large numbers. By 1980, Chinese Americans were considered the largest single Asian group in the United States. Although they no longer hold this position, as an ethnic group, Chinese Americans are deserving of specific consideration because of the discrimination and persecution they received during the early years of their settlement in America.

After the United States began to keep immigration records in 1820, only 43 Chinese immigrants were recorded from 1820 to 1849. However, this record excluded the West Coast, which was not a part of the Union at that time. In 1850 the population report for San Francisco included 787 Chinese.[3] In the next few decades, tens of thousands of Chinese, mostly young men, came to America. Twenty thousand arrived in 1852 alone.[4] California recorded approximately 25,000 for the state in 1852 and more than 50,000 in 1862.[5]

EARLY IMMIGRATION AND DISCRIMINATION

The background of this immigration was the political unrest of the 1800s in China, as well as the California gold rush and western expansion movement in America. As a portion of the immigrants moved to the South during the Reconstruction, some white planters reportedly hoped that the Chinese would replace black labor.[6] However, Chinese labor never played an important role in the economy of the South.

The Central Pacific Railway Company, in competition with the Union Pacific to build the first American transcontinental railroad, began to utilize the Chinese as laborers in 1865. The Central Pacific had to cross the solid granite of the Sierra Nevada range as well as the deserts of Nevada and Utah.[7] The Chinese laborer could earn thirty dollars a month working for the railroad. In China during that same time, he would earn three to five dollars a month.

By 1870, 77 percent of all the Chinese in America lived in California. It is believed by some that the Chinese built the agricultural industry of California.[8]

At first, Chinese immigrants were welcomed by the whites because they were willing to take lower-status jobs and provide cheap labor. However, anti-Chinese sentiment was already present during the late 1850s and very evident at the end of the 1860s as a result of economic pressures.

The depressed economy of the 1870s created an atmosphere in which the Chinese were blamed and persecuted for job shortages. Anti-Chinese meetings, called "sand-lot meetings," were frequent occurrences for unemployed whites. Gradually the Chinese were forced out of working on farms, railroads, or in factories and retreated into self-employment. "Ethnic antagonism" became the stimulus for stores, restaurants, and the American phenomenon of the Chinese laundry.

For several decades, Chinese carried a reputation as undesirables. In 1877, one Chinese community in San Francisco, the undisputed center of anti-Chinese agitation, was attacked by thousands of whites. In other towns, the entire Chinese population was forced to leave after threats of violence.

Justice was practically nonexistent because of a ruling that Chinese could not testify against a white person. An 1849 law, which prohibited testimony by blacks and Indians, was ruled to include the Chinese in 1854.

Some Chinese reacted to these circumstances by locating in urban Chinatowns. In California, thousands lived within the twelve-block boundary of San Francisco's Chinatown. Kinship networks developed which were called clans. The clans served as financial and political organizations to assist the Chinese. Assistance to start businesses and find employment was given. At the same time, cultural assimilation was discouraged and learning the English language was not considered important.

The late nineteenth-century immigration legislation injured the Chinese more than any other immigrant group.[9] In 1882, the United States government passed a series of laws which ended the immigration of Chinese. As the restriction went into effect, there were approximately eighteen males for every female in the 100,000 Chinese already in the United States. By 1920, the Chinese population had decreased to approximately 60,000.[10]

In 1943, the ban on Chinese immigration was lifted and Chinese Americans could become citizens. Labor was in short supply, and the immigrants were viewed in a more positive light. As a result, a period of cultural assimilation began. Many experienced upward social movement as they were able to get jobs with more prestige.

RELIGIOUS INFLUENCES

The early Chinese-American communities differed from the majority of immigrant groups in that churches did not play a prominent role. As a whole, the most important social organization was the family association or the clan.

During the nineteenth century, Chinese Americans held to their religious traditions, which were founded in Confucianism, Taoism, and Buddhism. The universe was viewed as a trinity of heaven, earth, and man:

> . . . heaven directs, earth produces, and man cooperates.
> When man cooperates, he prospers; on the other hand, if man
> does not cooperate, he destroys the harmonious arrangements

of the universe and suffers the consequences in the form of natural disasters, such as floods, droughts, and famines.[11]

There are a number of reasons why Christianity was often resisted by the Chinese in America. One was the loyalty they felt for their own religious traditions. Another reason was the inconsistency between church teachings and the American racism directed at the Chinese. A third reason is that some leaders within the Chinese community discouraged the acceptance of Christianity because they saw it as a threat to Chinese social institutions.[12]

Traditionally, religion in China has been nondenominational and has not been associated with conflict between groups. Loyalty to one church has not been emphasized, nor has membership lists. Instead, Chinese have shown a more relaxed attitude toward all groups, as well as a respect for all variations of religious belief. Although approximately one-third of the Chinese in Hawaii are estimated to be Christian, it is Christianity with a strong Chinese flavor.[13]

Social-Class Factors

In the 1980 census report, nearly half of all Chinese in the United States resided in three metropolitan areas: San Francisco/Oakland/Berkeley, New York/Newark/Jersey City, and Los Angeles/Long Beach. California has the largest Chinese population and Hawaii has the highest Chinese population percentage.[14] Living conditions, however, vary widely, as the Chinese-American community has become bipolar in its social class background. In 1980, the median household income for Chinese Americans was above the national average. Chinese Americans as a group have twice the proportion of college graduates as the average for America as a whole.[15] At the same time, large numbers of native-born Chinese Americans are living below the poverty level. Many Chinese-American males work in restaurants and the females have low-paying employment in the garment business.[16] The "silent" Chinese of San Francisco have been described as unemployed and living in substandard living quarters, while a suburban community in Monterey Park, California has become "America's first suburban Chinatown."[17]

The population of Chinese Americans nearly doubled between 1970 and 1980. About half of the immigrants who arrived during this time represented low-skilled workers, poverty, and crime. The media has covered stories of gang shootings in Chinatowns and the activities of the Triad Societies. As a result, the Chinese-American picture is becoming more bifurcated.

Some explain the above differences by dividing Chinese Americans into two groups: American-born Chinese (ABCs) and the recent fresh-off-the-boat immigrants (FOBs). Although all differences are not directly tied to these two categories, research does support this in certain areas. More and more of the ABCs are identified as better educated and more affluent. The FOBs are more likely to be poorly educated and work in lower paid service positions.[18]

At the same time, the Chinese Americans continue to be included with all Asian Americans in being referred to in terms of the "model minority" image. Remarkable achievement by Chinese Americans at every level of schooling has been given a great deal of attention by the media and social scientists. Since the 1920s they have equaled or surpassed whites on nonverbal intelligence tests. They have consistently earned the highest SAT scores of all ethnic groups in mathematics and science.[19] Different sources for this success have been touted, but most relate either directly or indirectly to the home environment and traditional Chinese values. An additional suggestion is that the high scholastic performance is related to the Confucian work ethic.[20]

Even though the model minority image is a positive one, it is still an act of stereotyping that is not appreciated by any ethnic group. Diana Fong summarizes well the contemporary status for Chinese Americans in a *New York Times* article that she entitled "America's 'Invisible' Chinese."

> We're still not fully integrated into the mainstream because of our yellow skin and almond eyes. Much has changed in 100 years [since the exclusion act], but we still cannot escape the distinction of race.[21]

FAMILY ROLES AND STRUCTURE

Studies which compare the family life of Chinese Americans with Americans from Western cultures find a number of differing factors. Children show more compliance to adult demands. Greater value is placed on kinship dependence than independent initiative. They are taught the values of sharing, noncompetitiveness, and control of violent outbursts. They show a sensitivity to group pressure. The space and ownership granted children by Western American parents was contrasted with shared rooms for Chinese-American children, both children and parents using one another's belongings. Chinese-American parents showed more strictness in areas such as weaning, toilet training, and the control of aggression.[22]

Chinese-American parents assume a strong parental role within a close-knit family structure. They work diligently at creating a strong motivation to learn. This "parental push" is based on the belief that education is necessary to achieve in competitive American society. If children do not perform adequately in the classroom or playground, parents have been known to apologize for the behavior of the child. Parents from other cultures are more likely to blame the school environment or the teachers in such circumstances.

The Western world has had a strong influence on the lives of Chinese-American women. At the same time, understanding the contemporary Chinese-American woman can only be done by considering the role prescribed for her by Chinese traditions. The basic principle was that women were subordinate to men. Within the Confucian doctrine, three obediences were outlined for women: "obedience to the father when yet unmarried, obedience to the husband when married, and obedience to the sons when widowed." In addition to this, four virtues were outlined: she knew her place, she did not talk too much, she would adorn herself to please the opposite sex, and she would willingly do all the chores in the home.[23]

A more equal status for women in China has been possible since the revolution in 1949. At the same time, male supremacy still governs many women's lives in China. Nevertheless, whether born in America or China, the role of the Chinese-American woman is gradually representing more and more equality.

Leslie concludes that "marriage as a fellowship of equals simply does not fit into the Eastern way of thinking about hierarchical relations in human society." He notes that in Chinese cosmology, the male element, Yang, is representative of positive and superior elements. However, the female element, Yin, is representative of the negative and inferior.[24]

Definite social changes are occurring in Asia, but the traditional roles can linger in various forms, even for families that have been in America for two or three generations. As women pursue higher education and seek professional careers, conflict between their traditional values and the contemporary society will continue. Even if the pursuit of a career is approved, the particulars may represent conflict. Helen Lee, an Asian-American student, relates how she and her parents did not talk with one another for one month after she told them that she had decided to drop her educational program in medicine to study for the ministry at Wheaton College. In addition to questioning her pursuit of ministry study, her unmarried status at twenty-four years of age was also an issue. Ms. Lee referred to twenty-five as the "witching age."[25]

The carry-over of tradition can cause a cultural conflict for the Chinese-American woman, even after experiencing Western socialization. Pressure is still put on Asian-American women to structure and maintain the family over their own individual development. In interviews with Asian-American women, Kwong found that they were "torn between reluctance to take on traditional roles and guilt over rejecting them, between the sense of independence American society offers and the sense of obligation they feel not only to their parents, but to their parents' cultural values."[26] In China, as well as in the United States, much improvement is needed before complete equality will be achieved in either country.

Three types of families have been identified among Chinese Americans. One is the *traditional* family which is representative of the family structure of families in China. Hierarchical in nature, the father plays a dominant role with highly structured roles for parents and children. The second type is the *bicultural* family which is usually typical of second- or third-generation families. This type is the result of the integration of two cultures, Chinese and American. They sense the advantages of learning American ways but at the same time wish to maintain certain traditions of the Chinese culture. Language is a prominent feature of this approach. Usually there will be a cautious maintenance of social relationships from both cultures. The third type is the *modern family* which is the result of seeking full acculturation. The result of their integration is more American than Chinese.[27]

However, we should not allow the above generalizations to cast a shadow over the image of the Chinese-American community as one with great diversity. The three types of families described above is just one example of the many differences that can exist. At the same time, one study found a tenacity in the Chinese Americans to resist the "melting pot" of America. The researcher concluded that Chinatowns "whether in the United States, Manila, Bangkok, Calcutta, or Liverpool have a remarkable similarity."[28] Most Chinese Americans, regardless of their differences, share the value of retaining their ethnic heritage and culture.

JAPANESE AMERICANS

Japanese first immigrated to the United States in significant numbers between 1890 and 1924. The 1924 Immigration Law, which specifically barred the Japanese from entering the states, remained in effect until 1952. However, from 1910 until 1970, the Japanese still represented the most numerous Asian-Pacific group in America. In the 1988 report compiled by the U.S. Bureau of the Census, the Japanese had declined to eighth in size of all Asian immigrant groups.[29]

The Japanese immigrated to the U.S. within the context of trade agreements under Commodore Perry following the Chinese Exclusion Act of 1882. Some came to Hawaii; others came to work on railroads, in mills, or in mines in the U.S. mainland; many were very active in farming. Prejudice increased dramatically following the 1905 defeat of Russia by Japan in the Russo-Japanese war.

The industriousness and knowledge of agricultural work put the Japanese into direct competition with native farmers who reacted with discriminatory actions. The California legislature passed a law in 1913 which prohibited any person ineligible for citizenship from owning land. Since their children who were born in America were automatically citizens, the Japanese put the land in their children's names. The California legislature then passed a law in 1920 which prohibited aliens from being guardians of a minor's property. In spite of this, by 1941 the Japanese raised 42 percent of truck crops in California.[30]

Although the anti-Japanese attitude may have originated in economic competition, its form has often occurred as a stereotype which questioned their "assimilability." This was sometimes explained by the lifestyle or general attitude of the Japanese.

One San Francisco reporter wrote about their lack of emotional expression, "This stoicism, however, is a distinguishing feature with the Japanese. It is part of their creed never to appear astonished at anything, and it must be a rare sight indeed which betrays in them any expression of wonder." Such so-called distinguishing features became a primary element in the anti-Japanese stereotyping used by journalists, politicians, novelists, and filmmakers.[31]

The mass evacuation of Japanese Americans following Japan's attack on Pearl Harbor was referred to as "our worst wartime mistake" in a 1945 *Harper's Magazine* article.[32] Roosevelt's Executive Order 9066 authorized the relocation of over 120,000 Japanese, the majority of whom were American citizens."[33] It should be noted that Caucasian vegetable growers and shippers pushed for this evacuation. Although the mass evacuation was presented as necessary for national security, it is interesting that it was not deemed necessary for the 150,000 Japanese living in Hawaii.[34]

GENERATIONAL DIFFERENCES

As immigrants, the Japanese community in America has been stratified according to four generations: the Issei, Nisei, Sansei, and Yonsei. Although all share the Japanese culture, they represent vastly different social classes, goals, acculturation, and even personalities, perceptions, and values.

The first generation Japanese immigrant is called the Issei. These were relatively homogeneous and generally young men with rural backgrounds. If still alive, they would represent senior citizen status. This group did not expect to become successful in America but were hopeful that their children would. Immigrants who entered the United States after 1954 are considered new Issei. They include a large number of war brides.

Second generation American-born children, called the Nisei, were born between 1900 and 1941. Their model of acculturation resulted in acquiring American ways, holding to the Japanese culture in only a minimal way. The Nisei were among those incarcerated in the many camps located in Utah, Idaho, Wyoming, Arizona, Arkansas, and California during the years of 1942–1945. The effects of this mass incarceration on the Japanese-American culture will possibly never be fully understood. This is due partially to a traditional Japanese view of fate, an orientation that suggests "it can't be helped" *(shikata ga-nai),* as well as a tendency to handle problems through internalization.[35]

As a group, the Nisei can be generalized as having achieved an above average degree of affluence, financial security, and education. Common problems include inadequate communication with both older and younger generations, having to deal with children who feel "liberated" from traditional Japanese patterns, and the possibility of interethnic and interracial marriages within their families. It is not expected that the Nisei will easily turn to counselors or church leaders for help in dealing with these problems. A couple methods which would encourage seeking help would be to have professionals available from their culture, as well as presenting assistance as "education" rather than counseling or therapy.[36]

During the 1930s it was not uncommon for some of the Nisei generation to return to Japan during their childhood years for education. They are called Kibei, although they are technically still Nisei. The Kibei returned to America with a strong Japanese affiliation.

The third generation is called the Sansei. They represent a large majority of the young adult population of Japanese Americans. The Sansei has experienced a high rate of outmarriage which is evidence of their assimilation, in rather stark contrast to the earlier stereotyped image of "unassimilability." Their children, the fourth generation, are labeled Yonsei. Both the Sansei and Yonsei tend to have assumed American mannerisms, values, and behaviors.

Either by force or choice, the Issei often lived in the United States in segregated communities with relatively little contact with the outside world. The Nisei and Sansei generations had more contact with the majority American culture and were not as withdrawn. However, they still were the recipients of an ethnic role definition that was often negative and stereotyped.

Harry H.L. Kitano, author of several books on racism and ethnic groups, notes methods of adaption that were used to deal with role conflict that resulted from the differences of being an American Japanese and a Japanese American.[37] One method was "role distance" that was sometimes utilized by Nisei and Sansei generations. In "role distance" the Japanese American would carry out the role prescribed by the dominant community, but maintain distance between the self and the role by functioning in certain ways when dealing with the majority community. "There may be an exaggerated politeness ('so sorry, please'), a passive conformity and playing out of stereotyped role ('all of us are good at gardening')." Kitano also noted specific phrases used to refer to this role distance such as "playing up to whitey," "jiving and gaming," "dealing with the goyim," and putting up with the "dumb Haole."[38]

Role distancing may also be used to place a distance between the individual and his or her ethnic community. Nisei adaptation was often in this category. The Japanese Americans may attempt to identify with Anglo values, norms, and lifestyles to the exclusion of their own ethnic culture. Members of their ethnic group might call such individuals a "banana," one who may look Japanese on the outside but are actually Anglo on the inside.

Individuals who retain a role distance from their own culture are more likely to seek professional counseling and therapy for this situation than for any other. Ministers and helping professionals within a Christian environment must realize that in order for the Asian American to participate flexibly in all possible contexts, the goal must be a multicultural one. A multicultural approach entails a shift from both a monocultural and a bicultural approach to one that is firmly anchored in an individual's primary culture. It involves integration and internalization of both cultures.[39]

SOCIAL FACTORS

The profile of the Japanese American has been one of excellence in a number of areas. They have generally outranked other minority groups in the areas of educational achievement, income, and employment.[40] Although there has been some increase in the rates of delinquency since the 1970s, the overall adult and juvenile crime rate has been lower than that of any other group.[41] Professionally, they are highly concentrated in managerial and technical occupations.[42]

Some have attributed this success to characteristics such as "conformity, aspiration, competitiveness, discipline and self-control."[43] In light of their early history of discrimination and hardship in America, Japanese Americans have made remarkable progress.

Family Structure

Following the evacuation and internment, Japanese Americans experienced a decline in their involvement in agricultural and small shopkeeper businesses. This caused a change in the traditional structure of the family. The patriarchal position of the father was weakened. In addition to this, the former family structure which was based on an economic production unit changed to the more independent nuclear family form which was typical of the mainstream American pattern.

Already in the late 1970s, Japanese-American women had begun to assume a more independent role. Most of the Nisei women were in their sixties and seventies and were feeling good about themselves as Japanese Americans within a Western culture. They found enjoyment in life by enrolling in classes, traveling, and taking the first steps in political activities or in working to support others in politics.

In studies to determine the degree of assimilation for Sansei women, characteristics differed from that found for Nisei. They showed less pressure to become Americanized when it involved losing their Japaneseness. Some showed a determination to counteract the tendency toward assimilation in order to pre-serve their culture. They were seeking an integration of the two cultures that represented a truly pluralistic society rather than Anglo-dominant society. In the terms of one Japanese-Ameri-can female working on a law degree:

> There comes a point in the lives of Asian women who pursue professional careers where they either choose to become to-tally assimilated in their white, yuppie culture or they con-sciously decide to maintain and foster their Asian identity. I hope that I can follow the latter course.[44]

Possibly the greatest change in family values and structure is due to the increase of intermarriage with Caucasians. The over-all level of intermarriage is a combination of low rates for Issei and Nisei, but relatively high rates for the Sansei in the 1960s and 1970s.

What is not known at this time is the overall effect which intermarriage will have on the Japanese-American culture. Studies have already found that Japanese Americans who marry Caucasians are less likely to participate actively in the ethnic community than those who have married within the ethnic group.

Communication between Japanese American family mem-bers can be expected to differ from that in dominant American families. When compared with non-Asian couples, Japanese-American spouses tend to make greater use of inferences and indirect communication. Child-rearing approaches follow a sim-ilar pattern. Asian parents will utilize techniques which gain the child's cooperation or shape behavior by outside stimuli, where-as mainline American parents utilize more direct confronta-tion.[45]

The traditional understanding of the role of the child is consistent with the hierarchical structure of the Japanese cul-ture. The image that is encouraged is "a child who is obedient, who relies on others, who recognizes, defers, respects and is polite to those in authority, who submerges individual wishes, needs and desires; who is generally non-aggressive; who obeys rules and can live in a world of restrictions and regulations."[46]

Educational Perspectives

Children from Japanese-American families are affected by differences in the classroom if they are newly arrived in America. Both their homes and their teachers have communicated in more indirect ways as described above. In their new schools in America, they may be urged to speak up in classrooms whereas this would likely have been discouraged in Japanese schools.

Education is a priority for Japanese parents. Of all groups in the United States, including the white majority, the Japanese have had the highest average of education since 1940.[47] A study comparing American and Japanese schools indicated that Japanese educational achievement was assisted by four elements: (1) Japanese place more importance on education in the home. (2) Formal education begins at an earlier age for most Japanese children. (3) Japanese children show greater discipline in school behavior than their American counterparts. (4) From high school through college, serious Japanese students do little but study and attend school.[48]

Japanese parents, along with their teachers, have been found to emphasize certain components that are not necessarily emphasized in U.S. schools. These are considered necessary for the future academic success of the child. Three which have been observed:

> (1) calculated arousal of learner motivation to acquire a specific skill and to become a member of its social setting (2) repeated practice of precisely defined basic component routines until they become automatic (3) development of self-monitoring of learning performance.[49]

The development of concentration skills and learning routines have prompted superior classroom management. Japanese first-grade children pay closer attention to the teacher when he or she is speaking and display generally better behavior. This has resulted in more actual teaching time in the classroom.[50] Although Asian schools are often perceived as "tension-filled intellectual factories," studies have found that Japanese students expressed less distress and fewer problems than the Americans.[51]

Value Orientation

Behavior norms for Japanese Americans are still primarily associated with a hierarchical structure. Values include acknowledgment of dependency, ascribed obligation, contractual obligation, loyalty to one's superior, and modesty in the presence of one's superior. Other preferences which have been noted include:

> situational orientation (rather than one based on absolutes and universals); a preference for indirection (rather than direct confrontation); remaining less visible in public through conformity; giving priority to "means" (the process and etiquette of actions) over ends (the final product); and a hard work, high achievement (especially in education) orientation.[52]

Connor and Kitano identified differences in psychological and behavioral orientations of the Japanese and Americans.[53] They are listed below in summary form.

Japanese	Majority Americans
collectivity	individuality
duty, obligation	will, freedom
hierarchical orders, dependency	self, egalitarianism, independence
shameful to "show off"	aggressive, assertive

The value orientation of Japanese Americans should also be considered in counseling and teaching situations. From a study of Asian-American social workers in Los Angeles, it was suggested that Japanese-American clients would best be treated in a more formal and less confrontational manner than Caucasian clients. Group sessions were not felt to be as successful. Counselors needed to learn to be patient in waiting for the Japanese Americans to talk about the real problem.[54]

Generation stratification is also a factor to consider in counseling. With the earlier generations, the Issei and older Nisei, indirect styles of communication are considered more effective. The young adult population, the Sansei, who are more likely to marry out of their cultural group, must often deal with problems of separation and dependency.[55]

KOREAN AMERICANS

The name "Korea" comes from the Koryo dynasty, which had ruled Korea from the tenth to the late fourteenth century. Its location between the powers of China and Japan caused it to be a transitional link which mediated concepts of religion and culture. This central location also caused Korea to be the scene of much military conflict as the larger powers waged war with each other.[56]

Starting in 1969, Koreans began arriving in America at an estimated average of 20,000 per year. In 1988 that estimate was changed to an average of 35,000 Koreans entering each year. The Korean immigrants, along with other Asian groups, have changed the predominantly white, Euro-American face of America to a diverse country with people of many colors.

HISTORY OF IMMIGRATION

One hundred years ago little was known about Korea in the West. In an 1881 study it is referred to as the "Hermit Nation."[57] Korea was "opened" by an 1876 treaty with Japan which allowed foreign trade. Diplomatic relations with America followed via the Shufeldt Treaty which opened Korea to the West in 1882. During the next thirty years, much Western thought entered Korea.

One important result of the new openness was permission for Christian missionaries to enter the country. After 1876, Christian missionaries were free to minister in Korea and were a strong influence in the country.[58] By 1904, approximately 175 Western missionaries from fourteen denominations were ministering. By 1909, the number had reached 205, almost all of which were Americans. Seventy-seven percent were Protestant.[59]

American missionaries started some of the first modern schools for girls in Korea. One of the earliest schools, started by American missionary, Mary Scranton, eventually became the largest women's university in the world. The mission schools graduated girls who went on to become active participants in the women's movement in Korea.

By the turn of the century, many Koreans were Christians. Because their conversion was due to the efforts of American missions, they viewed the United States as the hub of their religion. Consequently, most of the early Korean immigrants were recent converts to Christianity.

The first Korean immigrants were three men who arrived in the United States in 1885. Only one of the three, a physician, remained in America. Between 1890 and 1905, sixty-four students arrived. All had been encouraged by American missionaries to pursue their education in America.[60]

Large-scale immigration occurred between 1903 and 1905. Over 7,000 Koreans arrived in Hawaii as sugar plantation contract laborers. More than half of this number were Christians. About 2,000 of this group eventually moved to the mainland United States. Between 1910 and 1924, significant numbers escaped the poor working conditions and low wages of the plantations by moving to the urban areas. There they found work in service positions while those with sufficient capital started businesses such as laundries, barbershops, retail grocery stores, and restaurants.

During the early years of immigration, mainline Americans perceived Koreans as Japanese. For example, when anti-Japanese feelings were running high in California, a group of Korean laborers was attacked in Hemet Valley by a white mob that mistook them for Japanese workers.[61]

In 1907, almost all Korean immigration to Hawaii and the United States ceased for approximately forty years. This was due to Japanese influence following the Treaty of Portsmouth, which declared Korea a Japanese colony. Only the wives of Korean aliens already resident in the United States were allowed to enter. In 1910, only 461 Koreans were counted in the states. By 1940, this number had only increased to 1,711.[62]

Following the Korean War, a significant number of Korean women entered the United States as wives of non-Asian-American servicemen. In 1970, the Korean population was approximately 69,000. In 1980 it had increased to around 355,000. Since the mid-1980s, approximately 36,000 Korean immigrants arrive in the United States each year. This represents the second highest number of immigrants per year for any Asian group.[63]

Early Korean immigrants in both Hawaii and the U.S. mainland organized a religious community almost as soon as they arrived. As already mentioned, the majority were Christian which was a contrast to other Asian immigrants. By 1905, both Methodist and Episcopal services had been held. By 1918, the approximate 3,000 Korean Christians in Hawaii had organized 39 Korean Protestant churches.[64]

SOCIAL ADAPTATION

The large number of Korean Protestant churches in America have continued to play an important community role. As immigrants find themselves in an ethnic community, isolated from the mainstream of society, many turn to the church for support. Many Korean immigrants arrive in America as ministers or come for the purpose of preparing for the ministry. Even with the proliferation of Korean-American churches, some who desire to pastor have to select an alternative vocation due to competition for congregations.[65]

Historically, Korean-language schools were often operated through the church. Korean history and culture were taught in addition to their native language. In many cases, the pastor was the only person qualified to serve as a teacher. As the children began to attend local public schools, they developed fluency in the English language beyond that of their parents.[66]

Korean and Japanese languages belong to a language family different from Chinese. At the same time, Korean and Japanese languages are different from one another. Originally, Korean literature used classical Chinese form or style in which thousands of characters had to be memorized. The Korean language was much easier to learn after the "Korean script," Hangul, was invented. Although the upper classes continued to consider the Chinese system superior, Protestant missionaries encouraged the use of Hangul because it was easier to learn. The Korean alphabet consists of ten vowels and fourteen consonants. The Bible was soon translated into Korean, as were other books used by Christian schools and the church.[67]

A major hindrance to Korean immigrants has been the inability to speak the English language. A 1979 study found that only 10 percent of new immigrants to Los Angeles spoke English fluently. Korean is the primary language of 98 percent of Koreatown residents in Los Angeles. In the 1970 census, 76 percent of the national sample listed Korean as their native language.

Although this lack of language facility often impedes educational and occupational mobility, Korean Americans have still contributed to the "model minority" image by their accomplishments. Korean Americans are generously represented on faculties in American colleges and universities. About 20 percent of those born in Korea have professional or executive positions in the United States. They have developed numerous community institutions such as newspapers, schools, and churches, as well as cultural organizations.

In a study of demographics for Korean Americans, their profile is similar to other Asian groups in contributing to the model minority image. Korean family life is stable with the majority living in two-parent households. Parents are very concerned about the education of their children. Some have come to the United States specifically for that reason. The median income for Korean Americans is lower than that of Japanese and Chinese Americans but is higher than the average income for Filipinos or Vietnamese.[68]

Korean adaptation is different from that of domination and domestic colonialism. Early Koreans retained their traditional culture due to the hope that they would return to their homeland. Following annexation by Japan, their energy was aimed at maintaining their lost identity. Kitano suggests that the most appropriate title for this type would be the "government-in-exile" model and notes that the exile model usually lasts for only the original generation.[69]

The second generation of Koreans does not have the "we shall return" orientation and follows more traditional patterns of acculturation and integration. One factor that contributes to this is the higher than usual number of outgroup marriages. A study in the Los Angeles area found that 26 percent of the marriages involving Korean Americans were to non-Koreans.[70]

Some suggest that Koreans may integrate more rapidly into the American system than any other Asian group. To date, their pattern has not been established. However, many show a strong motivation to become Americanized. At the same time, there are those who are challenging Korean Americans to stress their Korean heritage. B.Y. Choy, author of *Koreans in America,* advises his fellow Korean Americans, "Don't try to be somebody you are not. Neither be Korean nor American. Just be yourself—Korean American. Only then you will feel at home with our heritage."[71]

In summary, a number of factors have made Korean immigration unique among Asian groups.

> (1) Early immigration was very brief, between 1902 and 1905, when the Japanese occupied their country.
> (2) Many immigrants were Christian, which meant that the church continued to be an important part of their community structure.
> (3) Although the early immigrants generally settled in Hawaii and the West Coast, the post-WWII immigrants were less restrictive in their locations so that Koreans are much more geographically dispersed than are the Chinese and Japanese.
> (4) Korea was never an enemy nation so that Koreans were not as subjected to demeaning stereotypes.[72]

SOUTHEAST ASIANS

Most Americans were introduced to the many traumas experienced by Cambodians through the movie *The Killing Fields.* The nightmare began when the Communist Khmer Rouge took over Cambodia, and thousands were forced to experience separation from their families and daily brutalities of public torture and executions.

Many of the Southeast Asians who immigrated to America endured unbelievable hardship. This is especially true for Vietnamese refugees, the Laotians, Cambodians, and premodern peoples such as the Hmong.

> Cambodians and Laotians left their countries under devastating conditions. Many endured boat crossings in unsafe vessels and experienced violence at the hands of sea pirates. They spent anywhere from a few months to a few years in refugee

camps in Thailand, Hong Kong and the Philippines. Obviously, these varied conditions of arrival had a significant impact
on the refugees' subsequent adaptation to American life.[73]

Many of the refugees have been insufficiently prepared to
deal with the modern urban society of America. Most came with
very little, some were stripped of what little they did have from
encounters with pirates. Approximately 4,000 Southeast Asian
immigrants were crowded into substandard housing in the one-
square-mile area known as Dallas' "Little Asia." All over the
country, similar enclaves developed. The majority of those who
arrived in poverty have continued to fight for economic survival.

In contrast with the poverty and substandard living conditions, of course, are the media stories of the Vietnamese child
who wins the spelling contest or receives some outstanding academic award. It cannot be discounted that there is also a successful segment of Southeast Asians present in America, especially among the Vietnamese. However, many of these came
from the more Europeanized part of Vietnamese society. As a
whole, Southeast Asians represent the more traditional disadvantaged minority groups than they do the stereotyped "model
minority" Asians.[74]

Ascher notes that the age of children in immigrating pro-
duces unique stresses. Infants of six months to two years seem
to adapt readily to America, although previous experiences and
recurring memories may produce nightmares and future problems.[75] Newcomers between twelve months and three years of
age experience language conflicts due to the changes experienced during a time of rapid linguistic development. Such children encountered changed linguistic systems before they were
old enough to "conceptualize the differences." This creates sus-
ceptibility to language-learning problems and "related neurotic
behavior."[76]

Southeast Asian adolescents who come to America have
special problems. The "three best predictors" of emotional distress to these youths are (1) being female, (2) not getting along
with American students, and (3) disagreeing with parents.[77]

In addition to this, adolescents who migrate have experienced increased pressures related to the task of identity devel-

opment. Southeast Asian adolescents operate out of four "identity systems" which may often be in conflict: (1) Southeast Asian, (2) American, (3) Refugee, and (4) Adolescent.[78] Some believe that the pressure is due to the fact that adolescents must simultaneously pass through the typical adolescent developmental crisis of "identity formation," as well as the historical crisis of becoming a refugee.[79]

Most of the teenagers of all Southeast Asian groups easily adopt the cultural styles of their American counterparts. Internally, however, they retain their specific ethnic identities as Hmong, Khmer, Vietnamese, Sino-Vietnamese, or Lao. They are not as likely to make friends with Americans or even with similar ethnic groups.[80]

Many Southeast Asian adults possess nontransferable skills. Among females there are the special complications of recent widowhood, the load of child-rearing in addition to working, and the possibility of being isolated at home in order to care for young children and others.[81]

Similar to other Asian groups, Southeast Asians are often stereotyped as exceptional in academics. An interesting example is the children of Southeast Asian boat people. After being here only three and a half years, and with parents who spoke no English, students reflected SAT scores almost three times higher than the national norm.[82] Americans who witness such academic prowess are inclined to label Asians as inherently superior in academics. While this makes them unique and reflects a "positive" stereotype, it may alienate them and cause them to be misunderstood.

A college student from Cambodia was asked by a fellow student why Asians were so smart and why he didn't have to study.

> I told him that being an Asian didn't make me smarter. But I also told him this—that sometimes Asian refugees will work very hard because, to us, school and studies mean life. He asked me what I meant and I told him we came here without language or education. Couldn't get any decent jobs. And if we can't work, we can't eat. If we can't eat, we will die. We are studying for our lives.[83]

Another stereotype is the persistent reference to Southeast Asians as "refugees." Wendy Tai, a newspaper reporter on minority affairs, observes, "With the Hmong, at what point do we stop calling them 'refugees'? Most have been here at least three years. They're Americans, at this point."[84]

Researchers Chinn and Plata noted the following characteristics for Southeast Asian children with a caution to avoid unwarranted generalizations.

1. They are sympathetic, gentle, polite, and reluctant to show anger or displeasure in a direct manner.

2. They are religious and conservative. They believe in fate, and their Buddhist beliefs suppress their aggressiveness.

3. They try to withhold their emotions from others, particularly strangers.

4. They tend to smile, perhaps more than most Americans, as an indication of their politeness and desire to please.

5. Being humiliated or made to "lose face," particularly in public, may evoke extreme and long-term bitterness and an unforgiving attitude.[85]

Paul Thai speaks for various civic groups in the Dallas area on the differences in family relationships between mainline Americans and the Indochinese. He gives the following characteristics for Indochinese families.

1. Family relationships are very close, including the extended family.

2. Often, three to five generations live in one home.

3. Older people live with younger family members and never in nursing homes.

4. Grown, unmarried children live at home with their parents.

5. The Indochinese family authority structure is very rigid.

6. The husband is the primary provider and is the final decision maker.

7. The Indochinese woman is the master of the home and the finances.

8. Family pressure is effective in keeping members in line.

9. Divorce is an unacceptable solution to marital problems.

10. Children are under strict control, corporal punishment is acceptable.

11. Children are expected to greet houseguests, be introduced, and then be dismissed.

12. Children are assigned household tasks only if their family is poverty-stricken.[86]

VIETNAMESE

In 1991 there were an estimated 875,000 Vietnamese in the U.S. and 130,000 in Canada. The majority of these arrived as refugees, rather than immigrants.[87] The number of Vietnamese that have arrived in America since the fall of Saigon in 1975 warrants a special look at this subgroup of Southeast Asian Americans.

Vietnamese have immigrated to the United States primarily in two waves: (1) following the fall of Saigon in April 1975 and (2) following 1978. The largest single group to arrive was the first wave of approximately 130,000 in 1975 following the fall of South Vietnam. A second group left after 1978. During the next ten years, over 750,000 Southeast Asians followed. "Some teenage refugee children arriving in this country entered school for the first time in their lives."[88]

A major part of the second wave were the "boat people" who attempted escape from the Communistic regime. It has been estimated that only half ever reached safety.[89] Approximately 269,000 boat people were admitted to the U.S. between 1979 and 1982. Since then, the number coming to the U.S. has been considerably smaller, averaging about 23,000 per year.[90]

Differences seem to exist between the waves of refugees. The first consisted of more well-to-do and educated classes while the second had less education and social standing. The majority of the latter were from the ethnic Chinese minority in Vietnam. Many of these now identify themselves as Chinese Americans.[91]

The psychosocial development of Southeast Asian children is greatly affected by the circumstances of their arrival. Some came with parents, others through Operation Babylift, and still others as unaccompanied minors. "The evidence suggests that the latter, mostly males, are particularly at risk. They tend to experience depression and behavioral problems, such as tantrums, withdrawal, and hyperactivity."[92]

Southeast Asian refugees show a decreasing dependence on welfare each year they are in this country. They have a far lower criminal record than the general population. Still, the new culture creates complications of depression, anxiety, hostility, paranoia, and similar stress responses.[93] Another group which suffers a special kind of disadvantage are the Amerasian children, Vietnamese-born, but with American fathers. These were shunned in their homeland and upon arrival to America suffer from the lack of a family unit.[94]

Vietnamese Americans stress the family rather than the individual and express an extended-family lifestyle. The majority are deeply attached to their families. They advocate strong discipline for children. "When we love our children, we give them a beating; when we hate our children, we give them sweet words."[95] Children feel a strong sense of duty and responsibility to their family.

Shyness is a characteristic often associated with Vietnamese. In actuality, the characteristic would be more accurately described as a reserved attitude toward strangers or those they do not know well. It is an attitude that shows politeness or respect, especially to elders or superiors. The Vietnamese would not use a public occasion to disagree openly. Instead, a subtle suggestion of alternatives might be made so that the one with an incorrect opinion does not lose face.

The value of modesty is a characteristic that has at times caused Vietnamese to be misunderstood. A Vietnamese motto suggests that saying less than what one actually knows is admirable. A common response to praise may be to deny it or say they do not deserve it. Such behavior would be seen as normal to other Vietnamese. Non-Asians often view the custom of remaining modest and humble as being passive or impolite.

As a sign of humbleness, Vietnamese will not want to call attention to themselves. Teachers in Christian education settings will find that Vietnamese students may be reluctant to ask questions and may seldom volunteer to give answers. If a teacher asks if they have been understood, Vietnamese will indicate that they did as a sign of politeness to the teacher that they hold in high respect. At the same time, teachers need to make sure that Vietnamese students understand that question and answer sessions are for the purpose of helping students understand the discussion and are not meant to embarrass anyone. The fact that everyone makes mistakes at some time needs to be emphasized since encouraging participation may place the Vietnamese in a situation in which they lose face.

When an answer is given, the Vietnamese speaking in English will often begin with the English word "yes." This is a translation of the polite form *da* in Vietnamese. The initial "yes" is simply an acknowledgment that the student is listening and should not be interpreted to mean either agreement or disagreement. The same might be true of the frequent smile. A handbook for teaching Vietnamese suggests that the smile may mean a number of different things such as a means to communicate interest, to please superiors, or as a polite screen to hide confusion or anger.[96]

The Confucian heritage of Vietnamese is apparent in their approach to social relationships.

> Vietnamese tend to be more formal and reserved in their style
> of relating to other people. They do not consider it polite to
> look someone straight in the eye or to disagree with them
> openly. They often smile or say "yes," when actually they are
> upset, so they will not hurt the other person's feelings.[97]

Vietnamese have shown a syncretistic approach to religion. Although most are Buddhist, others ascribe to Confucianism, Taoism, Roman Catholicism, and a number of less-known Eastern religions.[98]

Two primary religions are Buddhism and Catholicism. More than 80 percent of Vietnam was Buddhist. Today approximately 50 percent of Vietnamese in the U.S. claim this religion. Although only 10 percent of Vietnam was Catholic before the war, 40 percent of the first-wave were Catholic.[99]

Catholicism is the most prevalent religion among U.S. Vietnamese. Out of 100 Vietnamese Catholic communities, the largest is New Orleans (10,000 parishioners) followed by Port

Arthur-Beaumont and Houston, Texas. Smaller numbers of Vietnamese have become Protestant. An example is the Vietnamese Church of the Full Gospel.[100]

RELIGIOUS IMPLICATIONS

Churches and religious educational institutions are more likely to have contact with Asian Americans today than ever before. They represent one of the fastest growing ethnic groups in the United States. Although the influx has slowed down during the last decade, the total Asian culture is still highly representative of new immigrants. According to 1990 census figures, 4.6 million Asian Americans are foreign-born.[101]

Many have found their church home in what is casually referred to as "Asian churches" or in more specific terms such as "Chinese churches" or "Korean churches." These provide fellowship that is both spiritual and social. Services may be primarily in the native language and will almost always provide an extension of the events so that social activities are included. The exact nature of the services will vary and may represent differences of opinion in the congregation as to whether they should be more traditional or more Americanized.

Siang-Yang Tan believes that the worldview of Asians will usually involve the supernatural. He describes Asian Christians as more "evangelical in their theological convictions." In his discussion on counseling Asian Americans, he suggests some ways that the approach to counseling and care ministries can build on this distinction. One suggestion was to focus on the Holy Spirit and spiritual power. Along with this is his suggestion that ministers and counselors utilize "explicit integration," which is an approach to counseling that systematically utilizes the resources of prayer and Scripture in a "clinically competent and ethically responsible way."[102]

A primary problem in East-West encounters is communication. The situation is no less complex for Christian settings. An example of this is the missionary movement of the Christian church in Asia during the nineteenth and twentieth centuries. In addition to building churches, also constructed throughout the area were schools, hospitals, and social work centers. Kleinjans observes, "The missionaries used science the way St. Boniface used his axe on the holy Thunder Oak in Hesse, Germany."[103] The result was a victory of Western science followed by limited conversion. Again, Kleinjans notes, "The point is that the message received by the Asians was not the one which the missionaries had intended to get across."[104]

Arthur Schlesinger, Jr. contends that the missionary enterprise fits into the framework of American imperialism. "One fallacy," Schlesinger observes, "was the assumption by missionaries and their supporters that 'religion and other arts of civilization are portable commodities which it is our duty to convey to the backward nations, and that a certain amount of compulsion is justified in pressing their benefits upon people too ignorant at once to recognize them.' "[105]

Asians are well aware of EuroAmericans who perceive the Asian culture as somehow not "American." As one Asian American expressed it, "We know that it is not only whites who are Americans, but it is a reality that we are seen as Orientals and not as Americans." To deny that Asians are just as American as Irish or Germans is fallacious. More seriously, it negatively affects the very critical component of "identity formation."

It should not be true that those who are the easiest assimilated are the most deserving of acceptance as Americans. Asian Americans should not face the double bind of trying to take on all the values and customs of mainstream America and still not be accepted as "American" because they look different. America is a country of immigrants and cannot require conforming to any dominant culture in order to be a genuine American.

American-born Katherine Min wrote about this tension between being American and being Korean.

> Until I was nine, my childhood fantasy was that I would wake up one morning to discover that I had miraculously shed my straight black hair for golden curls, and that my eyes had turned round and blue. I imagined that I was really the daughter of an English count and a Korean princess. Later, I immersed myself in English history, convinced that through osmosis I could become Anglo-Saxon.[106]

Others have told how even their very close friends would ask when they planned to return to their mother country. The realization was that even for those born in America, they were perceived as foreigners. A Korean American offers the following challenge.

> Until now, white America has always considered those of us with Asian faces as "guests." It's up to us to change that by our greater participation in the mainstream and to educate those who are ignorant. Immigrants to this country came not only from the other side of the Atlantic, but the Pacific as well.[107]

This problem has been further compounded by the merging of white, American, and Christianity. Wesley S. Woo makes a telling accusation: "American Protestantism . . . has confounded the concepts of being Christian and being American and presumed the two to be virtually the same."[108] His point is the unspoken assumption that one cannot be Christian and American and maintain personal cultural values and traditions. Thus, Woo notes, many Asian Americans, especially youth, may feel ashamed or guilty concerning their cultural heritage.

Such feelings could be enhanced in a context in which the norm is that of Anglo-American culture. The practical goal, then, of the church congregation must be to avoid making the Asian-American family feel unwelcome or "strange" in the presence of community members.

Many Asians feel that methods of biblical interpretation should be an authentic expression of their culture. Stanley J. Samartha urges the development of cultural hermeneutics as an expression of growth and maturity: "To depend on rules of interpretation developed in countries alien to Asian life is a hindrance to the church's growth in maturity."[109]

CHRISTIAN EDUCATION

The larger Asian groups in this country do not differ significantly from their homelands in the practice and objectives of Christian education. This is due to the considerable influence America has had in the development of Asian Christianity. "Theory and praxis of religious education in America is quite visible in those countries as well as in Asian-American religious communities."[110]

There are at least two phenomena that seem to be distinctive of Asian-American religious education. (1) There is a "legacy of the nineteenth-century American Protestant churches' understanding of Christian education as a means of evangelism."[111] (2) There is an integration of religious education with language instruction in which religious education becomes a form of cultural orientation.[112]

The language barrier has been identified as a major communication problem in working with Asian-American families, especially for those who have more recently arrived in the United States. This can sometimes present a real challenge for ministers and teachers. Language problems do not disappear without special help and extra work. In some cases, the individual comes from a bilingual background. There may be cultural traditions and customs that restrict or impede verbal communication. It is suggested by some that Asian-American families may encourage one-way communication with their children so that the children do not receive sufficient practice with their new language. It is also possible that although English is the predominant language, the native language is used predominantly in the home and community.[113]

Of special concern is the effect on the individual's self-concept as the language problem plays out in daily life. A book of oral histories by Asian Americans includes the following account by Victor Merian, a Filipino-American reporter for the *Los Angeles Times*.

> Several of us would be taken to the attic of the school. The other people were there for stuttering and other impediments. I went because of my accent. Today, I still recall this vividly. I couldn't pronounce the r's. I grew up in an environment where my parents have strong Filipino accents. For instance, my father would call cockroaches, "COKE-ROACHES." I mean, that's the way it was pronounced. I grew up in the house like that.
>
> One time I had an oral report where I used the word, "COKE-ROACHES," and everyone burst out laughing. I had absolutely no clue what they were laughing at. I always

thought that's the way it was pronounced. I was having trouble saying r words, and so I would have to go to this attic a few times a week and I would have to crow like a rooster, to make the "er" sound. So I would say, "er-er-er-er-er." I remember sitting there and the teacher would come to me and say, "Well, how is the rooster coming?" I would say, "er-er-er-er-er-." Once the kids learned that that was why I was up there, people would greet me with rooster crows.[114]

Most Asian immigrants operate with the assumption that they need to know English to be successful in the United States. In some cases, a great deal of motivation is necessary to overcome the language deficiency to the point of becoming minimally competent. Encouragement and a secure environment must be provided to overcome serious deficiencies. Church programs can include such services without a full-scale program. Individuals can be trained to assist on a one-on-one basis, or if the situation demands it, a class could be offered.

Christian education should begin with the individual student and his or her unique needs. In dealing with any minority group a basic tenet is to relate to the group or individual on the basis of "felt need." We accept the fact that persons from all cultural groups share universal feelings. However, the expression of those feelings may be modified by cultural and social conditioning.

A stereotyped picture of the Asian child is that of being shy and quiet. In reality, this demeanor is more representative of a value orientation than a personality type. Most Asian cultures stress groupism more than individualism. Consequently, emphasis is placed on listening skills rather than on verbal skills and on cooperation rather than on competition. Children have been socialized to listen more than to speak and to speak in a soft voice.

In Asian countries, students would play a more passive role in the teaching-learning process than in America. Students respect their teachers and do not challenge those in authority. Students wait to be answered or to participate unless otherwise requested by the teacher. Teaching styles would commonly utilize memorization, copying, listening, taking notes, repetition, and recitation.[115] Even Asian-American children born in this country may value these activities if stressed by their parents. At the same time, more recent studies have found that Asian Americans demonstrate more assertiveness than is often assumed.

Asian Americans who spend all or most of their lives in America will not usually be representative of the traditional teaching styles used in Asian countries. However, if individuals attend Sunday School classes who have experienced schooling in their own Asian country, a gradual transition may be appropriate.

The American expectation for discussion and initiative should not be insisted upon. Extra time should be allowed to respond to questions. Present group work and group problem-solving activities in a manner that is nonthreatening and voluntary. Participation can be encouraged, but should not be required.

It would be wise for teachers to avoid any overemphasis upon physical touching or Western familiarity. In some religious circles, for example, it is common to pray over another by placing a hand upon the head. This would be most unwelcome to most groups of Asians.

Research has identified some differences between Asian Americans and Anglo Americans in personality development that have application to the teaching-learning process and other ministry opportunities. Researchers contend that Asian Americans tend to use a more practical and applied approach to life and life problems than Anglo Americans. Ideas will be evaluated more on the basis of the immediate practical application. Another difference identified in research is that Asian Americans "tend to prefer concrete, well-structured and predictable situations over ambiguous situations." Strong feelings were often restrained, the welfare of the family was considered more important than the welfare of the individual, and unquestioned obedience was given to family authority.[116]

Howard F. Van Zandt notes a number of behavior characteristics that enhance the art of negotiation between Japanese and non-Asians. Some are especially applicable to the local church setting. One is emotional sensitivity. Japanese Ameri-

~ans show a greater sense of emotional sensitivity than non-Asians. Perhaps maintaining their silence while mainline Americans are active and talking gives them an advantage.

Another characteristic is the value of friendship. Friendship is more valued as the length of contact is increased. The longer contact is valued more. It is expected that friends can be called upon for help. A third characteristic is the lack of any argumentative spirit. Silence will be the response, rather than a prompt retort or argument when a point is challenged. This is true even when the Japanese feels that he/she is right.[117]

Although Van Zandt was not addressing a Christian audience, the factors he presents provide a good model for relating to all cultures, including our own, and an excellent guideline for pastoral ministry, classroom teaching, and one-on-one counseling.

Finally, study groups could be utilized through the Christian education program to encourage discussion on the differences between Western and Eastern methods of communication and value orientations. This would provide an opportunity to exchange ideas about how the differences can be both recognized and validated.

MINISTERING TO ASIAN-AMERICAN YOUTH

The task of identity development can be especially stressful for members of Asian-American groups with a traditional value orientation such as the Asian culture exemplifies. Some speculate whether their identity should be more representative of Asian American or American Asian. One young girl whose parents came from Korea complained that her parents expected the same behavior from her that was expected of teenagers in the Korea they left over forty years ago. "They have come here and lived in isolation, not realizing that their own country has changed a lot by now," she stated.

One of the most often quoted studies regarding general personality characteristics of Asian Americans was completed by Sue and Sue. They concluded from their research that Asian-American youth, specifically Chinese Americans for their study, tend to give one of three reactions to culture conflict.[118] The categories identified by Sue and Sue were the traditional Chinese, the Chinese American, and the marginal or westernized Chinese.

Betty Chang has developed a variation of Sue and Sue's categories for health care that seems more appropriate for understanding Asian Americans as they participate in Christian ministries. She has expanded Sue and Sue's work with Chinese to apply to Asian Americans in general. Her conceptualization is a typology of four major characteristics of Asians in America as a result of their exposure to both Asian and the dominant Western values and behavior.[119]

Chang's first category is Traditional Asians who remain loyal to Asian values and behavior. Most often first-generation immigrants, they identify themselves very closely with the Asian culture in the more traditional sense. Some resist assimilation by maintaining traditional values and associating primarily with Asian Americans. The traditionalists do their best to meet the expectations of their family.

The second category, Asian Americans, have managed to balance traditional and Western values according to situations. They have integrated selected values and behavior from both cultures.

Individuals in the third category, Alienated Asians, have rejected the values of both traditional Asian and Western values and behaviors. Chang places street-gang practices and alternative lifestyles in this category. This category may include a form of racial self-hatred, demonstrated with words such as "I really resent being Korean. The Koreans I date are so passive. I definitely prefer Caucasians." This is often a developmental phase but may remain as a definite preference.

Chang's fourth category consists of Americanized Asians. Individuals in this category have generally adopted the dominant Western values and behaviors and express a desire for assimilation of the non-Asian American culture. They are often associated with white, middle-class America. The assimilation is sometimes preferred, but in other cases considered necessary. A Korean American described his assimilation in the following way: "Regrettably, I found I had to be completely 'American' to make friends and be accepted. This meant rejecting my native language, culture, and the Korean value of studious behavior."[120]

Somewhere between the two extremes of completely losing the Asian identity and tenaciously holding on to the traditional values, there should be room for intentional ethnic identity by which some variations are permissible. There should be room to develop a new identity by integrating aspects of other cultures and aspects of their ethnic heritage with their own unique experiences. Such individuals will be aware of environmental forces that have shaped their identity and will actively try to resolve cultural conflicts they experience. As one young adult female expressed it, "When you represent a hyphenated American culture, you are on your own. Somewhere there has to be a balance." This developmental task will be especially important for adolescents and young adults in the church but will continue throughout the adult years.

American-born teenager, Amy, whose parents were both born in India, wrote about her recent visit to India.

> India—where my so called "roots" are! It was frightening! Supposedly this was where I belonged, among my relatives. Then why did I feel so out of place? . . . They stared at me as if something was wrong with me. I wore my hair different and my clothes looked foreign to them. All around me I heard strange sounds. Voices seemed to communicate and yet I could not understand a word. The way they dressed, walked, even wore their hair seemed to look identical. It was so unlike home.[121]

Amy concludes with a vivid expression of compassion for an Indian girl her age who was begging on a street corner in New Delhi. It is possible the identification was influenced by her own ethnic heritage. Amy's essay is an eloquent illustration of the tension in ethnic identity development that can occur for the adolescent who attempts to bring together two cultures: one's roots and the birthplace of parents, and one's own unique cultural context in which experiences are similar to other teenagers in America.

Asian-American youth will experience the normal developmental tasks common to all adolescents. Nishioka suggests that in addition to this, there are some challenges which are unique to Asian-American youth. Ministers and youth workers should be sensitive to the following issues as Asian-American adolescents become members of their youth groups.

> 1) Asian American youth struggle with being members of a minority racial culture and what it means specifically to be Asian American.
> 2) Asian Americans struggle with expectations by their family and their teachers to live up to the "model minority" image that they have been given.
> 3) Asian Americans struggle to live up to the expectation that they will not bring shame upon their family and that they will make their ancestors proud.
> 4) Asian Americans struggle with forms of racism, prejudice or stereotyping, subtle or overt, that is associated with most minorities.[122]

In brief, Asian-American youth need assistance in both maintaining their identity as Asian American at the same time as they feel freedom to fully participate in the American culture. The Christian community setting must communicate that it is possible to do both.

MINISTERING TO ASIAN-AMERICAN FAMILIES

Asian-American families may be less expressive in their interactions than are middle-class white families, but they have their own means of communicating care and concern for one another. Betty Chang, in *Transcultural Health Care,* writes that one of these means is showing care and attention to one who is ill, even for minor conditions. She notes that hospital personnel sometimes express concern over the number of visitors an Asian-American patient receives, the extent to which family members want to stay in the room with children, and the amount of food brought to patients.[123] However, in the Asian culture this is an opportunity for the extended family and community to show concern. Such occasions would be an excellent opportunity for the church community to share in this expression. Not doing so may communicate a lack of care to the Asian-American family.

Using times of illness as an expressive opportunity may

change somewhat as the nuclear family becomes more common in the Asian-American culture. A religious sect in Hawaii, Tensho, is discouraging Asians from using the "sick role as a means of legitimizing one's dependency and affiliation needs." Traditionally, these occasions have provided opportunities for a wife or mother to show feelings of love and affection for male family members. Adherents of Tensho are more representative of the nuclear family than are Asian Americans in the states.

An increasing problem within the Asian-American community is the disparity that is sometimes being experienced between generations. This is especially apparent between members of the generation that represents immigration and their children who have been born and reared only in America. One Korean church in our community very intentionally employed a Caucasian youth leader to assist them in dealing with the strain between generations that was occurring.

After struggling with parents over the traditional Asian value orientation, some American-born Asian youth and young adults are consciously discarding the values their parents brought with them from Asia. A twenty-seven-year-old female who left Hong Kong in 1973 shared how she fought with her parents over leaving Chinatown to go to college. After doing so anyway, she was forced to return each weekend to work alongside her mother in a garment factory. She returned home after college because she had been taught that she had an obligation to take care of her family. However, she has now decided to discard the values her parents brought with them from China, including those regarding her role as a woman. She is contemplating graduate school rather than finding a husband.[124]

The differences between generations in Asian-American families may create obstacles to ministry within Asian churches as well. Tom Mathew, an American Keralite who has received recognition for his extensive publishing both in America and in India, advises leaders in Keralite churches to be aware of the differences in American Keralites. He identifies three different groups in America: (1) Kerala-born persons who have not accepted America as their own, (2) Americanized Keralites who are comfortable in both cultures, and (3) American-born

Keralites whose only culture is the American Keralite culture.[125]

Mathew notes that Keralite churches in America may function as though the only difference between the first and third groups is a linguistic difference. His concern is that leaders from the first group may restrict changes in the format of church ministry so that ministry needs of the third group will not be met. An additional problem Mathew observes is that Keralite pastors who have been trained for ministry in India, may be tempted to utilize a pre-immigration model for ministry to American-born Keralites in the church.

With the developing tension between generations in the Asian communities, it would be wise to encourage greater diversity in marital and parental interaction on the part of Asian Americans. Preventive programs through educational means could be provided as a regular offering in the church curriculum. The focus should be upon education and should be sensitive to the differences in family-life processes that exist in Asian-American groups. Adults who are closely tied to the more traditional approaches of their culture will need to feel that the problem is presented in a neutral manner.

The family-systems approach should be considered for dealing with family problems, as well as problems of individual family members. This strategy places the focus on the larger family unit rather than on individuals. The Asian-American emphasis on the collective unit would make this approach more effective than one-on-one counseling.

Tim Tseng suggests the theological themes of "healing" and "reconciliation" for generational tension. Families which are experiencing discord due to parental authoritarianism and adolescent resistance need to find assistance through the church ministries to reach harmony in Christ. This can come through the leadership, as well as counseling and educational programs. Tseng recommends that the subject of "Family Expectations" become a part of youth programming and gives a suggested session format in *Asian Pacific American Youth Ministry.*[126] This particular source is recommended for its many excellent youth program ideas provided for churches who work with Asian-American youth. Their sessions on racism could be adapted to work successfully with all youth groups regardless of ethnic makeup.

Due to the limitations of this work, the aspects considered relative to Asian Americans have been generalized beyond our preference. Approximately thirty groups could have been considered, each with their particular cultural, historical, and social distinctive. We recognize the injustice of not identifying the uniqueness of each. Of special note is the growing Asian-Indian population which has received relatively little research in relationship to some other Asian groups.

Readers are encouraged to seek out members of the specific groups and ask questions regarding their cultural traditions. Library resources are now plentiful for some of the primary groups, although more careful research is needed for subgroups.

Sumner Jones, managing editor of the *Minneapolis Spokesman,* an African-American weekly, feels that a specific voice is needed for minority groups. The coverage by the major media is often inaccurate and tends to focus on stereotypes. He gives a model of clear direction for church leaders with the following statement. "To serve the minority community, you have to be specifically attuned to them. The general does not serve the specific."[127]

CHAPTER ELEVEN

EXAMINING AFRICAN-AMERICAN CULTURE

Robert Leslie in his thoughtful monograph, *Counseling Across Cultures,* writes about the life of the noted African-American singer and writer, Maya Angelou. During a time when she was experiencing emotional distress, she made an appointment with a white psychiatrist who started the session by asking her if she was troubled. Leslie quotes Maya's feelings as she expressed them in "Singin' and Swingin' and Gettin' Merry Like Christmas."

> Yes, I was troubled; why else would I be here? But could I tell this man? Would he understand Arkansas, which I left, yet would never, could never leave? . . . How would he perceive another who, in a desperate thrust for freedom, left her only child who became sick during her absence? A mother who, upon her return, felt so guilty she could think of nothing more productive than killing herself and possibly even the child? . . . No, I couldn't tell him about living inside a skin that is hated or feared by the majority of one's fellow citizens or about the sensation of getting on a bus on a lovely morning, feeling happy, and suddenly seeing the passengers curl their lips in distaste or avert their eyes in revulsion. No, I had nothing to say to the doctor.[1]

Immigrants from many different countries have come to the United States in search of the "American Dream." African Americans differed from all other ethnic groups in that they did not willingly come to North America, nor was the "American Dream" made available to them. The predominant distinguishing factor for African Americans is the history of social, economic, and political oppression experienced because of color discrimination. This factor pervades every aspect of social institutions within which they participate. No aspect of the life of African Americans can be understood without giving consideration to the issue of racism that they have experienced.

From a contemporary perspective, black society has not gained the social equality intended through legislation and civil rights movements. In 1972 James Banks, currently director of the Center for Multicultural Studies at the University of Washington, made the sobering observation that

> the black man's status in relationship to whites has actually worsened in recent years. While the gap between whites and nonwhites is narrower in educational achievement than it was a decade ago, the gap in all other major areas—income, employment, health and housing—has increased in the last ten years, despite the symbolic and legal gains which accrued from the black revolt of the 1960s.[2]

More than twenty years later, African-American theologian James Cone sounds an even greater alarm.

> But despite the progress in middle-class black America, the black underclass are poorer today than they were in the 1960s. One half of black babies are born in poverty, and nearly twenty-five percent of the black men between the ages of nineteen and twenty-eight are in jails, prisons, or awaiting their day in court. With no respect for themselves or for anybody else, black youth are dropping out of school, having babies, joining gangs, selling drugs, and killing each other with a frequency that boggles the imagination.[3]

These obvious and continuing inequities demonstrate the unsettled and continuing tensions in North American society. In spite of this, black Americans experience continued advancement across a broad social front.

THE AFRICAN-AMERICAN CHURCH EXPERIENCE

One of the complex questions in the study of black religion is the issue of whether the black church is an expression of black culture itself, or whether it created a culture for a people which had been "decultured" through centuries of slavery. Until recently, most scholars have assumed that "almost all of the fundamental aspects of traditional African cultures" were extinguished in United States slavery.[4] An example would be the noted black sociologist E. Franklin Frazier, who observed, "An organized religious life became the chief means by which a structured or organized social life came into existence among the Negro masses."[5]

Opposed to this interpretation were W.E.B. DuBois and Melville Herskovits and, more recently, the ground-breaking work of C. Eric Lincoln and Lawrence H. Mamiya. The latter note that Frazier was raised in an atmosphere which viewed black society as having no independent culture or heritage. His view of the church in the black experience was negative. To Frazier, "Negro churches were a hindrance to the assimilation of Negroes into the mainstream of American life." He did not live to see the melting-pot concept replaced by the rainbow of African-American churches and leaders who created a new praxis of African-American faith in the civil rights struggle.[6]

Regardless of the final outcome of this discussion, the fact remains that the single institution that has had the greatest effect in maintaining cohesion in African-American society has been the black church.

Religion is viewed as an integral part of the African-American family life and is not limited to just a Sunday morning service. The African-American church has served as a very important socializing institution for individuals and as a means of leadership in the community. This was demonstrated by the high-profile role which black pastors played in the media coverage of the civil unrest following the Rodney King jury decision.

Black ministers have often been viewed as agents of change for the African-American culture. Martin Luther King, Jr. and Jesse Jackson are two familiar examples. However, American society has often focused on the church's role in the civil rights movement, and other political and civil causes, rather than the one played out daily in the social and family life of the black community.

The three largest black denominations are Methodist, Baptist, and Pentecostal in nature. While independent black Baptist and Methodist groups date from the eighteenth century, black denominations began in the nineteenth century. The African Methodist Episcopal Church (AME) and the African Methodist Episcopal Zion Church (AME Zion) were begun in 1816 and 1822 respectively. The third major black Methodist denomination, the Christian Methodist Episcopal (CME) began in 1870 as the Colored Methodist Episcopal, changing its name in 1854.[7]

Black Baptist churches are more recent with the National Baptist Convention, U.S.A., Inc., dating from 1895. A division in 1917 produced the National Baptist Convention of America followed by the Progressive National Baptist Convention, Ind., in 1961.[8]

The primary Pentecostal representative, the Church of God in Christ (COGIC), was founded in 1895 and has shown the greatest growth of any black group since World War II.[9] This group especially represents the racial divisions present in American society. As a legally incorporated church body, the Church of God in Christ contained scores of white ministers who had sought ordination. Between 1909 and 1913 there were as many white COGIC congregations as there were black. In April of 1914, however, white ministers left with the blessing of the denomination's founder, Charles H. Mason, to form a white denomination, the Assemblies of God.[10] The latter group has become the world's largest Pentecostal denomination, but has remained distinctively white in its composition. Out of 11,536 AOG congregations, only 121 have more than 51 percent black membership.[11]

Following the Civil War, Baptists multiplied in the South. During the 1870s thousands of black Methodists left the Methodist Episcopal Church, South and started the Christian Methodist Episcopal Church. Additional religious momentum was supplied by the African Methodist Episcopal Church and the

African Methodist Episcopal Zion Church. In 1880 the black National Baptists created their first national body. Grant S. Shockley claims, "By 1916 . . . more than 90% of all black Christians in the nation belonged to one of the seven nation-wide black denominations."[12]

One distinctive black contribution to American worship is the Azusa Street Revival, a series of meetings that took place in Los Angeles between 1906 and 1913. William J. Seymour, a black itinerant minister, held a series of meetings that emphasized the Pentecostal baptism in the Spirit and the ability to speak in tongues.[13] According to the *Dictionary of Pentecostal and Charismatic Movements,* "Indeed, nearly every Pentecostal denomination in the U.S. traces its roots in some way or other to the Apostolic Faith Mission at 312 Azusa Street."[14]

An additional factor in the black religious experience is the influence of Islam. Islam became an important symbol for black cultural development in the late 1960s. Originating in Detroit during the 1930s, the Nation of Islam expanded to fifty temples in twenty-two states and the District of Columbia by 1959.[15] By 1989 the *New York Times* had calculated that about 1 million of the 6 million Muslims in America were black and that "close to 90 percent of new converts are black."[16] Lincoln and Mamiya note the seriousness of this challenge to Christianity.

> It is already clear that in Islam the historic black church denominations will be faced with a far more serious and more powerful competitor for the souls of black folk than the white churches ever were. When is the question, not whether.[17]

While there are obvious theological differences between this movement and Christianity, churches must also respond to questions of whether Christians have matched Islamic efforts toward empowerment and enrichment of black society. In a multicultural society theology is often judged by praxis rather than doctrine.

THE AFRICAN-AMERICAN FAMILY

Research on the African-American family has taken three different approaches.[18] The first approach has been identified as the "cultural deviant approach." In this approach, black families are viewed as pathological. The controversial Moynihan report in 1965, in which the black family was viewed as pathological and at the root of the deterioration of black society, might be an example of this approach.[19]

The "cultural equivalent approach" followed the cultural deviant approach and represented much of the literature on African-American families from 1965 to 1979. In this view, black families were legitimate whenever their lifestyles conformed to middle-class family norms.

The third approach, the "cultural variant approach," is the more recent approach and has had its greatest exposure through predominantly black journals. In this approach, the black family is presented as a culturally unique, legitimate unit — as a different but functional family form.[20]

Ellison and Maynard note five themes that are present in research on the African-American family.[21] The *poverty-acculturation* theme compares the African-American family with the white middle-class family to determine its effective or ineffectiveness. The *pathology* theme views the African-American family as pathological because of specific conditions. Moynihan called particular attention to the number of black families which were headed by females and described this as a "tangle of pathology." A third model is the *reactive apology* theme which was an attempt to counteract the pathology theme with the view that black and white families are essentially the same when the effects of racism, poverty, and oppression have been omitted. The fourth theme, the *black nationalist,* views the black family in a more selective manner, focusing primarily on positive aspects only. Finally, the *proactive-revisionist* theme attempts to take a holistic approach with attention given to the current social forces acting upon the family, as well as the family's reactions to these forces. This theme has included the influence of African values upon the black family.

One of the first things that must be noted is that there is no such thing as "the black family." African Americans represent many different countries and ethnic backgrounds, each with wide variation in lifestyles, customs, and values. Even though the largest group is of African origin, they too represent diversity as a result of factors such as age, geographic differences, religious background, and socioeconomic status. The discussion that follows is with the acute awareness that the research presented is applicable to some black families and cultures but certainly cannot be generalized as representative of African Americans in all parts of the United States and across all socioeconomic groups.

THE KINSHIP NETWORK OF AFRICAN-AMERICAN FAMILIES

In spite of this diversity, a sense of unity, cooperation, and mutual responsibility is present among African Americans. James R. King identifies it as *Oneness of Being* in which there is relating to the whole black community, whether across generations or economic levels. King speculates that this perception of *peoplehood* has developed as a result of the struggle by African Americans to combat social, economic, and political hardships in America.[22] Hale-Benson suggests that this strong sense of community could possibly also have originated from the survival of the tribe. She notes that the common use of words such as "sister," "brother," or "cousin" for those without actual kinship are instrumental in modeling this loyalty for the children of each generation.[23]

In the traditional African pattern of family life, "family" was not limited to two people who were married to each other. Instead of marriage uniting two people, it united two families with a network of extended kin. This network not only influenced individual family members but assumed responsibility for their economical and emotional well-being.[24]

A history of oppression for African Americans has often required the assistance of "significant others" in carrying on household and child-rearing responsibilities. During slavery, grandmothers or relatives would help rear children whose parents had been sold. It has been suggested that the extended family served an economical purpose both during slavery and in the years that followed.[25] Consequently, even when contemporary society might not require it, this arrangement has continued in various degrees. It is not uncommon for African-American children to be reared in the household of grandparents or to experience a form of cooperative parenting from uncles and aunts. This is especially true in cases in which a parent is lost due to death or divorce.

Researchers lament the fact that black inner-city adolescents have separated marriage from childbearing.[26] The black single mother is twelve times more likely than her white counterpart to have never been married. At the same time, Howard and Wanda Jones claim that the percentage of pregnancies that end in an abortion is considerably lower for African-Americans than it is for white women.[27] King simply writes that in the "black community there is no such thing as an illegitimate child." His explanation is that every child in the black community belongs to the entire black community.[28]

Ethnic minority families differ from the majority culture in their dependence on the extended family. The idea of an extended family for the African American can be traced back to the pattern of family in West Africa. Their family pattern is not limited to biological parents but includes all relatives, both legal and biological.

The extended family for the African American might simply be described as all those who see themselves as one. Although the prevalent Western concept of the nuclear family will give a number of variations to the black family, the prevalent spirit will be reflective to some degree of the African culture.[29]

In times of stress, the extended family can serve as a buffer. In many minority groups, this expanded network has served as a means of filtering out or reinterpreting racist messages that the children may receive during their formative years. Bobby, an African-American seminarian, expressed the following regarding his childhood.

> Back in 1963 in our little town, everything was segregated. The only time I was in the same place with whites was in the stores. You know what is strange? As a child, I did not know there was even a problem with that. In looking back and reflecting on my childhood, I find that this was a very secure time for me. I think it is because we not only had immediate family members but also extended family members. Since all

of these people played an active part in my development, I felt safe and loved. Our parents and family provided the important things in life so that if we didn't have something, we never knew it.

The extended family is viewed as having certain roles for its members. However, in its struggle for survival the black family has been required to make a number of adaptations in its traditional family structure. Generally the male's role is to provide economic resources for the purpose of giving the family stability. This simple model has not always worked well for the black family when faced with discrimination and oppression in the workplace. Consequently, the black woman has often been forced to take an active role in giving the family financial stability, more so than has been true for white women.[30]

Comer and Poussaint, professors of psychiatry at Yale and Harvard respectively, argue in *Raising Black Children* that race and economic problems create additional problems for black parents and make it a more difficult task to rear emotionally healthy children.[31] McAdoo found in his research on black families that the extended family network has helped many black parents manage despite adverse social conditions. This has been especially true when assistance was provided by way of financial resources and cooperative or surrogate parenting.[32]

A pattern of intergenerational relationships that is common among African-American families is identified by Bengston, Rosenthal, and Burton as *matrilineal*.[33] An example of the matrilineal pattern is when older black women serve as the "other parent" for their grandchildren, usually due to their child's single-parent status. In 1986, approximately one-half of all births to African Americans involved an unmarried female.[34] In such cases, the mother/grandmother is likely to share her household and to provide financial assistance.[35] The matrilineal pattern can provide assistance and family structure in a situation that could otherwise be restrictive for both mother and child.

DEMOGRAPHICS OF THE BLACK AMERICAN FAMILY

Research has shown differences between minority and nonminority families. Some of those differences as they related specifically to the African-American family are noted below. Once again, attention must be directed back to our earlier statements that there is wide variation within any one minority group and that it does a great disservice to any such group when we label or assign static conditions. It is with this reiteration that we include some aspects identified in research as factors present in the black family.

African-American children have consistently faced greater social adversities than white children. The 1985 study "Black and White Children in America: Key Facts" showed that African-American children were three times more likely than white children to live in poverty and five times more likely to live in a family supported by welfare.[36] Only 3 percent of poor families are considered persistently poor, but 62 percent of them are African American in makeup.[37]

The African-American family is more likely to be a single-parent family than will be true of families in the general population. Approximately 70 percent of all African-American children will be reared by a single mother and 40 percent of all African-American families will be headed by a woman.[38] One-half of black adolescents will remain with a single parent through adolescence in comparison to 15 percent for white American adolescents.[39]

With the single-parent status, it is more likely that family members will experience limited resources of time and money. Although studies have shown that such circumstances can prompt early autonomy in the children, at the same time, the parent will be limited in the energy available to provide supportive and intricate parenting. Studies have found poor school performance to be related to single parenting when accompanied by poverty.[40]

Similar to other American ethnic minority groups, blacks are more likely than whites to have large and extended families. In a study of American adolescents, it was found that adolescents from both African-American and Hispanic-American cultures experience more interaction with grandparents, uncles, aunts, and cousins, as well as more distant relatives, than is true for white American adolescents.[41]

Statistics have shown that a large number of African-American children are victims of child abuse. However, it must be kept in mind that reported cases of family abuse are disproportionately represented by poor and ethnic families so that comparative studies with the majority culture may be inaccurate. Some feel that this is the case for African-American children.[42]

African Americans are more likely to represent the working class of America. Studies in child rearing have found that in comparing middle-class and working-class families, the latter often value obedience and neatness whereas the former will emphasize self-control and delay of gratification. Middle-class parents will be more likely than working-class parents to give verbal praise and to utilize explanation and reasoning.[43]

Age has traditionally been given greater respect in the black culture than in the white. This may be changing somewhat as the younger generation is looked to as the ones who will bring equality and acceptance in the predominant white culture. James R. King notes that in the American South it has not been considered out of line for an older black person to discipline black children, even when there is not a direct connection with the family.[44] Within the biological family, black elders especially serve in directing, counseling, and teaching roles. An important function which they are given is to transmit the history and culture of their people. They are also viewed as a source of religious instruction for the family. These functions in turn cause the children to recognize the wisdom and role of the older relatives and to grant them positions of respect.

At the same time, being African American, female, and old in America may represent a position called "triple jeopardy"—ageism, sexism, and racism. Over one-third of older African-American women live in poverty as compared to approximately 13 percent of older white women and 10 percent of both male and female older white Americans. Fifty-five percent of elderly black American women who live alone, live on less than $5,300 per year. Most older African-American women are widowed and three out of five live alone. Elderly individuals of all minority ethnic groups are more likely to become ill but less likely to receive medical treatment than are their elderly white American counterparts.[45]

Despite the fact that elderly African-American women represent the most economically handicapped group in America, their status in the black family and culture is one of power and respect. Their survival strategy has included family support, the American work ethic, and their religious faith.[46] It is believed that the black church has provided a source of strength for the African-American woman that can be traced back to the years of slavery.

It should be noted that the differences found in many of the above areas are due more to the condition of economics than it is to ethnicity. In a review of literature, it would be noted that while significant differences are found among ethnic groups, the groups compared were often white Americans from middle-class backgrounds and minority Americans from low-income backgrounds.

FAMILY ROLES AND RELATIONSHIPS

Roles within the black family must be viewed as having developed from an interplay of three factors: the African heritage, their mode of accommodation into mainstream America, and their method of coping with years of oppression.[47] The effect of these three factors has already been observed above in the extended family network and the nonfamily additions to that network. A similar association is apparent within the nuclear family.

An unfortunate stereotyped image of the black male has been created for contemporary America. Although its origin might have been for the purpose of calling attention to the needs within the black family, the outcome has possibly been more negative than positive. Statistics related to the large population of black males who are unemployed or incarcerated have been quoted too frequently and applied too freely to situations that are often not directly related. While the need that does exist cannot be overlooked, nor should we overlook the large population of black males who have very successfully carried out their roles as sons, fathers, husbands, and professionals.

When changes occur in the traditional roles of women, it

can be expected that accompanying changes will occur in the roles of men. With the rethinking of women's roles in contemporary culture, for both Christian and non-Christian settings, the roles of men have become less defined in the minds of many. There is an attempt to find a mediating position which empowers women while at the same time remaining faithful to traditional biblical understandings. Changes on the part of one side in the male-female relationship have a direct effect on the other side of the relationship. In no culture has this been more apparent than with the black culture, although it currently is a struggle for persons from all backgrounds.

The black male as father and spouse will vary within the black community according to factors such as education and economic level. For the black male, as is true for males in general, self-identity is associated with the ability to provide economically for their family. This presents a challenge to families when cultural influences are working in opposition to success in this area.

Black male heads of households only earn 70 percent of the income made by their white counterparts. Black males in the U.S., regardless of age, are three times as likely to live in poverty than are white males.[48] Black males have one of the highest job loss rates. Their jobs often require longer hours to provide the necessary finances to meet family obligations. Such circumstances contribute to a picture of "peripheralness" for the male within the black family.

The absence of fathers in homes is becoming increasingly characteristic of all American families, regardless of cultural background. Although the absent father is characteristic of some black families, it cannot be generalized to all. In some cases, the employment of the mother has resulted in an adjustment in which the father becomes a "Mr. Mom." This may be a solution on a practical level, but when it is perceived as necessary because black women have more opportunities than black men, it will not contribute to either a healthy family setting or an adequate male self-image.

In research conducted by Hoffman and Manis, "becoming a parent" was the reply given for women across all cultures when asked to indicate the most important event in making them feel like an adult. This was also the response given by European-American men who were fathers. However, African-American fathers identified "supporting yourself" as the most important event, the same response as given by European-American men and women who did not have children. African-American couples who were not parents were more likely to choose "marriage" as the event which they felt indicated the achievement of adulthood.[49]

Sources on the black family vary in their opinions as to whether the male should assume the primary role of family leader. This is not different from the variation in views one would find regarding the American culture as a whole, both from a Christian and a non-Christian perspective. Hines and Boyd-Franklin, of Rutgers Medical School, feel that although an understanding of the role of the male varies, the black male is "likely to demand and to receive recognition as head of household from their wives and children."[50] Hannah describes the extended black family as promoting an egalitarian view of sex roles and maintains that in the African-American family, the rigid sex role approach is rejected, acknowledging instead "the complementary and interchangeable roles of the sexes."[51] She sees this as predating the feminist movement. Hines and Boyd-Franklin agree with this, stating: "The Women's liberation [movement] is not a new concept to the average black woman, regardless of social class."[52]

In *Heritage and Hope: The Legacy and Future of the Black Family in America,* Howard Jones, a black evangelist formerly associated with the Billy Graham Evangelistic Association, and his wife, Wanda, reiterate Robert B. Hill's five basic strengths of the black family, one of which is "adaptability of family roles." The Jones' note that this primarily involves egalitarian decision-making which is "more characteristic of black families than the popular image of matriarchy or wife-dominance."[53]

Within the black family, the female is especially likely to be seen as assuming more of the responsibility for running the household. Again, Hines and Boyd-Franklin suggest that the role of the African-American female may be misunderstood as dominant—whether or not it is—because of her need to assume some tasks which women as a whole in the larger culture may not. In some instances, this would be due to the disproportionate number of men to women in the black community, as high as forty-four to one in certain geographical areas.[54]

In order for role reversals to be acceptable and to strengthen a family, both economically and psychologically, certain concessions must be made. Mirra Komarovsky's *Dilemmas of Masculinity* provides interesting insight into men's lives. She found that although men complained about inadequate parent nurturance in their own lives, they did not expect to be required to share the responsibility for this task with their own children. Equal sharing would be perceived as role reversal which is consistently rejected by most.[55]

Komarovsky maintains that for a true egalitarian pattern to exist, men and women must have equal access to educational and vocational opportunity. This should certainly be true for the black culture. Some believe that black women are given opportunities that black men currently are not. For example, in the area of education, there has been a larger increase in the number of black women receiving doctorates than black males. In 1986, 499 black women earned doctoral degrees, which represents an increase of 16 percent over the number earned in 1977.[56] Simply put, our society cannot afford to feel relaxed regarding the opportunities available for minority groups if it provides for only a segment of that group. This is especially true when it contributes to an imbalance in the most basic of all social institutions, the American family.

EDUCATIONAL PERSPECTIVES

Education has been highly valued in the African-American culture. This is evident in current statistics which show an increase in the number of blacks completing educational degrees now that limitations are not as prevalent. However, the overall increase in higher education for African Americans has been more directly a result of females both enrolling in and graduating from institutions of higher learning. An obstacle for both males and females has been the knowledge that there may be limitations for the use of their degrees once they enter the job market. In the America of "equal opportunity" whether or not a satisfactory position is obtained is not in direct relationship to the individual's skills, talents, and preparation.

African-American children face a daily dilemma that they share with other minorities. They must live in two cultures: the culture of the home and neighborhood and the culture of the majority with its schools and other social institutions. Prior to a multicultural awareness, the indirect message given by social institutions was often that the minority culture was "wrong" or inferior. With the increased sensitivity to diversity in our communities, the message which needs to be conveyed through social institutions is that "different" does not imply "wrong."

For the African-American child, the feeling that "different" is "wrong" has contributed to academic settings in which success is more difficult to attain. The results have been seen in below average academic achievement and lower self-concepts, often directly due to racism and daily inequalities.

Contemporary classrooms are attempting to reshape this picture, and even though the residual is present, progress is being made. Again we must reiterate the need to avoid perpetuating a stereotyped image of the African-American learner. Although statistics have documented differences between the African American and other groups, consideration must always be given to geographic, socioeconomic, and individual differences.

A difference in learning styles between African-American youth and their multicultural counterparts has been studied by some researchers. Janice E. Hale-Benson has described African-American youth as more relational than analytical in their learning style.[57] As per our earlier discussion regarding learning styles, relational would be similar to Witkin's learning style that considers the entire field. This is promoted by a family pattern that socializes members to be relational, consequently encouraging a more personal approach to learning. It has also been speculated that this more relational approach may be traced to a historical background which required individuals to be very in "tune with the moment-to-moment moods of others" for survival purposes.[58]

Shade has suggested that the person-oriented lifestyle and worldview of African Americans differs from the usual object-oriented cognitive style required for success in public schooling.[59] The typical approach in a classroom will be the teacher calling attention to specific objects such as a letter of the alphabet or a rule of mathematics.

The person-oriented approach also applies to counseling African Americans. In his interesting monograph on counseling across cultures, Leslie suggests that counseling methods with a more personal approach will be more successful with African-American clients. He shares a counseling event in which a minister used a method that was considered unorthodox to the counseling discipline, but which showed a great deal of concern and caring. He observed that the parishioner valued this approach much more than if he had experienced "all this talk stuff."[60]

MULTICULTURAL ISSUES

Churches which intend to reach the whole community for Christ must decide to act with intentionality in addressing multicultural issues. This can be accomplished in five ways. *First,* they must avoid what Martin Luther King called the "myth of time." King referred to this as the "strangely irrational notion that there is something in the very flow of time that will inevitably cure all ills."[61] Whites often assume that Christian teaching will eventually conquer evil so that social unrest or political turmoil will become a thing of the past. King resisted this, observing that "time is neutral. It can be used either destructively or constructively."[62]

> I am coming to feel that the people of ill will have used time much more effectively than the people of good will. We will have to repent in this generation not merely for the vitriolic words and actions of the bad people, but for the appalling silence of the good people.[63]

The *second* objective for active churches is to carefully refine the content of teaching materials. This involves the issue of whether materials and methodology should be Afrocentric or multicultural. The latter approach attempts to correct the presence of ethnocentrism by creating an awareness of diversity. The former, conversely, attempts to correct ethnocentrism by emphasizing one particular people and history.[64]

Many African-American educators feel that the only way to truly empower and enable black youth is to provide a distinctively black approach to content and teaching. Joseph Crockett maintains that

> it is necessary for Christian education to uphold cultural integrity for African Americans. Christian education for the Black church involves, fundamentally, process of teaching scripture in light of the experiences and traditions of African Americans. Christian education involves the processes of teaching the scriptures with respect for the experiences and traditions of particular cultures, so that the person may become transformed and share in God's transforming activity in history.[65]

A requisite element in this approach is the "exodus strategy" of education in which sociopolitical analysis becomes the "primary process for teaching Scripture."[66] The assumption is that there are inherent parallels between African-American experiences and that of the ancient Hebrews.

A common ingredient of Afrocentric curriculums is the assumption that the Western traditions of Christianity have devalued African culture and history. Black theologians such as Cain Hope Felder feel that the American church must arrive at a renewed and more comprehensive understanding of the black religious experience. The first step in this process is to "recognize the total inadequacy and racial bias of the West's intellectual tradition in its endeavors to provide allegedly 'universal' conceptual and religious norms."[67] Felder contends that

> determining the meaning of the Bible for the Black religious experience involves the following: 1. an international "African" identity; 2. a new skepticism about prevailing Eurocentric exegesis, hermeneutics, and historiography; 3. a renewed commitment to the New Testament vision of liberation as a self-perpetuating process, continued self-critique, and the establishment of shared power, first for a "beloved Black community," but also for all.[68]

While the distinctiveness of all cultures is to be honored, the concept of an "Afrocentric" curriculum presents some questions which Christian educators should carefully consider. Foremost would be the issue of a monocultural solution which could work against the interests of a truly multicultural approach. Diane Ravitch expresses a concern that such reinforcements of ethnicity may produce negative results: "If we teach children to identify only with members of their own race or ethnic culture, we run the risk of promoting and sanctioning ethnocentrism and prejudice. Under no circumstances," Ravitch cautions, "should the curriculum be patterned to stir ethnocentric pride or to make children feel that their self-worth as human beings is derived from their race or ethnic origin."[69]

Another concern is whether such an approach blurs the distinction between culture and ethnicity. Richard Beswick cautions that educators must beware of needlessly confusing the two. "Ethnicity" deals with "generational heritage and history," while "culture" consists of the "ideas, customs, and art of a people's living present." When these are confused, the outcome can be cultural relativity.

> In this view, equal value is posited for all cultural and religious expressions. In contrast, good education allows students to pursue objective criteria for determining what is good or bad, valuable or useless in any particular culture. Racism may affect the way one regards another's culture or religion. But it does not follow that every articulated cultural or religious preference is racist.[70]

The point is that culture and ethnicity are inseparably bound together. Whether European, African, or Asian, every person is a mix between ethnic heritage and social history. The attempt to somehow separate the two for curricular interests will always deny part of the total person. An African American is both an African and an American. An Asian American is both an Asian and an American.

Third, churches which act with intentionality regarding multiculturalism will carefully examine themselves concerning oft-repeated accusations of Eurocentrism. Michael Warren observes that in the name of the Gospel we often "hand on to young people the vision of the dominant culture, covered over with a thin religious veneer."[71]

Hale-Benson notes that Christian educators once assumed that "American culture was inherently consistent with Christian ideals. A major function was then to teach in order to support the republic and democracy."[72] A truly multicultural approach will demand that this assumption be reexamined.

> This assumption has had to be challenged and enlarged. Christianity may include elements that are consistent with the democratic ideal; however, Christianity is in no way limited to current or ideal practices of democracy. The character of Christian education has to allow for its own evaluation.[73]

She goes on to remind us that "Christian education must allow for increasing numbers of persons with cultural differences to study the scripture and encounter the God of all creation in light of their particular experience."[74]

It is true that Christianity consists of basic truths which are not diluted by time. The sacred text does contain a "transcultural" meaning and the primary purposes of biblical authors can be clearly perceived. At the same time, the issues facing the church are as much sociological as theological. Unwarranted relationships can exist between Christianity and the dominant culture.

Fourth, churches must develop a multicultural approach that glorifies and reaffirms diversity. In the early days of slavery, white missionaries were constantly puzzled about the demonstration of black religious experience. Emotional worship and happy attitudes were often viewed as being somehow in opposition to true Christian worship. However, as Gayraud S. Wilmore observes, "what whites regarded as incapacity and childishness was more often a completely different approach to religion, a different view of the world, and a studied avoidance of white control."[75] Ethnicity means diversity. Differences should be glorified and affirmed as a total expression of the body of Christ. Consider the vitality of African culture and the contribution it makes to Christian religious experience.

No culture comes as close to the cultures depicted in Scripture as African cultures. The church needs to examine ancient African cultures in the light of Scripture, and determine whether, by restoring certain aspects of it, the African American family can be equipped to overcome the dilemma it now faces.[76]

George and Yvonne Abatso suggest that Christian educators seek to restore basic components of traditional African culture into the C.E. program of their churches. One of the foremost of these is a harmony of the sacred and the secular.

One question which Christian educators have to ask themselves is whether the practice of Western Christianity has been to create a separation between the sacred and the secular which inhibits a truly multicultural approach to ministry. In practical terms, the impression is often conveyed that being a Christian is simply a matter of repeating a formula or attending a weekly service.

An example of this practice is the tendency to develop formulas whereby a person merely confesses his/her sins, accepts Jesus Christ, is baptized, and memorizes a few Scriptures. They learn to quote a few key verses and then they try to look sanctimonious on Sunday morning and/or Wednesday night. However, their moral behavior during the week does not shift from seeking profit at the expense of others. The problem for American life and for African American family life today, is that there is no harmony between the spiritual and what are considered secular aspects of life.[77]

Additional components to be emphasized are harmony between male and female roles, a sense of community, and next-life preparation.[78]

A *fifth* way in which churches can be truly multicultural is to expand spiritual horizons to include social ministry. This means discovering the thrill and challenge of empowering others to achieve the fullest existence possible. "Empowerment . . . means the enabling and supporting process with which racial and ethnic peoples may become authentic human beings in the fullness of God."[79]

One large and influential denomination has made tremendous progress in missions, to the point that 80 percent of its membership lives outside the United States. Yet the leadership of the denomination consists almost entirely of white American males. These people are not hypocrites; none would claim to be racists, nor would any deny the value of human advancement and equality. In order for empowerment to occur, however, something else has to happen. Good feelings and positive attitudes are not enough. True multiculturalism demands that those who have the power give it up to those who truly represent their constituency. This is especially difficult because all one has to do to retain power is—nothing. Conversely, the decision to empower must always be accompanied by action, and by sacrifice!

It is in this area that the North American church has a chance to make its voice heard in the strongest possible way. Cecil "Chip" Murray, the senior pastor of First African Methodist Episcopal Church in Los Angeles, states it most effectively: "White evangelicals need an at-risk Gospel for at-risk people in an at-risk society."[80]

MINISTRY CONSIDERATIONS

Cultural and environmental considerations have often received only lip service in ministry settings. In practice, they may receive little attention. For the church to provide a ministry that enhances the life of individuals within the black community, it must act with intentionality. The following suggestions are only a few of the many applications that might be made for a ministry setting.

1. The church must resolve to actively do what is possible to diminish the adverse social conditions which the African American faces.

Empathy and awareness is not sufficient at this point. Continued conditions of oppression must not be tolerated. Churches can become involved in numerous services that will be helpful for the black community, as well as other minority groups. Examples of such ministries include:

1. Ministry through literacy training.
2. Ministering by equipping grandmothers and grandfathers.

3. Ministering through day care.
4. Ministering by developing apartment complexes for single and low-income parents.
5. Ministering by acquiring federal funds.
6. Ministering by teaching entrepreneurial skills.[81]

2. Careful attention must be given to the manner in which problems of the African-American families are presented.

The unique problems must be clearly articulated in order to initiate programs and activities for solutions and to develop a greater awareness by the society at large. At the same time, awareness and articulation can result in further preconceptions and racism. Martin Luther King, Jr. gave a warning regarding this in 1967.

> As public awareness of the predicament of the Black family increases, there will be danger and opportunity. The opportunity will be to deal fully rather than haphazardly with the problem as a whole, as a social catastrophe brought on by many years of oppression. The danger is that the problems will be attributed to innate Black weaknesses and used to justify further neglect and to rationalize continued oppression.[82]

3. Church planning and programming should include intentional modeling by "significant others."

James Banks writes, "We are not going to progress significantly in augmenting the black child's self-concept until we either change the racial attitudes and perceptions of white Americans or create new 'significant others' for black children."[83] A multicultural perspective will certainly include the important goal of changing racial attitudes, but a more specific project may be to provide "significant others."

There is an acute need for modeling the Christian walk today. This need exists first within the family, and second within the church as a supplement to the family. Modeling can only effectively occur through relationship with "significant others."

One of the greatest lessons the black church can teach its white counterparts is the value and meaning of the church as a family. Theologian J. Deotis Roberts notes that in the black community the family is not limited to blood relationships. There is instead a sense of belonging by all. According to Roberts:

> We believe that this type of consciousness and deep sense of kinship should be encouraged and cultivated. The experience of belongingness of a people who are oppressed by racism leads to health, sanity, and wholeness. It is thus that we are able to walk tall in spite of all we must endure.[84]

The church has the responsibility to supplement families within the church whenever these role models are missing. An illustration of how powerful such modeling can be is supplied by the Lawndale Community Church, a Chicago congregation which reflects a multicultural, holistic ministry. The founding pastor, Wayne Gordon, "a white farm boy from Iowa," sensed the perception of a "white leader" syndrome as well as the lack of a strong African-American leader for his congregation. His solution? Gordon recruited a capable black pastor, Carey Casey, while he concentrated on leadership of the church community outreach programs. The fact that the black community could see that power was not coveted, but shared, continues to produce a powerful evangelical witness in the community of Lawndale.[85]

In forming such a ministry, black males could be recruited to develop a relationship with children from homes in which a father is missing. Both male and female professionals could be utilized in career day programs or in one-on-one counseling or fellowship opportunities to encourage children and teenagers to set vocational goals. Mentoring programs could be initiated that either directly or indirectly pair youth with adults in a relationship that supports youth educational and vocational decisions.

Media coverage was recently given to Henry Gaskins when he received the President's Volunteer Action Award at the White House. He has initiated a home-based academy that serves as an after-school tutorial program for four hours every weeknight and all day Saturday. In addition to the tutoring, Gaskins and his wife, plus some volunteers, help students develop personal goals and lead them to commit themselves to succeed. It is apparent that the success of this tutoring program is as much a result of the personal relationship approach, if not more than the specific assistance with school work.

Another example is Madeline Cartwright, an African American who became principal of an elementary school in one of the most devastated inner-city areas of North Philadelphia. She has turned the school around by setting an example in some very basic areas such as giving children the opportunity to have clean clothes to start each day. She and her staff personally wash children's clothes at the beginning of the day so that each has the "opportunity to feel better about themselves." She has asked the state of Pennsylvania to set up "mentor houses" in which families can mentor families in how to develop more healthy family patterns and relationships.[86]

Within every African-American community are local representative role models such as Gaskins and Cartwright. However, examples on a national level can also inspire young blacks in the local church. John Perkins, whose varied ministries continue to impact minorities nationwide, currently the publisher of *Urban Family*, a magazine that seeks to promote minority role models, and Peggy L. Jones, senior pastor of the multiracial Macedonia Assembly of God Church in St. Paul, Minnesota, a consultant to churches wanting to deal with multiracial diversity, are two nationally known leaders who regularly mentor the greater African-American church community.

A study of biographies of contemporary African Americans who are leaders in religious institutions, government, and the arts can be utilized to serve as surrogate mentoring. The lives of these individuals can inspire others with the message that "it can be done" and "our little bit can make a difference." Such messages are especially important for African-American adolescents who face the task of developing identities and making educational and vocational plans with the awareness that they will probably experience the discrimination and obstacles that are present in a race-conscious world.

4. The church should address the role it might take in working toward the removal of barriers to academic achievement for African-American children and youth.

Hale-Benson notes that churches must confront the educational challenges black children face in school.

It is our thesis that black children do not enter school disadvantaged. They emerge from school as disadvantaged youth. For this reason the church must evaluate its ministries to black youth based in part on an accurate assessment of the core causes of the challenges they face. It necessitates confronting the difficulties children and youth experience in negotiating the school.[87]

Hale-Benson suggests that churches should attempt to design programs or networks especially for the purpose of encouraging African Americans to achieve academically. This will take place as they are encouraged to complete high school and to enroll and graduate from college. She also feels that ministry should have a special focus for the black adolescent male, using as a beginning point the cultural values and attitudes already present in the African-American culture.[88]

5. *White ministers and church leaders should be candid in discussing the issue of racism.*

This is a factor that will often permeate experiences that the African American has in both the church and the larger society. Church leaders must assume their biblical responsibility for making it known that this is a justice issue that must be discussed.

Although it is now accepted that race is not a valid way to categorize people, prejudice based on race is still a prevalent social practice. Financial resources, educational and professional opportunities, and cultural rights are still very determined by an individual's membership in a specific "racial" group. In America, racism is largely based on color so that even cultural assimilation does not eliminate it.

Ministers sometimes question whether open discussion of racism is an appropriate method for the church. Often this hesitation is a means of masking personal discomfort on the part of leadership and/or members of the congregation in dealing with the problem.

Stereotypes and biases that are the basis of racism are primarily associated with personal experiences. Too often, time is not taken to honestly examine the impact that these experiences have had on us. A beginning point is for leadership to develop a self-awareness of feelings and experiences related to their own personal biases.

Church groups and Sunday School classes should be encouraged to discuss racism in an open and reflective manner. Hopson and Hopson in *Different and Wonderful* give several excellent suggestions for role-play between parents and children that could be adapted for the church setting.[89]

6. *A family ministry in the local church can take the initiative to present opportunities for the development and enhancement of intergenerational relationships.*

Historically, as local churches became aware of the need for family ministry, various types of so-called family programs were provided. A common form was to have "something for everyone," a form of specialized program in which each member of the family received age-level programming. This was an expected approach for a society that had become highly specialized. However, in the process, the family was ministered to separately rather than as a unit. Even more important, the pattern of segregating the age-levels was continued so that each seldom had contact with other generations, and then often on only a closely graded basis.

The extended network of the black family is a reminder for local church programming that contact across generations needs to be "reinvented" for the church. All ethnic minority groups stress the extended family more than the majority white culture. The benefits which minority groups have experienced from this family pattern would be helpful for all families. While geographic limitations have often made the nuclear family pattern a necessity, church families interacting with church families could initiate lasting intergenerational relationships.

7. *Last, and possibly the most important guideline for ministry to any culture, the church must contribute to the strengthening of family life in the African-American community.*

More than the number of parents present in the home, more than the amount of money available in the home, more than the educational level or social class of the family members, the most important factor is the character of the family culture. An active and progressive family ministry is needed to assist the family to become a more healthy "whole" by developing new and more effective methods of relating and by enhancing their present family strengths.

A recent "Peanuts" cartoon shows Linus and Charlie Brown in conversation at the park. Linus asks, "Does having a dog make your life better?" Charlie Brown answers, "Absolutely! Dogs protect you, give you comfort, love, joy and companionship—that's their job." The cartoonist concludes with a picture of Snoopy sitting on the bench thinking, "Talk about stress . . . !

The stress placed on the family today may be similar to the function assigned to the little dog. It is expected to make up for all the losses of contemporary society. The truth is that families cannot survive alone. Churches have the opportunity to fulfill the Gospel mandate by becoming a Family to families.

One way to accomplish this is to follow the example of the African kinship family pattern in which every member of the group is included and is considered to be of vital importance. There are no solitary Christians. The meaning of community is essential to the Christian way of life. African-American culture is a continuing lesson to those contemporary churches which desire a spiritual identity congruent with the early church of the New Testament.

CHAPTER TWELVE

OUR MULTICULTURAL OPPORTUNITY

BACKGROUND

Arthur Ashe, the world renowned tennis player and role model for thousands of youths, fought against a background of racial misunderstanding and prejudice. Sports writer Kenny Moore recounts how

> every Sunday, Arthur Jr. had to go to church, either to First Presbyterian or Westwood Baptist, where his parents had met and where he would look up at a picture of Christ with blond hair and blue eyes and wonder if God was on his side.[1]

This example is only one of thousands illustrating one of the basic challenges not only to the world of education, but also to evangelical Christianity. Dallas Theological Seminary professor Dan Wallace observes that, "Most of the power brokers of evangelicals, since the turn of the century, have been white, obsessive-compulsive males."[2] He goes on to make a frank but honest appraisal:

> Not only have we ignored the powerful testimony of the Black church, we have also failed to listen to the women of the

church. If the imago Dei is both male and female, by squelch-
ing the contribution of women we distort that very image
before a watching world.[3]

SOME PRACTICAL GUIDELINES

This refreshing but frank appraisal presents evangelicals with
two challenges: (1) how can we become more inclusive, and (2)
yet remain loyal to the tenets of our faith? Christians must be
especially careful that their environment not become the sub-
stance of an ethnocentric message. At the same time, attempts
to be inclusive cannot compromise the Christian message.
There are at least three guidelines which may help us in recon-
ciling these seemingly opposing principles.

First, we must review and reaffirm our commitment to the
authority of Scripture. Bible scholars are fond of saying that
every religious question ultimately becomes a question of
hermeneutics. It is the same with multiculturalism. To approach
the question of diversity without a clear commitment to the
authority of Scripture is to risk a hermeneutic of relativity that
will leave little more than story-telling for the basis of Christian
belief.

Speaking at a recent conference on "Reclaiming the Bible
for the Church," Yale scholar Brevard Childs noted the necessity for rediscovery of the exegetical tradition of the church. According to Childs the question is "whether the Bible in any form
can be anything more than an expression of time-conditioned
human culture . . . whether any ancient text has a determinate
meaning." He goes on to make an observation which directly
applies to the contemporary multicultural debate: "The issue of
whether the Christian community of faith can claim a special
relation to its scriptures as a guide to faithful living has been
met by a challenge which would recognize only sociological
forces at work as various communities seek to establish their
identities with warrants from the past.[4]

The point is that even the most sincere desire for equality
must have more than a sociological reference point. Many of
the tensions prompted by multiculturalism come about because

of pluralistic assumptions. It is far too easy (and inaccurate) to simply assume that because there are many cultures, truth must also be pluralistic and that Christian doctrine is merely an accident of cultural evolvement.

Consider the issue of the substitutionary atonement. Some theologians have argued that the picture of Christ's death as a sacrifice to appease an angry God comes from the medieval construct of Anselm in the eleventh century. Serfs lived in an atmosphere where service to a lord and avoidance of wrath or punishment were primary objectives of daily life. Accordingly this view is often criticized as outmoded and irrelevant to the needs of modern people.

To be sure, the view of Anselm is far from perfect. It is true, for example, that he concentrates upon the wrath and appeasement of God to the exclusion of clearly connecting personal salvation with Christ's death. But to simply discard the themes of sacrifice and wrath against sin as being fragments of medieval thought is to miss the clear teaching of Scripture. In the final analysis, the Bible has to settle the question. Does the Bible present Christ's death as a sacrifice? Does Scripture portray God as being angry (outraged, actually) at sin? The clear answer is yes. Any view which leaves out these themes would be seriously deficient. The fact that Anselm may have applied similar categories in the eleventh century is supplemental, but in the final analysis, incidental to the witness of our primary authority.

The practical application of this principle is that we cannot satisfy social needs by recasting Christian belief in terms of contemporary social commentary. The Christian solution for humanity was, is, and will remain the Cross on Golgotha.

Second, Christians must emphasize the social and psychological implications of a unified view of human creation. If humanity is a special creation of God, and if we bear His image within us, our communications with each other can be assumed to conform to common patterns of communication and meaning. The Gospel becomes not the expression of one ethnic group or tradition, but rather the proclamation for all humanity. The fact that we all have died in Adam, and can be made alive in Christ, is transcultural.

This principle becomes especially important in dealing with other cultures. Many times Eastern thought is presented as being "qualitatively" different from that of the West. Other societies are pictured as existing outside Western categories of meaning.

There is also a great deal of truth in this assumption. The history of the doctrine of the Trinity is a clear testimonial to how the East and West can think differently. Still, the fundamental laws of human logic seem applicable to all groups. Anyone who has studied comparative religions, for example, will quickly admit that the law of contradiction is present in all religions. Without it they would not exist. The point is that the message of Christ is the same for all, and the same salvation can be experienced by all. The fact that Christ came to die for sinners, "of whom I am chief," has the same meaning for us that it did for the Apostle Paul.

Another ramification of this principle is that all humans are truly personal beings with the same inherent rights and privileges. There is no room in Christianity for division into "classes" or privileged groups. Within the context of Christianity it is truly possible to realize the meaning of human rights and freedoms.

Not only are we truly personal, in Christ we are also truly spiritual. There is a higher part of our being which gives an even greater meaning to the concept of equality. When we mistreat one another, or when racism or class oppression occurs, we are mistreating and oppressing creatures made in God's own image. To deny equal rights is to deny God.

Finally, a unified view of creation also recognizes the gravity of human sinfulness. The struggle for human rights is not merely sociological or political, it is part of the spiritual warfare portrayed by Paul in Ephesians 6:12. A Christian view of human rights will not spend needless time or resources searching for an illusory "great society." The path to racial and social reconciliation will always begin in the confessional. Each of us must face the fact that we are sinners, that we are prejudiced, and that we have failed in many ways to present the image of the kingdom needed for our society.

Third, churches must implement a model of practical servanthood. This constitutes an especially serious challenge for today's church. For the past century we seem to have operated within what might be called the savior paradigm. The church was understood as the ark of salvation and its primary purpose was to spread the message to the lost. This paradigm affected ministry in a number of ways. In many cases, churches were viewed as "soul-saving stations" with the primary responsibility of bringing in those from without so that minister and staff might perform the saving function.

Such churches also became exclusive in that those brought in were to assume the distinctives characteristic of the group. Church teaching was characterized by indoctrination, and newcomers were responsible to learn the language of the group as well as think the same thoughts.

The focus of church efforts became naturally associated with self-interest. A particular confession or tradition was attempting to survive in the midst of competitors. Church activities and programs catered to the preservation and enhancement of the individual congregation.

Churches also tended to promote and accept nuclear families. Programs and educational curriculums related to traditional family structures. There was little if any room for those who did not conform to the middle-class social profile. Such churches became inherently monocultural. Congregations of similar social backgrounds naturally assumed racial and social compositions consistent with their exclusivistic emphasis.

There was some theological justification for this approach. Since the battle of *The Fundamentals,* evangelical Christians have experienced conflicts with systems which attempt to solve the social ills of society while at the same time denying or negating basic Christian beliefs. Many raised in conservative Christianity have little patience for explanations of the human dilemma which do not begin with a biblical anthropology.

TOWARD A PARADIGM

This leads to the suggestion that there may be an alternative paradigm, more promising for contemporary needs. We would call this the "servant" church. Viewed from this motif, the role of the church in a multicultural society assumes the vocation of support and service. This does not mean that salvation is left out, or that the "saving" motif is discarded; rather, it means that churches must develop a servant identity. The goal of the church is to minister rather than be ministered to. The congregation assumes the responsibility of *diakonia,* of serving others in the best sense of the example supplied by the Jerusalem congregation.

Such a church will necessarily become inclusive rather than exclusive. Congregations will take on the character and constituency of the people around them. What is there about your church, for example, that might make people feel uneasy or unwelcome? What makes an outsider feel like an "outsider"? Answering that question will go far toward a true fulfillment of the evangelistic task.

The ministry of the servant church will be enlarged through the theme of empowerment. To "empower" is simply to help others improve their lives by overcoming social, economic, and educational obstacles which have hindered their full participation in the benefits of society. There is, however, one very critical clarification that must be made. We cannot "empower" without being willing to give up some of our power (in the case of Christians, all of it).

It is very easy to think of "empowering" in terms of programs and outreach to the disadvantaged. But that kind of empowerment is actually a misnomer. Attempting to improve the life-situation of others by providing goods and services is no more than gift-giving. True empowerment comes when we actually convey power to others, when we enable others to make choices and take advantage of opportunities previously denied them.

This brings up an additional issue. Empowerment must also be more than an attitude. True sharing of power must always be planned and intentional. Action must follow words. Empowerment cannot be something that just "happens"; it will not wander into our churches like a desert traveler. If empowerment is truly to occur, church and denominational leaders must identify specific problems and launch direct solutions. Equality can only come by sacrificing what is perhaps the most desired human possession—power.

Churches should also be aware that they are being closely watched to see if, indeed, actions follow words. This is an area of great frustration among minorities. Some feel that racism is so entrenched that no solution is in sight. Glandion Carney, associate director of missions for InterVarsity Christian Fellowship, remains pessimistic concerning the future of racial relations.

> There has been very little fruit from the pledges of racial reconciliation made by evangelical groups, such as the National Association of Evangelicals and other major Christian agencies. These organizations continue to be white in their structure and avoid issues that concern the cities.[5]

Robert Lupton, President of Family Consultation Services Urban Ministry, notes that the black community feels whites have not put forth the necessary effort to overcome racial divisions. According to Lupton:

> [The black community] would want us to be neighbors. If we still segregate our lives, what are we saying? A church reconciled has to be a Body reconciled, and that involves every aspect of our living. This will require a practical theology of reconciliation and a strategy of creating reconciliation in our neighborhoods.[6]

Multicultural churches will also be holistic in their outreach. This means that we minister not only to the spiritual, but to the physical, psychological, emotional, and economic needs of those around us. Day cares can be provided, English lessons can be taught, jobs can be provided, and loans can be secured. All of these areas contain critical needs for disadvantaged minorities.

In the process of ministry the church will become an extended family in which all will feel welcome regardless of sociological profile. Churches which have a true openness toward others will experience many ethnic groups and backgrounds in their congregations. This does not mean that churches have to contain differing ethnic components to be true churches; rather, it means that all will be welcome and that some churches will naturally take on a multicultural identity as they reach out to their communities.

An additional clarification is needed at this point. We are not saying that it is wrong for churches to be monocultural. North America is covered with monocultural congregations that are authentic representatives of their surrounding community. Many such congregations express only the strongest witness for Christ within the context of their community. The question is whether we are being true to the mission of our church in our local situation. A monocultural church in a multicultural community should ask itself how it might become more inclusive. The question is how the needs of the community can be met. Conversely, in both cases, however, the need is for sensitivity—a truly multicultural burden which seeks to address every need in the name of Christ. More than anything else, a truly universal outreach of the Christian message must begin with a change of our attitudes. Churches which primarily represent one cultural group are not necessarily biased or lacking in dedication.

The point should also be made that the issue of monocultural congregations is hardly confined to those who feel that they represent a "majority." "Minority" Christians can be equally guilty in preserving the status quo of separatism. Stanley K. Inouye observes that "the minority Christian is as much at fault as the majority Christian. The sin is the same. They both define belonging as sameness and therefore do not contribute to each other or work together as they ought."[7] According to John Perkins, "There is no biblical basis for a black, white, Hispanic, or Asian church."[8]

A REVISED SELF-UNDERSTANDING

Finally, to be truly multicultural the church must come to a new understanding of how Christianity should function in a democracy. We do not mean to do wrong, not for one moment would we knowingly violate the civil or human rights of another person; yet, in spite of good intentions the attempt to assist in making the kingdom just a little more visible can produce extremely negative results. Wesley S. Woo contends that

> American Protestantism has confounded the concepts of being Christian and being American and presumed the two to be virtually the same. This intermingling of ideas and values has been racially and culturally oppressive in suggesting that one could not be Christian or American and hold on to one's own cultural values and traditions.[9]

While we as evangelicals accept all who wish to join us without reservation, we must ask the question whether we are actually advancing a monocultural society in the name of Christianity. If we are truly to be multicultural we must never forget that we live in a democracy. Attempts to return to the Old Testament or to "reconstruct" society according to a biblical model may be in many ways admirable, but they also ignore the nature and purpose of the church in the world. If we are going to truly minister to all of society, we must recognize the plurality inherent in America and consequently emphasize the spiritual nature of the church which exists within it as a sojourner. This world is not our home. Attempts to make it such will ultimately violate the spiritual nature and saving purpose of the church.

Part of the problem is that we as Christians might very well die for the protection of individual rights and freedoms. This is why many groups are justly irritated at accusations of Eurocentrism or ethnocentrism. After all, one of the primary goals of any ethnocentric group, religious or otherwise, is the protection of individual rights which have been perceived as being denied.

For the Christian church to operate in a holistic manner, however, there must be a genuine awareness of corporate rights as well as personal rights. S.D. Gaede speaks of the category of "socializing communities," that is, families, schools, churches, and any other learning communities which attempt personal formation. Gaede observes that

> the bottom line is that such communities must have the opportunities and resources necessary to nurture the next generation according to the truths they believe. As long as we recognize only individual rights and largely ignore the rights and

responsibilities of socializing communities, we will not have truth-bearing communities.[10]

Continuing, Gaede states:

American Christians have the tendency to worship with those who are like them—ethnically, economically, and so on. If we approach community along those same stratified lines and our "socializing institutions" turn out to be white and middle-class, then our communities will not represent the body of Christ; they will not have all the insights and gifts of the body; and we will not wind up teaching the whole, life-changing truth of Scripture.[11]

Christians must be willing to relinquish desire for societal control and let those who wish otherwise follow their own life path. This is very difficult, but we are reaching a point in our society where the church must decide whether its role is to be servant or conqueror.

Those of us who are concerned with human rights and equality would like nothing better than to find an effective, simple, and quick solution to the problem. In fact, we have no quick solutions. Social scientists have noted that children seem remarkably free of negativism toward those who are different. As the school years advance, however, prejudice seems to make an increasing impact until by the high school years definite divisions have occurred. The ultimate source of such feelings will be a matter of continuing debate among students of human behavior. The plain truth is, however, that all of us have prejudice. It is somehow part of our being.

For this reason, we argue that the critical place to begin is not with programs or finances, but with our feelings. We must develop a sensitivity which will recognize not only the rights of others but also the presence of inferior feelings within ourselves. A large part of the answer is simply imitating Christ.

Reuben Brooks warns that "Christians tend to theologize their cultures into a deception that theirs is the most 'biblical.' "[12] The message of faith, however, is always centered in the person of Christ: "It is He who transcends all ethnicities and transforms any cultures from within: not by our tampering with structural forms from without, but by transforming mankind from within."[13]

The mere decision to follow Christ's example, however, is not enough by itself. Decision must be followed by action. We should enhance our sensitivity by engaging in a number of practical steps that will help us to make cultural awareness a reality. An example of such action is the recent decision of the Pentecostal Fellowship of North America to form a new multiracial association. After seventy years of racial separation, the previously all-white group voted to disband and form a new multiracial body, the Pentecostal-Charismatic Churches of North America. The group has an executive committee of six whites and six blacks. Pentecostal historian Vinson Synan terms the decision "a decisive turning in the history of the Pentecostal movement."[14]

Near the close of his impassioned defense of Native Americans, Bartolomé Las Casas makes an especially significant observation.

> The Indians are our brothers, and Christ has given his life for them. Why, then, do we persecute them with such inhuman savagery when they do not deserve such treatment? The past, because it cannot be undone, must be attributed to our weakness, provided that what has been taken unjustly is restored.[15]

It is the latter part of this statement that is of critical importance for the evangelical church in a multicultural world. If we say that we have not sinned, we deceive ourselves. "The past cannot be undone." Now, however, a divided society is closely watching our claims of mission and purpose. "What has been taken unjustly must be restored." This means soul searching, giving, and sacrificing on both the personal and corporate levels.

One of the best biblical examples of the integration of faith and action is the sacrifice of Isaac by Abraham. Many have wrestled with the account of James in which Abraham is mentioned as having been justified by works. What is easily overlooked, however, is that the sacrifice of Isaac came a generation after Abraham first believed and God "reckoned it to him as righteousness" (Gen. 15:6). James is teaching that the reality of Abraham's faith was authenticated by his performance in an hour of great trial. His works reflected the true nature of his faith.

As evangelicals we are like Abraham. We have preached and witnessed to the reality of a faith that is biblical and saving.

Past generations were times of doctrinal and spiritual warfare in which the truth of the Gospel was advanced at great cost. Now, however, a new generation has arisen. This generation demands to see our faith carried out in our actions. They want to see our faith lived. It is this challenge that awaits us as we minister in and to a multicultural world.

CONCLUSION

In the St. Louis Art Museum hangs an intriguing painting by the African-American artist John McCrady. The work, entitled *Swing Low Sweet Chariot,* portrays the end of life's journey among a poor farming family. The family is gathered around the deathbed of a woman of advanced age. What they do not see is a golden chariot descending from heaven, accompanied by angels, rapidly descending upon their small, isolated home. The interesting thing is that all of the figures are black. A black soul is going home; black angels are leading the chariot; a black family is grieving. Yet none can doubt the painting's powerful message of ultimate hope which transcends all races.

Another work, *Tidings of Great Joy,* by the German painter Bernhard Plockhorst, portrays the joyful announcement of that ultimate hope. In this work the humble shepherds, the angels and cherubs are all obviously white. Yet there can be no doubt of the universal joy and spiritual strength expressed by the artist.[16]

So what color is your God? The truth is we all see God with eyes that have been conditioned by a multitude of factors which constitute that complex thing we call culture. In Jesus Christ, however, all of the beautiful diversity still speaks of a unity — of a unified hope for us all. In neither of the above pictures do we see God, and perhaps that is for the best. There is an ultimate reality which none can fully portray or comprehend. The expression of that reality has been given to us in a thousand different ways (and colors). But as we joyfully celebrate our hope through Christ we can and will come to an ever increasing realization of our unity in Him!

➤ NOTES

Chapter 1: Our Multicultural Challenge

1. Gordon Aeschliman, *GlobalTrends* (Downers Grove, Ill.: InterVarsity, 1990), 71.

2. Michael Meyer, "Another Lost Generation," *Newsweek,* 4 May 1992, 70–71.

3. Ray Bakke, *The Urban Christian* (Downers Grove, Ill.: Inter-Varsity, 1987), 181.

4. Meyer, "Another Lost Generation," 71.

5. Jo Kadlecek, "The Coloring of the American Church," *National & International Religion Report,* 19 April 1993, 3.

6. Ibid.

7. Richard J. Mouw, *When the Kings Come Marching In* (Grand Rapids: Eerdmans, 1983), 16.

8. Ibid., 20–21.

9. Jacquelyn Grant, "A Theological Framework," in *Working with Black Youth: Opportunities for Christian Ministry,* ed. Charles R. Foster and Grant S. Shockley (Nashville: Abingdon, 1989), 74.

10. Dennis P. Hollinger, "The Church: A Social Institution? *TSF Bulletin* 10 (January–February 1987): 20.

11. Frances E. Kendall, *Diversity in the Classroom* (New York: Teachers College Press, 1983), 20.

12. Ibid.

13. Ibid., 21.

14. Richard H. Niebuhr, *Christ and Culture* (New York: Harper Torchbooks, 1951), 32–34.

15. Millard J. Erickson, *Christian Theology* (Grand Rapids: Baker, 1985), 112–20.

16. Jacquelyn Grant, "Teaching Scripture with Cultural Specific-

ity," in *Working with Black Youth: Opportunities for Christian Ministry,* ed. Charles R. Foster and Grant S. Shockley (Nashville: Abingdon, 1989), 56.

17. Ibid., 57–58.

18. Erickson, *Christian Theology,* 121.

19. William J. Larkin, *Culture and Biblical Hermeneutics* (Grand Rapids: Baker, 1988), 97.

20. Aeschliman, *GlobalTrends,* 76.

21. John E. Kyle, ed., *Urban Mission: God's Concern for the City* (Downers Grove, Ill.: InterVarsity, 1988), 75.

Chapter 2: A Conceptual Framework of Culture

1. Robert J. Schreiter, *Constructing Local Theologies* (Maryknoll, N.Y.: Orbis, 1986), 45–49.

2. See Jeffrey C. Alexander and Steven Seidman, eds., *Culture and Society: Contemporary Debates* (Cambridge: Cambridge Univ. Press, 1990), for a more complete discussion.

3. Claude Lévi-Strauss, *Structural Anthropology,* vol. 2, trans. Monique Layton (New York: Basic, 1976), 142–44.

4. Robert C. Ulin, *Understanding Cultures* (Austin, Texas: Univ. of Texas Press, 1984), 116–17.

5. Clifford Geertz, *The Interpretation of Cultures* (New York: Basic, 1973), 350–51.

6. Ibid., 357.

7. Ibid.

8. Schreiter, *Local Theologies,* 55.

9. Ibid.

10. Richard K. Fenn, quoted by David Lyon, *Sociology and the Human Image* (Downers Grove, Ill.: InterVarsity, 1983), 12.

11. E.B. Tylor, *The Origins of Culture* (New York: Harper and Row, 1958), 1.

12. Ibid.

13. Ward H. Goodenough, *Culture, Language, and Society* (Menlo Park, Calif.: Benjamin/Cummings, 1981), 48.

14. Ibid., 48–49.

15. Ibid., 49.

16. Antonio Gramsci, "Culture and Ideological Hegemony," in *Culture and Society: Contemporary Debates,* ed. Jeffrey C. Alexander and Steven Seidman (Cambridge: Cambridge Univ. Press, 1990), 48.

17. Gwynn Williams, "The Concept of 'Egemonia' in the Thought of Antonio Gramsci: Some Notes on Interpretation," *Journal of the History of Ideas* 21 (1960): 587, quoted in Ronald Takaki, *Iron Cages: Race and Culture in 19th Century America* (New York: Oxford Univ. Press, 1990), vi–vii.

18. Note that "hermeneutics" is not limited to a religious context. Properly it refers to any interpretation framework used in analyzing cultures and languages.

19. Kevin J. Vanhoozer, "The World Well Staged?" in *God and Culture,* ed. D.A. Carson and John D. Woodbridge (Grand Rapids: Eerdmans, 1993), 22.

20. Ibid., 29.

21. Justo L. González, *Out of Every Tribe and Nation: Christian Theology at the Ethnic Roundtable* (Nashville: Abingdon, 1992), 31.

22. Noted in Hollinger, "The Church," 21.

23. Quoted in Schreiter, *Local Theologies,* 40.

24. Schreiter, *Local Theologies,* 39.

25. Paulo Freire, *Education for Critical Consciousness* (New York: Continuum, 1993), 33–34.

26. C.R. North, "The World," in *The Interpreter's Dictionary of the Bible,* ed. George Arthur Buttrick (Nashville: Abingdon, 1986), 4:874.

27. "Animism" may best be defined as the worship of the forces of nature. To ancient peoples the most obvious form would involve procreation, hence an inherent emphasis on sexuality as part of worship.

28. Eugene A. Nida, *Message and Mission* (New York: Harper & Row, 1960), 215.

29. William Hendricksen, *The Gospel of Matthew* (Grand Rapids: Baker, 1973), 243.

30. Gregory Jao, "Culture in the Flow of Biblical History: A Mandate for Ethnic Identity-Affirming Ministries" (Unpublished paper, April 1992), 13.

31. "Epistle to Diognetus" in *The Ante-Nicene Fathers,* ed. Alexander Roberts and James Donaldson (Grand Rapids: Eerdmans, 1979, reprint), 1:26–27.

32. "1 Clement" in *The Ante-Nicene Fathers*, ed. Alexander Roberts and James Donaldson (Grand Rapids: Eerdmans, 1979, reprint), 1:11.

33. "Epistle of Ignatius to the Philadelphians" in *The Ante-Nicene Fathers*, ed. Alexander Roberts and James Donaldson (Grand Rapids: Eerdmans, 1979, reprint), 1:81–82.

34. Martin Luther, "The Freedom of a Christian," in *Luther's Works,* vol. 31, ed. Harold J. Grimm, trans. W.A. Lambert (Philadelphia: Fortress, 1957), 344.

35. Paul G. Hiebert, "Metatheology: The Step Beyond Contextualization," in *Reflection and Projection: Missiology at the Threshold of 2001*, ed. Hans Dasdorf and Klaus W. Mueller (Bad Liebenzell, Germany: Verlag der Liebenzeller Mission, 1988), 384.

36. William A. Dyrness, *Learning About Theology from the Third*

World (Grand Rapids: Zondervan, 1990), 31.

37. Ibid., 32.

38. Schreiter, *Local Theologies,* 28.

39. Sidney Rooy, "Historical Models," in *New Alternatives in Theological Education,* ed. C. René Padilla (Oxford, U.K.: Regnum, 1988), 70.

40. Hiebert, "Metatheology," 388.

41. Ibid., 390.

42. Ibid.

43. Ibid., 392.

44. Arlin C. Migliazzo, "The Challenge of Educational Wholeness: Linking Beliefs, Values, and Academics," *Faculty Dialogue* (Winter 1993): 3–5.

45. Lyon, *Sociology and the Human Image*, 31–32.

46. Ibid.

47. Ibid., 32.

48. Bartolomé Las Casas, *In Defense of the Indians,* trans. Stafford Poole (DeKalb, Ill.: Northern Illinois Univ. Press, 1992), xvi.

49. Ibid., 72.

Chapter 3: Communicating a Theology of Cultural Awareness

1. Arthur M. Schlesinger, Jr., *The Disuniting of America: Reflections on a Multicultural Society* (New York: W.W. Norton, 1991), 10.

2. Dinesh D'Souza, *Illiberal Education: The Politics of Race and Sex on Campus* (New York: Vintage, 1991), 238.

3. Ronald Takaki, *A Different Mirror* (Boston: Little Brown, 1993), 427.

4. Gerald Graff, *Beyond the Culture Wars* (New York: W.W. Norton, 1992), 5.

5. David J. Hesselgrave, "Contextualization of Theology," in *Evangelical Dictionary of Theology,* ed. Walter A. Elwell (Grand Rapids: Baker, 1974), 271.

6. "Praxis" derives from Greek and may be understood as a synonym for "practice," the common experience of a community in living its daily life. According to Poling and Miller, the term refers to the "unity of purposeful activity and the thoughtful consideration of that activity" (James N. Poling and Donald E. Miller, *Foundations for a Practical Theology of Ministry* [Nashville: Abingdon, 1985], 65). "Rather than search for a single, true interpretation of the Bible for all times, scholars are asking what a particular text meant in a particular community and how that meaning changes as the community context changes" (p. 22).

7. Hesselgrave, "Contextualization," 271.

8. Charles H. Kraft, *Christianity in Culture* (Maryknoll, N.Y.: Orbis, 1991), 21.

9. Mr. Michael Ntow, interview with authors, 7 December 1993.

10. Louis Luzbetak, *The Church and Cultures: New Perspectives in Missiological Anthropology* (Maryknoll, N.Y.: Orbis, 1988), 78.

11. Ibid.

12. Hesselgrave, "Contextualization," 272.

13. Luzbetak, *The Church and Cultures,* 79.

14. Kraft, *Christianity in Culture,* 269.

15. Ibid., 120.

16. P.I. McCary, *Black Bible Chronicles: From Genesis to the Promised Land* (New York: African American Family, 1993).

17. Paul Blanckenberg Watney, "Contextualization and Its Biblical Precedents" (Ph.D. diss., Fuller Theological Seminary, 1985), 1.

18. William A. Dyrness, *Learning About Theology from the Third World* (Grand Rapids: Zondervan/Academie, 1990), 20–21.

19. Erickson, *Christian Theology,* 105ff.

20. Ibid., 120.

21. Gabriel Fackre, "The State of Systematics," address to the American Theological Society, Princeton Theological Seminary, N.J., 12 April 1991.

22. Joseph V. Crockett, *Teaching Scripture from an African-American Perspective* (Nashville: Discipleship Resources, 1990), xiii.

23. Ibid., 40.

24. Quoted in Dean William Ferm, *Contemporary American Theologies: A Critical Survey* (New York: Seabury, 1981), 73.

25. Charles R. Foster and Grant S. Shockley, eds., *Working with Black Youth: Opportunities for Christian Ministry* (Nashville: Abingdon, 1989), 57.

26. Ibid., 57–58.

27. Quoted in Merle English, "Bible Stories Are Getting an Afrocentric Focus," *The Dallas Morning News,* 31 December 1993, 11c.

28. Erich Martel, "How Valid Are the Portland Baseline Essays?" *Educational Leadership* (December 1991/January 1992): 20.

29. Ibid., 20.

30. Frank Yurco, quoted in Martel, "Portland Baseline Essays?" 20.

31. In the following paragraphs we are relying on Kraft's explication of Wilson's ideas; see his *Christianity in Culture,* 304–5.

32. Dorothee Söllee, "Peace Needs Women," in *Faith That Transforms: Essays in Honor of Gregory Baum,* ed. Mary Jo Leddy and Mary Ann Hinsdale (New York: Paulist, 1987), 116.

33. Quoted in Ferm, *Contemporary American Theologies,* 61.

34. Joe Klein, "Whose Values?" *Newsweek,* 8 June 1992, 19.

35. See Donald Dayton, *Discovering an Evangelical Heritage* (New York: Harper and Row, 1976).

36. "A Theology for Confronting the Cultural Captivity of Evangelicalism," *Academic Alert*, IVP's Book Bulletin for Professors, vol. 2, no. 1 (Winter 1993), 1–2, 4.

37. Bernard Ramm, *The Evangelical Heritage* (Waco, Texas: Word, 1973), 13.

38. "Apophatic" theology is the attempt to describe God by what He is not rather than what He is (cataphatic theology). The method is especially associated with Eastern Orthodoxy and Christian mysticism. See Vladimir Lossky, *The Vision of God*, trans. Asheleigh Moorhouse (Bedfordshire, England: American Orthodox Book Service), 1963.

39. Philip Schaff, *The Creeds of Christendom* (Grand Rapids: Baker, 1983), 1:206–7.

40. Ferm, *Contemporary American Theologies*, 117.

41. David J. Hesselgrave, *Communicating Christ Cross-Culturally*, 2nd ed. (Grand Rapids: Zondervan, 1991), 105.

42. Stanley K. Inouye, "The Mirror of God," *Christianity Today*, 3 March 1989, 27.

Chapter 4: Coming to Terms with Multiculturalism

1. Marianne Corey and Gerald Corey, *Becoming a Helper*, 2nd ed. (Pacific Grove, Calif.: Cole, 1993), 109.

2. James S. Wurzel, ed., *Toward Multiculturalism* (Yarmouth, Maine: Intercultural, 1988), 1.

3. Ibid., 2.

4. Sara Bullard, "Sorting Through the Multicultural Rhetoric," *Educational Leadership* 49 (December 1991/January 1992): 3, 5.

5. Diane Ravitch, "A Culture in Common," *Educational Leadership* 49 (December 1991/January 1992): 10.

6. Ibid.

7. J.A. Banks, *Teaching Strategies for Ethnic Studies*, 2nd ed. (Boston: Allyn & Bacon, 1979), 69–70.

8. Charles Zastrow and Karen Kirst-Ashman, *Understanding Human Behavior and the Social Environment* (Chicago: Nelson-Hall, 1990), 525.

9. Willard A. Williams, *Educational Ministries with Blacks* (n.p., The Board of Discipleship of the United Methodist Church, 1974), 6.

10. Wilma Longstreet quoted in Kendall, *Diversity in the Classroom*, 13.

11. Mary Jane Collier, "Conflict Competence within African, Mexican, and Anglo American Friendships," in *Cross-Cultural Interpersonal Communication*, ed. Stella Ting-Toomey and Felipe Korzenny

(London: Sage, 1991), 135.

12. Ibid.

13. Milton M. Gordon, *Assimilation in American Life: The Role of Race, Religion, and National Origins* (New York: Oxford Univ. Press, 1964), 27–28.

14. Deirdre Meintal, "What Is a Minority?" *The Unesco Courier,* June 1993, 10–13.

15. Ibid., 10.

16. Asa G. Hilliard III and Mona Vaughn-Scott, "The Quest for the Minority Child," in *The Young Child, Reviews of Research,* vol. 3, ed. Shirley Moore and Catherine Cooper (Washington, D.C.: National Association for Education of Young Children, 1982), 177.

17. Ibid.

18. John H. Westerhoff, "Enculturation," in *Harper's Encyclopedia of Religious Education,* ed. Iris V. Cully and Kendig Brubaker Cully (New York: Harper and Row, 1990), 217.

19. James W. White, *Intergenerational Religious Education* (Birmingham, Ala.: Religious Education Press, 1988), 136.

20. Westerhoff in Cully, *Encyclopedia of Religious Education,* 217.

21. John H. Westerhoff, "Fashioning Christians in Our Day," in *Schooling Christians: "Holy Experiments" in American Education,* ed. Stanley Hauerwas and John H. Westerhoff (Grand Rapids: Eerdmans, 1992), 269.

22. Westerhoff in Cully, *Encyclopedia of Religious Education,* 217.

23. Ibid., 269.

24. Ibid., 270.

25. Ibid., 217.

26. Charles Zastrow and Karen Kirst-Ashman, *Understanding Human Behavior and Social Environment* (Chicago: Nelson-Hall, 1990), 520.101.

27. Banks, *Teaching Strategies,* 23.

28. Molefi Kete Asante, Eileen Newmark, and Cecil A. Blake, *Handbook of Intercultural Communication* (London: Sage, 1979), 158.

29. Westerhoff, "Fashioning Christians," 264–65.

30. Larry A. Samovar and Richard E. Porter, *Intercultural Communication: A Reader,* 6th ed. (Belmont, Calif.: Wadsworth, 1991), 6.77.

31. Banks, *Teaching Strategies,* 79.

32. Alister McGrath, *Christian Theology: An Introduction* (Oxford: Blackwell, 1994), 103.

33. Ibid.

34. Richard J. Mouw and Sander Griffioen, *Pluralisms and Horizons* (Grand Rapids: Eerdmans, 1993), 92.

35. Ibid., 176.

36. Banks, *Teaching Strategies,* 69.

37. Ibid.

38. Ibid., 71.

39. Robert Merton, "Discrimination and the American Creed," in *Discrimination and National Welfare,* ed. Robert M. MacIver (New York: Harper, 1949), 47.

40. Becky W. Thompson and Sangeeta Tyagi, eds., *Beyond a Dream Deferred, Multicultural Education and the Politics of Excellence* (Minneapolis: Univ. of Minnesota Press, 1993), 54.

41. White, *Religious Education,* 138–39.

42. Ibid., 139.

43. Ferm, *Contemporary American Theologies,* 63.

44. Ibid.

45. White, *Religious Education,* 139.

46. Williams, *Ministries with Blacks,* 6.

47. Gajendra K. Verma and Christopher Bagley, eds., *Race Relations and Cultural Differences* (New York: St. Martin's, 1984), 57.

48. Sara Bullard, "Sorting Through the Multicultural Rhetoric," 5.

49. Banks, 1979, 3.

50. James A. Banks and Cherry A. McGee Banks, *Multicultural Education: Issues and Perspectives,* 2nd ed. (Boston: Allyn and Bacon, 1993), 3.

51. Ibid., xiii.

52. Christine E. Sleeter and Carl A. Grant, "An Analysis of Multicultural Education in the United States," *Harvard Educational Review,* 57:4 (November 1987): 422.

53. Quoted in Bullard, "Sorting Through the Multicultural Rhetoric," 5.

54. Sohan Modgil, Gajendra K. Verma, Kanka Mallick, and Celia Modgil, eds., *Multicultural Education: The Interminable Debate* (London and Philadelphia: Falmer, 1986), 5.

55. Ibid.

56. Manuel Ramírez III and Alfredo Casteñeda, *Cultural Democracy, Bicognitive Development, and Education* (New York: Academic, 1974), 6.

57. Ibid.

58. C. Carter, *Non-native and Nonstandard Dialect Students: Classroom Practices in Teaching English, 1982–83* (Urbana, Ill.: National Council of Teachers of English, 1981), xi.

Chapter 5: Multiculturalism in the Church Setting

1. Arthur M. Schlesinger, Jr., *The Disuniting of America: Reflections on a Multicultural Society* (New York: W.W. Norton, 1992), 64.

2. D'Souza, *Illiberal Education,* 244–45.

3. Tony Mecia, "External Review Deconstructs Duke's English Department," *Campus* (Spring 1994): 7, 10.

4. Ibid., 7.

5. D'Souza, *Illiberal Education,* 240.

6. Schlesinger, *The Disuniting of America,* 10.

7. John F. Wilson, "Liberal Education in a Multicultural Democracy: the Roles of Texts, Minds, and Hearts," in *Academic Literacies in Multicultural Higher Education,* ed. Thomas Hilgers, Marie Winch, and Virgie Chattergy (Mañoa, Hawaii: Univ. of Hawaii at Mañoa/Center for Studies of Multicultural Higher Education, 1992), 24.

8. D.A. Carson, "Christian Witness in an Age of Pluralism," in *God and Culture,* ed. D.A. Carson and John D. Woodbridge (Grand Rapids: Eerdmans, 1993), 32–33.

9. Ibid., 33.

10. William J. Larkin, Jr., *Culture and Biblical Hermeneutics* (Grand Rapids: Baker, 1988), 192.

11. Ibid., 200.

12. David Augsburger, *Pastoral Counseling Across Cultures* (Philadelphia: Westminster, 1986), 19.

13. S.D. Gaede, *When Tolerance Is No Virtue* (Downers Grove, Ill.: InterVarsity, 1994), 64.

14. Ibid., 67–69.

15. James W. Fowler, *Weaving the New Creation: Stages of Faith and the Public Church* (San Francisco: Harper, 1991), 151.

16. Grinberg and Grinberg, quoted in Marcelo M. Suarez-Orozco and Carola E. Suarez-Orozco, "Renegotiating Cultural Diversity in American Schools," in *Hispanic Cultural Psychology: Implications for Education Theory and Research,* ed. Patricia Phelan and Ann Locke Davidson (New York: Teachers College Press, 1993), 116.

17. Morris A. Inch, *Doing Theology across Cultures* (Grand Rapids: Baker, 1982), 29.

18. Ibid., 96.

19. Thom Hopler, *A World of Difference* (Downers Grove, Ill.: InterVarsity, 1981), 86.

20. Richard Pratte, *Pluralism in Education: Conflict, Clarity, and Commitment* (Springfield, Ill.: Charles C. Thomas, 1979), 12.

21. Ibid.

22. Quoted in Pratte, *Pluralism in Education,* 13.

23. Quoted in Sohan Modgil et al., *Multicultural Education: The Interminable Debate* (London/Philadelphia: Falmer, 1986), 7.

24. Ibid.

25. Fowler, *Weaving the New Creation,* 156.

26. James Garbarino, *Children and Families in the Social Environment,* 2nd ed. (New York: Aldine De Gruyter, 1992), 180.

27. Reuben H. Brooks, "Cross-Cultural Perspectives in Christian Education," in *Foundations of Ministry: An Introduction to Christian Education for a New Generation,* ed. Michael J. Anthony (Wheaton, Ill.: Victor/BridgePoint, 1992), 113.

28. Brooks, "Cross-Cultural Perspectives," 107–8.

29. Rebecca Peña Hines, Lillian Phenice, Verna Hildebrand, and Mary McPhail Gray, "Helping Families Understand Their Diversity," National Association for the Education of Young Children 1992 Annual Conference, New Orleans, 11–14 November 1992.

30. González, *Out of Every Tribe,* 102.

31. Fowler, *Weaving the New Creation,* 156.

32. Stanley Hauerwas, "On Witnessing Our Story," in *Schooling Christians: "Holy Experiments" in American Education,* ed. Stanley Hauerwas and John H. Westerhoff (Grand Rapids: Eerdmans, 1992), 230.

33. Max DuPree quoted in Bill J. Mowry, "A Contextualized/Transactional Model for Leadership Development," *Christian Education Journal* 13:1 (Autumn 1992), 62.

34. Robert C. Serow, *Schooling for Social Diversity* (New York: Teachers College Press, 1983), 96.

35. Fowler, *Weaving the New Creation,* 147. For more on the concept of civility, see the helpful work by Richard J. Mouw, *Uncommon Decency: Christian Civility in an Uncivil World* (Downers Grove, Ill.: InterVarsity, 1992).

36. G. Contreras, "Irrelevance and Bias in Multicultural Curricula" in *Early Childhood Bilingual Education, A Hispanic Perspective,* ed. Theresa H. Escobedo (New York: Teachers College Press, 1983), 109.

37. Ibid.

38. Darlene Powell Hopson and Derek S. Hopson, *Raising the Rainbow Generation* (N.Y.: Simon and Schuster, 1993), 12.

39. Fenn in Lyon, *Sociology and the Human Image,* 12.

40. James A. Banks, "Multicultural Education: Nature, Challenges, and Opportunities," in *Multicultural Education for the 21st Century,* ed. Carlos Diaz (Washington, D.C.: National Education Association, 1992), 33.

41. Ibid., 43.

Chapter 6: Parameters of Diversity

1. Charles Wagley and Marvin Harris, *Minorities in the New World: Six Case Studies* (N.Y.: Columbia Univ. Press, 1958), 4–11.

2. Theresa H. Escobedo and Johanna H. Huggans, "Field De-

pendence-Independence: A Theoretical Framework for Mexican American Cultural Variables?" in *Early Childhood Bilingual Education, A Hispanic Perspective,* ed. Theresa H. Escobedo (New York: Teachers College Press, 1983), 119.

3. F.R. Kluckhohn and F.L. Strodtbeck, *Variations in Value Orientations* (Evanston, Ill.: Row, Peterson, 1961).

4. Celia Jaes Falicov, "Mexican Families," in *Ethnicity and Family Therapy,* ed. Monica McGoldrick, John K. Pearce, and Joseph Giordano (New York: Guilford, 1982), 153.

5. John W. Santrock, *Life-Span Development* (Dubuque, Iowa: Brown and Benchmark, 1995), 14.

6. Susan S. Stodolsky and Gerald Lesser, "Learning Patterns in the Disadvantaged," in *Challenging the Myths: The Schools, the Blacks, and the Poor,* Harvard Educational Review Reprint Series, no. 5 (Cambridge: Harvard Education Review, 1975), 43.

7. Howard Gardner, *Frames of Mind* (New York: Harper Collins, 1983).

8. Karen Swisher, "Learning Styles: Implications for Teachers," in *Multicultural Education for the 21st Century,* ed. Carlos Diaz (Washington, D.C.: National Education Association, 1992), 73.

9. Karen Swisher and Donna Deyhle, "The Styles of Learning Are Different, but the Teaching Is Just the Same: Suggestions for Teachers of American Indian Youth," *Journal of American Indian Education, Special Issue* (August 1989), 1.

10. Asa G. Hilliard, "Teachers and Cultural Styles in a Pluralistic Society," *NEA Today* 7 (June 1989): 67.

11. Manuel Ramírez III and Alfredo Castañeda, *Cultural Democracy, Bicognitive Development, and Education* (New York: Academic, 1974), 70.

12. Rosalie Cohen, "Conceptual Styles, Culture Conflict, and Nonverbal Tests of Intelligence," *American Anthropologist* 71 (1969), 828–56.

13. Janice E. Hale-Benson, *Black Children, Their Roots, Culture, and Learning Styles* (Baltimore: Johns Hopkins Univ. Press, 1982), 30–31.

14. Herman A. Witkin, *Psychological Differentiation* (New York: Wiley, 1962).

15. Swisher, "Learning Styles," 75.

16. Antoine M. Garibaldi, "Preparing Teachers for Culturally Diverse Classrooms," in *Diversity in Teacher Education,* ed. Mary E. Dilworth (San Francisco: Jossey-Bass, 1992), 26.

17. Stephan Thernstrom, Ann Orlow, and Oscar Handlin, eds., *Harvard Encyclopedia of American Ethnic Groups* (Cambridge: Harvard Univ. Press, 1980).

Chapter 7: Examining Hispanic-American Culture

1. Linda Chavez, "Out of the Barrio," in *Taking Sides: Clashing Views on Controversial Issues in Race and Ethnicity,* ed. Richard C. Monk (Guilford, Conn.: Dushkin, 1994), 224.

2. Manuel Ortiz, *The Hispanic Challenge: Opportunities Confronting the Church* (Downers Grove, Ill.: InterVarsity, 1993), 25.

3. Baruth and Manning, *Multicultural Education,* 115.

4. Rafael Valdivieso, "Demographic Trends of the Mexican-American Population: Implications for Schools" (ERIC Digest, September 1990): 1.

5. Ibid., 2.

6. Richard R. Valencia, ed., *Chicano School Failure and Success* (New York: Falmer, 1991), 16.

7. Thernstrom, Orlow, and Handlin, *Harvard Encyclopedia,* 282–83.

8. *Population Profile of the United States,* Bureau of the Census, Current Population Reports, Special Studies Series p–23, no. 159 (Washington, D.C.: U.S. Government Printing Office, 1989), 38.

9. Banks, *Teaching Strategies,* 311.

10. Thernstrom, Orlow, and Handlin, *Harvard Encyclopedia,* 697.

11. Kitano, *Race Relations,* 159.

12. Arthur Tenorio, "The Mexican Americans," in *In Praise of Diversity: A Resource Book for Multicultural Education,* ed. M.J. Gold, C.A. Carl, and H.N. Rivlin (Washington, D.C.: Teacher Corps/Association of Teacher Educators, 1977), 184.

13. Elia Jaes Falicov, "Mexican Families," in *Ethnicity and Family Therapy,* ed. Monica McGoldrick, John K. Pearce, and Joseph Giordano (New York: Guilford, 1982), 136.

14. Banks, *Teaching Strategies,* 323.

15. Ibid., 327.

16. Joseph P. Fitzpatrick, " 'Returning' to the United States," in *Race and Ethnic Relations 91/92,* ed. John A. Kromkowski (Guilford, Conn.: Dushkin, 1991), 75.

17. Edward W. Christensen, "Counseling Puerto Ricans: Some Cultural Considerations," in *Understanding and Counseling Ethnic Minorities,* ed. George Henderson (Springfield, Ill.: Charles C. Thomas, 1979), 270.

18. Kenneth R. Johnson, *Teaching the Culturally Disadvantaged* (Palto Alto, Calif.: Science Research Associates, 1970), 78.

19. Thernstrom, Orlow, and Handlin, *Harvard Encyclopedia,* 864.

20. Ortiz, *Hispanic Challenge,* 34.

21. Banks, *Teaching Strategies,* 348.

22. Kitano, *Race Relations,* 182

23. Baruth and Manning, *Multicultural Education,* 122.

24. Baruth and Manning, *Multicultural Education,* 122.

25. Thernstrom, Orlow, and Handlin, *Harvard Encyclopedia,* 866–67.

26. Joseph Fitzpatrick and Lourdes Travieso, "The Puerto Ricans," in *In Praise of Diversity: A Resource Book for Multicultural Education,* ed. M.J. Gold, C.A. Carl, and H.N. Rivlin (Washington, D.C.: Teacher Corps/Association of Teacher Educators, 1977), 202–3.

27. Ortiz, *Hispanic Challenge,* 36–37.

28. Kitano, *Race Relations,* 191.

29. Guillermo Bernal, "Cuban Families," in *Ethnicity and Family Therapy,* ed. Monica McGoldrick, John K. Pearce, and Joseph Giordano (New York: Guilford, 1982), 189.

30. Thernstrom, Orlow, and Handlin, *Harvard Encyclopedia,* 257.

31. Bernal, "Cuban Families," 189.

32. Kitano, *Race Relations,* 98.

33. Fitzpatrick, " 'Returning' to the United States," 76.

34. Banks, *Teaching Strategies,* 376.

35. Marcelo M. Suarez-Orozco and Carola E. Suarez-Orozco, "Hispanic Cultural Psychology: Implications for Education and Research," in *Renegotiating Cultural Diversity in American Schools,* ed. Patricia Phelan and Ann Locke Davidson (New York: Teachers College Press, 1993), 109.

36. Fitzpatrick, " 'Returning' to the United States," 76.

37. Bernal, "Cuban Families," 191.

38. Banks, *Teaching Strategies,* 386.

39. Bernal, "Cuban Families," 192.

40. Ibid., 191–93.

41. Falicov, "Mexican Families," 142–43.

42. Ibid., 138.

43. John Dacey and John Travers, *Human Development Across the Lifespan,* 2nd ed. (Dubuque, Iowa: Brown and Benchmark, 1994), 44.

44. Falicov, "Mexican Families," 140.

45. Monica McGoldrick, "Ethnicity and Family Therapy: An Overview," in *Ethnicity and Family Therapy,* ed. Monica McGoldrick, John K. Pearce, and Joseph Giordana (New York: Guilford, 1982), 10.

46. Ana Marie Schuhmann, "Learning to Teach Hispanic Students," in *Diversity in Teacher Education,* ed. Mary E. Dilworth (San Francisco: Jossey-Bass, 1992), 97–98.

47. Alba N. Ambert and Clare S. Figler, "Puerto Ricans: Historical and Cultural Perspectives," in *Puerto Rican Children on the Mainland: Interdisciplinary Perspectives,* ed. Alba N. Ambert and María Alverez (New York: Garland, 1992), 25.

48. Baruth and Manning, *Teaching Strategies,* 122.

49. Banks and Banks, *Multicultural Education,* 337.

50. Amy Stuart Wells, "Hispanic Education in America: Separate and Unequal," no. 59 (ERIC/CUE Digest, 1990): 1.

51. Ibid., 2.

52. Ibid., 3.

53. Fernandez and Guskin in Wells, *Hispanic Education in America,* 3.

54. Wells, *Hispanic Education in America,* 4.

55. Betty Gould, "Methods of Teaching Mexicans" (M.A. thesis, University of Southern California, 1932; reprint, R & R Research Associates, San Francisco, 1973).

56. Schuhmann, "Learning to Teach Hispanic Students," 94–95.

57. Baruth and Manning, *Multicultural Education of Children and Adolescents,* 137–38.

58. Lois V. Edinger, Paul L. Harris, and Dorothy V. Meyer, *Education in the 80's, Curricular Challenges* (Washington, D.C.: National Education Association, 1981), 119.

59. Smith and Caskey, *Promising School Practices,* 8–16.

60. Thomas Weyer, *Hispanic U.S.A. Breaking the Melting Pot* (New York: Harper and Row, 1988), 51–52.

61. Baruth and Manning, *Multicultural Education of Children and Adolescents,* 261–62.

62. Ibid., 262.

63. Henry Sioux Jackson and William J. Hernandez-M. *Educating the Mexican-American* (Valley Forge, Pa.: Judson, 1970), 36.

64. Manuel Ramírez III and Alfredo Castañeda, *Cultural Democracy, Bicognitive Development and Education* (New York: Academic, 1974), 64.

65. Nieto, *Affirming Diversity,* 112.

66. Manuel Ramírez, "Cognitive Styles and Cultures Democracy in Action," in Wurzel, *Toward Multiculturalism,* 201–2.

67. Edinger, Harris, and Meyer, *Education in the 80's,* 117.

68. Falicov, "Mexican Families," 140.

69. C.H. Mindel, "Extended Families among Urban Mexican Americans, Anglos and Blacks," *Hispanic Journal of Behavioral Sciences,* 2 (1980): 21–34.

70. C.J. Falicov and B.M. Karrer, "Cultural Variations in the Family Life Cycle: The Mexican-American Family," in *The Family Life Cycle: A Framework for Family Therapy,* ed. E.A. Carter and M. McGoldrick (New York: Gardner, 1980).

71. Santrock, *Life-Span Development,* 489.

72. Marina A. Herrera, "Hispanic Americans," in *Harper's Encyclopedia of Religious Education,* ed. Iris V. Cully and Kendig Brubaker Cully (New York: Harper and Row, 1990), 293.

73. Ortiz, *Hispanic Challenge,* 129.

74. Grant, "Theological Framework," 61.

75. Paulo Freire, *Pedagogy of the Oppressed* (New York: Continuum, 1990), 81–84.

76. Washington Padilla, "Non-Formal Theological Education," in *New Alternatives in Theological Education,* ed. C. René Padilla (Oxford, U.K.: Oxford/Regnum, 1988), 128.

77. Ortiz, *Hispanic Challenge,* 166.

78. Gloria S. Boutte, Sally LaPoint, and Barbara Davis, "Racial Issues in Education: Real or Imagined?" *Young Children* 49 (November 1993): 20.

79. Louise Derman-Sparks and the A.B.C. Task Force, *Anti-Bias Curriculum, Tools for Empowering Young Children* (Washington, D.C.: National Association for the Education of Young Children, 1989), 57–58.

80. Jack O. Balswick and Judith K. Balswick, *The Family: A Christian Perspective on the Contemporary Home* (Grand Rapids: Baker, 1991), 28.

81. Mary Ellen Goodman, *Race Awareness in Young Children* (New York: Collier, 1964).

82. Derman-Sparks, *Anti-Bias Curriculum,* 5.

Chapter 8: Examining Native-American Culture

1. David Murray, *Forked Tongues: Speech, Writing & Representation in North American Indian Texts* (Bloomington, Ind.: Indiana Univ. Press, 1991), 58.

2. J.A. Axelson, *Counseling and Development in a Multicultural Society* (Monterey, Calif.: Brooks/Cole, 1985), 27.

3. Edward H. Spicer, "American Indians," in *Harvard Encyclopedia of American Ethnic Groups* (Cambridge: Harvard Univ. Press, 1980), 62.

4. Angie Debo, *A History of the Indians of the United States* (Norman, Okla.: Univ. of Oklahoma Press, 1970), 15.

5. Spicer, "American Indians," 58.

6. The variation in number reported is probably due to the minimum population of a tribe required for a source to recognize it. Some tribes have a very small membership list. The United States Bureau of Indian Affairs reported 500 according to Joseph E. Trimble, "Value Differentials and Their Importance in Counseling American Indians," in *Counseling Across Cultures,* ed. Paul P. Pedersen et al. (Honolulu: Univ. of Hawaii Press, 1976), 206.

7. Debo, *A History of the Indians,* 143–45.

8. Ibid.

9. Parillo, *Strangers to These Shores,* 255.

10. Kenneth R. Johnson, *Teaching the Culturally Disadvantaged* (Palo Alto, Calif.: Science Research Associates, 1970), 87.

11. Ibid.

12. Ibid., 88.

13. Ibid., 89.

14. Suzanne Dame Porter, "From the Cherokees to Columbus: Examining Bias; Creating Anti-Bias," 1992 Annual Conference: National Association for the Education of Young Children, New Orleans, 11-14 November 1992.

15. Gerald Murphy, "About the Iroquois Constitution," *The Cleveland Free-Net,* Distributed by the Cybercasting Services Division of the National Public Telecomputing Network, n.d.

16. Maria Estela Allende Brisk, "Language Policies in American Education," *Journal of Education* 163 (Winter 1981): 3.

17. Curtis Emanuel Jackson, "Identification of Unique Features in Education at American Indian Schools" (Ph.D. diss., University of Utah, 1965), 38.

18. Francis Paul Prucha, *The Indians in American Society* (Los Angeles: Univ. of California Press, 1985), 6–10.

19. Roy Harvey Pearce, *Savagism and Civilization* (Baltimore: Johns Hopkins Univ. Press, 1965), 73.

20. John H. Holst, "Educational Developments and Trends," in *The Indian in American Life,* ed. G.E.F. Linquist (New York: Friendship, 1944), 96.

21. Jackson, "Identification of Unique Features," 53.

22. Dwight W. Hoover, *The Red and the Black* (Chicago: Rand McNally, 1976), 272–73.

23. Jon Reyhner and Jeanne Eder, *A History of Indian Education* (Billings, Mont.: Eastern Montana College, 1989), 122.

24. Axelson, *Counseling and Development,* 39.

25. Carolyn Attneave, "American Indians and Alaska Native Families: Emigrants in Their Own Homeland," in *Ethnicity and Family Therapy,* ed. Monica McGoldrick, John K. Pearce, and Joseph Giordano (New York: Guilford, 1982), 63.

26. Axelson, *Counseling and Development,* 40.

27. E.T. Seton, *The Gospel of the Red Man* (New York: Doubleday, 1936), 19.

28. Axelson, *Counseling and Development,* 40.

29. Vincent N. Parrillo, *Strangers to These Shores: Race and Ethnic Relations in the United States* (Boston: Houghton Mifflin, 1980), 236.

30. Attneave, "American Indians and Alaska Native Families," 62–65.

31. Ibid., 63.

32. Trimble, "Value Differentials and Their Importance," 208.

33. Axelson, *Counseling and Development,* 42.

34. R.G. Lewis and M.K. Ho, "Social Work with Native Americans," in *Counseling American Minorities*, 3rd ed., ed. Donald R. Atkinson, George Morten, and Derald Wing Sue (Dubuque, Iowa: W.C. Brown, 1983), 67.

35. Axelson, *Counseling and Development,* 39.

36. Ibid.

37. Ibid., 40–41.

38. John G. Red Horse, et al., "Family Behavior of Urban American Indians," in *Understanding and Counseling Ethnic Ministries,* ed. George Henderson (Springfield, Ill.: Charles C. Thomas, 1979), 310.

39. Ibid., 311–12.

40. Ibid., 313.

41. Ibid., 312–13.

42. Axelson, *Counseling and Development,* 40.

43. Harry L. Saslow and Mary J. Harrover, "Research on Psychological Adjustment of Indian Youth," in *Understanding and Counseling Ethnic Minorities,* ed. George Henderson (Springfield, Ill.: Charles C. Thomas, 1979), 302–4.

44. Ibid.

45. LeRoy G. Baruth and M. Lee Manning, *Multicultural Education* (Needham Heights, Mass.: Allyn & Bacon, 1992), 43.

46. A. Brown, "Cherokee Culture and School Achievement," *American Indian Culture and Research Journal* 4 (1980): 55–74.

47. Lewis and Ho, "Social Work with Native-Americans," 65–72.

48. Swisher and Deyhle, "The Styles of Learning Are Different, but the Teaching Is Just the Same," 1–14.

49. K. Swisher and B. Page, "Determining Jicarilla Apache Learning Styles: A Collaborative Approach" (Paper delivered at the Annual Meeting of the American Educational Research Association, Boston, Mass., 18 April 1990).

50. D. Sanders, "Cultural Conflicts: An Important Factor in the Academic Failure of American Indian Students," *Journal of Multicultural Counseling and Development* 5 (1987): 81–90.

51. Karen Swisher and Donna Deyhle, "Adapting Instruction to Culture," in *Teaching American Indian Students,* ed. Jon Reyhner (Norman, Okla.: Univ. of Oklahoma Press, 1992), 83–85.

52. O. Werner and K. Begishe, "Styles of Learning: The Evidence for Navajo." Paper presented at Styles of Learning in American Indian Children Conference. (Stanford, Calif.: Stanford Univ. Press, 1968), 1–2.

53. Baruth and Manning, *Multicultural Education,* 50.

54. Swisher and Deyhle, "Adapting Instruction to Culture," 87–88.

55. Attneave, "American Indians and Alaska Native Families," 81–82.

56. Red Horse et al., "Family Behavior in American Indians," 314.

57. Ibid., 311–15.

58. Taylor McConnell, "Native Americans," in *Harper's Encyclopedia of Religious Education,* ed. Iris V. Cully and Kendig Brubaker Cully (New York: Harper & Row, 1990), 447–48.

59. Baruth and Manning, *Multicultural Education,* 467.

60. Parrillo, *Strangers to These Shores,* 250.

61. Joyce Moss and George Wilson, *Peoples of the World, North Americans* (Detroit: Gale Research, 1991), 148.

62. Baruth and Manning, *Multicultural Education,* 44.

Chapter 9: Examining Asian-American Culture

1. Sam Sue, "Growing up in Mississippi," in *Asian Americans,* ed. Joann Faung Jean Lee (New York: New, 1992), 3.

2. Sucheng Chan, *Asian Americans: An Interpretive History* (Boston: Twayne, 1991), 3.

3. Thompson and Tyagi, *Beyond a Dream Deferred,* 7.

4. Baruth and Manning, *Multicultural Education,* 88–89.

5. Thernstrom, Orlow, and Handlin, *Harvard Encyclopedia,* 150.

6. Donald Ng, ed., *Asian Pacific Youth Ministry* (Valley Forge, Pa.: Judson, 1988), 7.

7. "Cultural Crosscurrents," *Dallas Morning News,* 16 February 1994, sec. 1C, 16C.

8. U.S. Bureau of the Census, *Statistical Abstract of the United States,* 109th ed. (Washington, D.C.: U.S. Government Printing Office, 1989), 10.

9. Roger Daniels, *Coming to America* (New York: HarperCollins, 1990), 352.

10. Banks, *Teaching Strategies,* 352.

11. Thea Lee, "Trapped on a Pedestal," in *Race and Ethnic Relations 91–92,* ed. John A. Kromkowski (Guilford, Conn.: Dushkin, 1991), 95–96.

12. Chan, *Asian Americans,* 3–4.

13. Janine Bempechat and Miya C. Omori, "Meeting the Educational Needs of Southeast Asian Children," ERIC/CUE Digest, no. 68.

14. Baruth and Manning, *Multicultural Education,* 92.

15. Chan, *Asian Americans,* 71.

16. Ibid., 74–75.

17. Ibid., 73.

18. Wesley Woo, "Protestant Work among the Chinese in the San Francisco Bay Areas, 1880–1920" (Ph.D. diss., Graduate Theological Seminary, Berkeley, 1983).

19. C. Kim, "Asian Americans," in *Harper's Encyclopedia of Religious Education,* ed. Iris V. Cully and Kendig Brubaker Cully (New York: Harper and Row, 1990), 43.

20. Ibid.

21. Baruth and Manning, *Multicultural Education,* 98.

22. Betty Chang, "Asian-American Patient Care," in *Transcultural Health Care,* ed. George Henderson and Martha Primeaux (Menlo Park, Calif.: Addison-Wesley, 1981), 260.

23. "Cultural Crosscurrents," *Dallas Morning News,* 16C.

24. Baruth and Manning, *Multicultural Education,* 99.

25. Karen Chia-Yu Liu, "Every Child Is Special," *First Teacher* 10 (October 1990).

26. Baruth and Manning, *Multicultural Education,* 98.

27. Karen Chia-Yu Liu and Margaret B. Roth, "Bridges to Crosscultural Understanding — Communicate Effectively with Asian Families and Children." Workshop presented at the annual meeting of the National Association for the Education of Young Children, New Orleans, 13 November 1992.

28. Duong-Thank Binh, *A Handbook for Teachers of Vietnamese Students* (Arlington, Va.: Center for Applied Linguistics, 1975), 8–10.

29. Ann Hagen Griffiths, *The Korean Americans* (New York: Facts on File, 1992), 53.

30. "Cultural Crosscurrents," *Dallas Morning News,* 1C, 16C.

31. Yongsook Lee, "Koreans in Japan and the United States," in *Minority Status and Schooling,* ed. Margaret A. Gibson and John U. Ogbu (New York: Garland, 1991), 131.

32. William Petersen, "Success Story, Japanese American Style," *New York Times Magazine,* 6 January 1966, 21ff.

33. Roger Daniels, *Asian America: Chinese and Japanese in the United States since 1950* (Seattle: Univ. of Washington Press, 1988), 317–22.

34. Duane Elmer, *Cross-Cultural Conflict* (Downers Grove, Ill.: InterVarsity, 1993), 52.

35. Chang, "Asian-American Patient Care," 266.

36. Robert C. Leslie, *Counseling Across Cultures,* UMHE Monograph Series (New York: UMHE Communication Office, 1979), 12.

37. Ibid., 11.

38. S. Sue and D.W. Sue, "Chinese-American Personality and Mental Health," in *Asian Americans: Psychological Perspectives,* ed. S. Sue and N.N. Wagner (Palo Alto, Calif.: Science & Behavior), 111–24.

39. Chang, "Asian-American Patient Care," 271.

Chapter 10: Selected Asian Groups

1. Kim, "Asian Americans," 43.

2. Harry H.L. Kitano and Noreen Matsushima, "Counseling Asian Americans," in *Counseling across Cultures,* ed. Paul B. Pedersen et al. (Honolulu: Univ. Press of Hawaii, 1981), 174.

3. Henry Shih-shan Tsai, *The Chinese Experience in America* (Bloomington, Ind.: Indiana Univ. Press, 1986), 2.

4. Joan May Cordova, "Historical and Cultural Conflict," in *Asian Pacific Youth Ministry,* ed. Donald Ng (Valley Forge, Pa.: Judson, 1988), 26.

5. Harry H.L. Kitano, *Race Relations* (Englewood Cliffs, N.J.: Prentice Hall, 1985), 219.

6. Daniels, *Asian America,* 40–41.

7. Tsai, *The Chinese Experience,* 15.

8. Ronald Takaki, *Different Mirror: A History of Multicultural America* (Boston: Little, Brown, 1993), 193–94.

9. Tsai, *The Chinese Experience,* xii.

10. John J. Macionis, *Sociology* (Englewood Cliffs, N.J.: Prentice Hall, 1989), 303.

11. Tsai, *The Chinese Experience,* 42.

12. Ibid., 44.

13. Kitano, *Race Relations,* 229.

14. Tsai, *The Chinese Experience,* 153–56.

15. Macionis, *Sociology,* 303.

16. Banks, *Teaching Strategies,* 413.

17. Roger Daniels, *Coming to America* (New York: HarperCollins, 1990), 354.

18. Ibid.

19. Ibid., 163.

20. Ellie McGrath, "Confucian Work Ethic," *Time,* 28 March 1983, 52.

21. Diana Fong, "America's 'Invisible' Chinese," *New York Times,* 1 May 1982.

22. Tsai, *The Chinese Experience,* 162–63.

23. Ibid., 157–58.

24. Leslie, *Counseling Across Cultures,* 13.

25. "Cultural Crosscurrents," *Dallas Morning News,* 16 February 1994, 16C.

26. Ibid.

27. Kitano, *Race Relations,* 224.

28. Ibid., 223.

29. Lee, *Asian Americans,* 55.

30. Parrillo, *Strangers to These Shores,* 285.

31. Ibid., 283.

32. Eugene V. Rostow, "Our Worst Wartime Mistake," *Harper's Magazine,* September 1945, 191.

33. Cordova, "Historical and Cultural Context," 28.

34. Parrillo, *Strangers to These Shores,* 285–88.

35. Harry H.L. Kitano, "Counseling and Psychotherapy with Japanese Americans," in *Cross-Cultural Counseling and Psychotherapy,* ed. Anthony J. Marsella and Paul B. Pedersen (New York: Pergamon, 1981), 231.

36. Steven P. Shon and Davis Y. Ja, "Asian Families," in *Ethnicity and Family Therapy,* ed. Monica McGoldrick, John K. Pearce, and Joseph Giordano (New York: Guilford, 1982), 227.

37. Kitano, "Counseling and Psychotherapy with Japanese Americans," 233.

38. Ibid., 235.

39. Farah A. Ibrahim, "A Course on Asian-American Women," *Women's Studies Quarterly* 20 (Spring/Summer 1992): 46–47.

40. Kitano, "Counseling and Psychotherapy with Japanese Americans," 229.

41. Parrillo, *Strangers to These Shores,* 292.

42. Banks, *Teaching Strategies,* 422.

43. Parrillo, *Strangers to These Shores,* 291–92.

44. Mei Nakano, *Japanese American Women: Three Generations 1890–1990* (Berkeley, Calif.: Mina, 1990), 226.

45. Kitano, *Race Relations,* 252.

46. Kitano, "Counseling and Psychotherapy," 238.

47. Parrillo, *Strangers to These Shores,* 291.

48. Donald B. Irwin and Janet A. Simons, *Lifespan Developmental Psychology: Instructor's Course Planner* (Madison, Iowa: Brown and Benchmark, 1994), 171.

49. Lois Peak, "Training Learning Skills and Attitudes in Japanese Early Educational Settings," in *Early Experience and the Development of Competence,* ed. William Fowler (San Francisco: Jossey-Bass, 1986), 114.

50. Ibid., 115.

51. Santrock, *Life-Span Development,* 304.

52. Harry H.L. Kitano, *Japanese Americans* (Englewood Cliffs, N.J.: Prentice Hall, 1976), 120–36.

53. Kitano, "Counseling and Psychotherapy with Japanese Americans," 237.

54. Ibid., 238.

55. Ibid.

56. Ann Hagen Griffiths, *The Korean Americans* (New York: Facts on File, 1992), 21.

57. Ibid., 23.

58. Ibid., 33.

59. Cordova, "Historical and Cultural Context," 28.

60. Thernstrom, Orlow, and Handlin, *Harvard Encyclopedia,* 602.

61. Kitano, *Race Relations,* 197.

62. Thernstrom, Orlow, and Handlin, *Harvard Encyclopedia,* 602.

63. Daniels, *Coming to America,* 365.

64. Sucheng Chan, *Asian Americans,* 73.

65. Thernstrom, Orlow, and Handlin, *Harvard Encyclopedia,* 605.

66. Ibid., 602.

67. Griffiths, *Korean Americans,* 28–31.

68. Daniels, *Coming to America,* 367.

69. Kitano, *Race Relations,* 201.

70. Ibid.

71. Griffiths, *Korean Americans,* 91.

72. Kitano, *Race Relations,* 195–96.

73. Janine Bempechat and Miya Omori, "Meeting the Educational Needs of Southeast Asian Children," ERIC/CUE Digest, no. 68, 2.

74. Daniels, *Coming to America,* 369.

75. Carol Ascher, "The Social and Psychological Adjustment of Southeast Asian Refugees," ERIC/CUE Digest, no. 21.

76. Ibid.

77. Ibid.

78. Carol Ascher, "Southeast Asian Adolescents: Identity and Adjustment," ERIC/CUE Digest, no. 51.

79. J.F. Nidorf, "Mental Health and Refugee Youths: A Model for Diagnostic Training," in *Southeast Asian Mental Health, Treatment, Prevention, Services, Training and Research,* ed. T. Owan and E. Choken (Washington, D.C.: Department of Health and Human Services, Office of Refugee Resettlement, 1985).

80. Ascher, "Southeast Asian Adolescents."

81. Ascher, "Social and Psychological Adjustment."

82. Dudley Barlow, "Restoring Faith" (Conversations in the Teacher's Lounge), *Education Digest* 57 (April 1992): 23.

83. Fiffer, *Imagining America,* 189.

84. Stacy Nelson, "Media Stereotype Asian-Americans as 'Model Minority'" (Delphi Computer Information Service), 13 April 1990, 11.

85. Philip C. Chinn and Maximino Plata, "Perspectives and Educational Implications of Southeast Asian Students" in *Exceptional Asian Children and Youth,* ed. Margie K. Kitano and Philip C. Chinn (Reston, Va.: The Council for Exceptional Children, 1986), 21.

86. Fiffer, *Imagining America,* 128–29.

87. Susan Auerbach, *Vietnamese Americans* (Vero Beach, Fla.: Rourke, 1991), 2–3.

88. Chinn and Plata, "Perspectives," 12.

89. Auerbach, *Vietnamese*, 4.

90. Daniels, *Coming to America*, 353.

91. Ibid.

92. Bempechat and Omori, "Meeting the Educational Needs."

93. Ascher, "Social and Psychological Adjustment."

94. Bempechat and Omori, "Meeting the Educational Needs."

95. Auerbach, *Vietnamese*, 22.

96. Duong-Thanh Binh, *A Handbook for Teachers of Vietnamese Students* (Arlington, Va.: Center for Applied Linguistics, 1975), 17–18.

97. Auerbach, *Vietnamese*, 23.

98. Paul James Rutledge, *The Vietnamese Experience in America* (Bloomington, Ind.: Indiana Univ. Press, 1992), 47.

99. Auerbach, *Vietnamese*, 7.

100. Ibid., 19.

101. "Cultural Crosscurrents," *Dallas Morning News*, 16C.

102. Sian-Yang Tan, "Counseling Asians," in *Healing for the City*, ed. Craig W. Ellison and Edward S. Maynard (Grand Rapids: Zondervan, 1992), 114–15.

103. Everett Kleinjans, "Communicating with Asia," in *Intercultural Communication: A Reader*, ed. Larry A. Samovar and Richard E. Porter (Belmont, Calif.: Wadsworth, 1972), 263.

104. Ibid.

105. Arthur Schlesinger, Jr., "The Missionary Enterprise and Imperialism," in *The Missionary Enterprise in China and America*, ed. John K. Fairbank (Cambridge, Mass.: Harvard Univ. Press, 1974), 336, 339.

106. Griffith, *Korean Americans*, 80.

107. Ibid., 90.

108. Wesley S. Woo, "Theological Dimensions," in *Asian Pacific Youth Ministry*, ed. Donald Ng (Valley Forge, Pa.: Judson, 1988), 15.

109. R.S. Sugirtharajah, ed., *Voices from the Margin: Interpreting the Bible in the Third World* (Maryknoll, N.Y.: Orbis, 1991), 38.

110. Kim, "Asian Americans," 43.

111. Ibid.

112. Ibid., 43–44.

113. Baruth and Manning, *Multicultural Education*, 105.

114. Victor Merian, "Visiting the Homeland," in *Asian Americans*, ed. Joann Faung and Jean Lee (New York: New, 1992), 45–46.

115. Chia-Yu Liu and Roth, "Bridges to Cross-Cultural Understanding."

116. Baruth and Manning, *Multicultural Education*, 103.

117. Howard F. Van Zandt, "How to Negotiate in Japan," in *Intercultural Communication: A Reader*, ed. Larry A. Samovar and

Richard E. Porter (Belmont, Calif.: Wadsworth, 1972), 267–72.

118. Derald Wing Sue and Stanley Sue, "Counseling Chinese Americans," *Personnel and Guidance Journal* 50 (1972): 637–45.

119. Betty Chang, "Asian-American Patient Care," 275.

120. Griffiths, *Korean Americans,* 88.

121. Amy Mathew, quoted in "The Beggar in My Prayer," *Lantern,* September 1992, 19.

122. Rodger Y. Nishioka, "Developmental Characteristics of Youth," in *Asian Pacific American Youth Ministry,* ed. Donald Ng (Valley Forge, Pa.: Judson, 1988), 46–47.

123. Chang, "Asian-American Care," 261.

124. "Cultural Crosscurrents, *Dallas Morning News,* 16C.

125. Thompson K. Mathew, "Ministering to the ABK's," *Impact* (Spring 1994): 1–2.

126. Tim Tseng, "Family Expectations" in *Asian Pacific American Youth Ministry,* ed. Donald Ng (Valley Forge, Pa.: Judson, 1988), 97–103.

127. Sumner Jones as quoted in Nelson, "Media Stereotype Asian-Americans," 11.

Chapter 11: Examining African-American Culture

1. Leslie, *Counseling Across Cultures,* 1.

2. James A. Banks, "Racial Prejudice and the Black Self-Concept," in *Black Self-Concept: Implications for Education and Social Science,* ed. James A. and Jean D. Crambs (New York: McGraw-Hill, 1972), 6.

3. James H. Cone, "Demystifying Martin and Malcolm," *Theology Today* 51, no. 1 (April 1994): 28.

4. Lawrence W. Levine, *Black Culture and Black Consciousness* (New York: Oxford Univ. Press, 1977), 4.

5. Edward Franklin Frazier, *The Negro Church in America* (New York: Shocken, 1963), 30.

6. C. Eric Lincoln and Lawrence H. Mamiya, *The Black Church in the African American Experience* (Durham, N.C.: Duke Univ. Press, 1990), 125.

7. Gerald David Jaynes and Robin M. Williams, Jr., eds., *A Common Destiny: Blacks and American Society* (Washington, D.C.: National Academy, 1989), 174.

8. Ibid.

9. Ibid.

10. Joe Maxwell, "Healing the Rift between the Races," *Charisma,* April 1993, 18–24.

11. Ibid., 21–22.

12. Grant S. Shockley, "Historical Perspectives," in *Working with Black Youth,* ed. Charles R. Foster and Grant S. Shockley (Nashville: Abingdon, 1989), 11.

13. C.M. Robeck, Jr., "Azusa Street Revival," in *Dictionary of Pentecostal and Charismatic Movements*, ed. Stanley M. Burgess and Gary B. McGee (Grand Rapids: Zondervan/Regency, 1988), 33.

14. Ibid., 35.

15. Jaynes and Williams, *A Common Destiny,* 193.

16. Lincoln and Mamiya, *Black Church,* 390.

17. Ibid., 391.

18. W. Allen, "Black Family Research in the United States: A Review, Assessment and Extension," *Journal of Comparative Family Studies* 9 (Summer 1978): 167–89.

19. Daniel Moynihan, *The Negro Family: The Case for National Action,* Office of Policy Planning and Research, United States Department of Labor (Washington, D.C.: U.S. Government Printing Office, 1965).

20. Robert Staples and Alfredo Mirance, "Racial and Cultural Variations among American Families: A Decennial Review of the Literature on Minority Families," in *Family in Transition,* ed. Arlene S. Skolnick and Jerome H. Skolnick (Boston: Little Brown, 1983), 498–99.

21. Craig W. Ellison and Edward S. Maynard, *Healing for the City: Counseling the Urban Setting* (Grand Rapids: Zondervan, 1992), 128–29.

22. James R. King, "African Survivals in the Black American Family: Key Factors in Stability," in *Understanding and Counseling Ethnic Minorities,* ed. George Henderson (Springfield, Ill.: Charles C. Thomas, 1979), 46.

23. Janice Hale-Benson, *Black Children: Their Roots, Culture, and Learning Styles* (Baltimore: Johns Hopkins, 1986), 49.

24. Andrew Billingsley, *Black Families in White America* (New York: Touchstone, 1988), 39.

25. H. Gutman, *The Black Family in Slavery and Freedom 1750–1925* (New York: Vintage, 1976).

26. Carolyn B. Thompson-Wallace, "Black Inner-City Teenagers" in *The Black Family,* ed. Lee N. June (Grand Rapids: Zondervan, 1991), 77.

27. Howard and Wanda Jones, *Heritage and Hope* (Wheaton, Ill.: Victor, 1992), 26.

28. King, "African Survivals in the Black American Family," 48.

29. Darlene B. Hannah, "The Black Extended Family: An Appraisal of Its Past, Present, and Future Statuses," in *The Black Family,* ed. Lee N. June (Grand Rapids: Zondervan, 1991), 36–37.

30. Billingsley, *Black Families,* 25.

31. James P. Comer and Alvin E. Poussaint, *Raising Black Children* (New York: Plume, 1992).

32. H.P. McAdoo, ed., *Black Families* (Newbury Park, Calif.: Sage, 1988).

33. V. Bengston, C. Rosenthal, and L. Burton, "Families and Aging: Diversity and Heterogeneity," in *Handbook of Aging and the Social Sciences,* ed. R.H. Binstock and L.K. George (San Diego: Academic, 1990).

34. Santrock, *Life-Span Development,* 567.

35. M.N. Wilson, "The Black Extended Family: An Analytical Consideration," *Developmental Psychology* 22 (1986): 246–56.

36. M.W. Edelman, *Families in Peril* (Cambridge, Mass.: Harvard Univ. Press, 1987).

37. Grace J. Craig, *Human Development,* 6th ed. (Englewood Cliffs, N.J.: Prentice Hall, 1992), 482.

38. Ibid.

39. Santrock, *Life-Span,* 392.

40. Ibid.

41. Ibid., 235.

42. Joan A. Ganns, "Sexual Abuse: Its Impact on the Child and the Family," in *The Black Family,* ed. Lee N. June (Grand Rapids: Zondervan, 1991), 176.

43. Santrock, *Life-Span,* 240.

44. King, "African Survivals in the Black American Family," 52.

45. Santrock, *Life-Span,* 560.

46. C.M. Perry and C.L. Johnson, "Families and Support Networks among African American Oldest-Old," *International Journal of Aging and Human Development* 38 (1994): 41–50.

47. Paulette Moore Hines and Nancy Boyd-Franklin, "Black Families," in *Ethnicity and Family Therapy,* ed. Monica McGoldrick, John K. Pearce, and Joseph Giordana (New York: Guilford, 1982), 88.

48. Santrock, *Life-Span,* 333.

49. L.W. Hoffman and J.D. Manis, "The Value of Children in the United States: A New Approach to the Study of Fertility," *Journal of Marriage and the Family* 41 (1979): 589.

50. Hines and Boyd-Franklin, "Black Families," 88.

51. Hannah, "The Black Extended Family," 43.

52. Hines and Boyd-Franklin, "Black Families," 90.

53. Jones, *Heritage and Hope,* 24.

54. Hines and Boyd-Franklin, "Black Families," 89.

55. Mirra Komarovsky, *Dilemmas of Masculinity* (New York: W.W. Norton, 1976).

56. Santrock, *Life-Span,* 333.

57. Hale-Benson, *Black Children,* 42.

58. James A. Vasquez, "Teaching to the Distinctive Traits of Minority Students," *Clearing House* 63 (March 1990): 299–304, 300.

59. Swisher, "Learning Styles," 78.

60. Leslie, *Counseling Across Cultures,* 2.

61. Martin Luther King, Jr., *Why We Can't Wait* (New York: Mentor, 1963), 86.

62. Ibid.

63. Ibid.

64. Carol Ascher, "School: Programs for African American Males," ERIC/CUE Digest (1991), no. 72.

65. Joseph V. Crockett, *Teaching Scripture from an African-American Perspective* (Nashville: Discipleship Resources, 1990), xiii.

66. Ibid., 40.

67. Cain Hope Felder, *Troubling Biblical Waters: Race, Class, and Family* (Maryknoll, N.Y.: Orbis, 1989), 8.

68. Ibid.

69. Ravitch, "A Culture in Common," 11.

70. Richard Beswick, "Racism in America's Schools," ERIC Digest Series, no. EA49 (1990), 5.

71. William R. Myers, *Black and White: Styles of Youth Ministry* (New York: Pilgrim, 1991), 69.

72. Hale-Benson, *Black Children,* 59.

73. Ibid.

74. Ibid.

75. Gayraud S. Wilmore, *Black Religion and Black Radicalism* (Maryknoll, N.Y.: Orbis, 1984), 13.

76. George and Yvonne Abatso, *How to Equip the African American Family* (Chicago: Urban Ministries, 1991), 13.

77. Ibid., 19.

78. Ibid., 18–21.

79. Willard A. Williams, *Educational Ministries with Blacks* (n.p.: The Board of Discipleship of the United Methodist Church, 1974), 10.

80. Cecil Murray, "Needed: an At-risk Gospel," in "The Myth of Racial Progress," *Christianity Today,* 4 October 1993, 20.

81. Abatso, *How to Equip,* 200–205.

82. Santrock, *Life-Span,* 241.

83. James A. Banks and Jean D. Grambs, eds., *Black Self-Concept: Implications for Education and Social Science* (New York: McGraw-Hill, 1972), 8.

84. J. Deotis Roberts, *Roots of a Black Future: Family and Church* (Philadelphia: Westminster, 1980), 11.

85. "Passing on the Power," *Christianity Today,* 4 October 1993, 21.

86. Santrock, *Life-Span,* 306.

87. Janice Hale-Benson, "Psychosocial Experiences," in *Working with Black Youth: Opportunities for Christian Ministry,* ed. Charles R. Foster and Grant S. Shockley (Nashville: Abingdon, 1989), 34.

88. Ibid., 30–54.

89. Darlene Powell Hopson and Derek S. Hopson, *Different and Wonderful: Raising Black Children in a Race-Conscious Society* (New York: Simon & Schuster, 1990), 58–61.

Chapter 12: Our Multicultural Opportunity

1. Kenny Moore, "Sportsman of the Year: The Eternal Example," quoted in Kelly Brown Douglas, *The Black Christ* (Maryknoll, N.Y.: Orbis, 1994), 5.

2. Dan Wallace, "Who's Afraid of the Holy Spirit?" *Christianity Today,* 12 September 1994, 38.

3. Ibid.

4. "Reclaiming the Bible for the Church," Evangelical Lutheran Church in America News Release, 17 June 1994.

5. Glandion Carney, "I'm Pessimistic" in "The Myth of Racial Progress," *Christianity Today,* 4 October 1993, 20.

6. Quoted in Kadlecek, "The Coloring of the American Church," 4.

7. Inouye, "Mirror of God," 28.

8. John Perkins, "Something Is Wrong at the Root" in "The Myth of Racial Progress," *Christianity Today,* 4 October 1993, 18.

9. Woo, "Theological Dimensions," 15.

10. S.D. Gaede, *When Tolerance Is No Virtue* (Downers Grove, Ill.: InterVarsity, 110–11.

11. Ibid., 111.

12. Reuben H. Brooks, "Cross-Cultural Perspectives in Christian Education," in *Foundations of Ministry,* ed. Michael Anthony (Wheaton, Ill.: Victor/BridgePoint, 1992), 108.

13. Ibid.

14. "Pentecostals Move to End Racial Split," *Chicago Tribune,* 20 October 1994, sec. 1.

15. Las Casas, *In Defense of the Indians,* 362.

16. Cynthia Pearl Maus, *Christ and the Fine Arts* (New York: Harper and Row, 1959), 59.

➤ SELECT INDEX

A

Acculturation **59, 74, 120, 184–86, 195, 221**
Additive multiculturalism **75**
Aeschliman, Gordon **17**
African-American Baseline Essays **48**
African-American family **220–21, 225, 229**
  cultural deviant approach **221**
  cultural equivalent approach **221**
Allport, Gordon **61**
Anabaptists **36**
Anti-Bias Curriculum **126**
Apes, William **130**
Ashe, Arthur **244**
Asian-American family **162, 171, 205–6, 212**
Assimilability **185**
Assimilation **59, 89, 114, 134, 143, 179, 187, 189, 210, 218, 241**
Augsburger, David **71**
Augustine **24, 32, 38**
Auster, Lawrence **56**
Azusa Street Revival **220**

B

Bakke, Ray **9**
Balswick, Jack and Judith **127**
Banks, James **64, 217, 238**
Bernstein, Helen **10**

Biculturalization **59**
Bilingual education **107, 113, 115**
Black Bible Chronicles **44**
Bloesch, Donald **51**
Bloom, Allan **69**
Boas, Franz **23**
Bonhoeffer, Dietrich **33, 45**
Brooks, Reuben **77, 253**
Bullard, Sarah **63**
Bultmann, Rudolf **45**

C

Calvin, John **32**
Carney, Glandion **250**
Carson, Donald A. **69**
Catholicism, Roman **109, 161, 202**
Chavez, Linda **100**
Chicano Movement **104**
Childs, Brevard **245**
City of God **32**
Clement **31**
Cognitive style **96–97, 116, 149, 232**
Collective family **172**
Collective unity **155**
Communication style **149**
Cone, James **217**
Confucianism **162, 179, 202**
Conscientization **62**
Consensual collateral **137**
Contextualization **41–42**

Crockett, Joseph **46, 233**
Cross-cultural communication **20,
  60**
Cultural family pattern **92**
  situational stress patterns **93**
  transcultural patterns **92**
Cultural relativism **60**
Culture **14, 22–26**
Curriculum **36, 48, 56, 67, 80,
  84–85, 97, 114, 118, 122–24,
  126–28, 214, 233–34**

D

D'Souza, Dinesh **40, 68–69**
Daly, Mary **50**
Deconstructionism **60**
Discrimination **58, 61–62, 78, 82,
  103, 105, 107–8, 128, 158, 167–68,
  174, 177, 188, 217, 224, 240**
Dynamic equivalence **43**
Dyrness, William A. **34, 44**

E

Empowerment **80, 87, 126–27, 220,
  236–37, 249**
Enculturation **58–59, 62**
Enryo syndrome **169–71**
Epistle of Ignatius **31**
Epistle to Diognetus **31**
Erickson, Millard **11, 15, 45**
Ethnic identity **73, 109, 140, 211**
Ethnicity **46, 56–59, 74, 79, 227,
  234–35**
Ethnocentrism **59–60, 82, 233–34,
  252**
Eurocentrism **16, 40, 234, 252**
Extended family **110–11, 118–20,
  142, 144, 152, 162, 174, 201,
  212, 222–25, 242**

F

Facelina, Raymond **25**
Fackre, Gabriel **45–46**

Falicov, Celia Jaes **120**
Family patterns **90, 93, 98, 110,
  143, 163, 240**
Family roles **92, 118, 127, 227**
Felder, Cain Hope **233**
Fenn, Richard K. **22, 84**
Ferm, Deane William **52**
Field-dependent **96–97, 116**
Field-independent **96–97, 116**
Filial piety **171–72**
Fiorenza, Elizabeth **50**
Fowler, James W. **72, 75, 79–80**
Freire, Paulo **26, 122**

G

Gadamer, Hans-Georg **22**
Gaede, S.D. **72, 252–53**
Gardner, Howard **94**
Geertz, Clifford **21**
González, Justo L. **25**
Goodman, Mary Ellen **128**
Graff, Gerald **41**
Graham, Billy **10, 229**
Gramsci, Antonio **23**
Grant, Jacquelyn **15**
Green, Thomas **60**
Griffioen, Sander **60**
Guevara, Che **50**

H

Half-way pluralism **60**
Harris, Marvin **58**
Hauerwas, Stanley **79**
Hegel, Georg **23**
Hendriksen, William **30**
Herskovits, Melville Jean **59**
Hiebert, Paul **34–36**
Hierarchical structure **189, 191**
Hilliard, Asa III **48**
Hispanic-American family **119,
  121**
Hollinger, Dennis P. **13**
Hopler, Thom **73–74**

I

Identity systems **198**
  adolescent **198**
  American **198**
  refugee **198**
  Southeast Asian **198**
Inch, Morris **73**
Individualism **138, 207**
Inouye, Stanley K. **54, 251**
Insular pluralism **60**
Interethnic communication **60**
Interethnic relations **77–78, 82**
Intergenerational connectedness **112**
Intermarriage **105, 188**
Iroquois League **16, 131, 133**
Issei **185–87, 189, 191**

J

Jerusalem Council **31**

K

Keralite **213–14**
King, Martin Luther Jr. **218, 232, 238**
Klein, Joe **51**
Kluckhohn, Clyde **90**
Kraft, Charles **41, 43, 49**
Kuyper, Abraham **33**
Kyle, John E. **17**

L

Larkin, William J. **16, 70**
Las Casas **38, 254**
Learning patterns **90, 94–95**
Learning styles **78–79, 95–97, 116, 148, 231**
  field independent **96–97**
  field dependent **96–97**
Lévi-Strauss, Claude **20**
Liberation **15, 17, 34, 41–43, 45–47, 49, 51, 62–63, 122, 229, 233**
Life cycle **112**
Lincoln, C. Eric **218, 220**
Lupton, Robert **250**

Luther, Martin **32–33, 35**
Luzbetak, Louis **42**
Lyon, David **37**

M

Malinowski, Bronislaw **20**
Mamiya, Lawrence H. **218, 220**
Marginality **146**
Marx, Karl **32**
Marxism **17, 50–51**
Matrilineal **224**
McCary, P.I. **44**
Mead, Margaret **59**
Melting pot **65, 161**
Mentoring **125, 239–40**
Meintel, Dierdre **58**
Merton, Robert **61**
Migliazzo, Arlin C. **36**
Migration **73, 102, 106, 108, 110, 119**
Model minority **159, 168, 181, 195, 197**
Monoculturalism **128**
Montagu, Ashley **57**
Mouw, Richard J. **12, 60**
Moynihan report **221**
Multicultural education **63–64, 84**
  additive approach **85**
  contextual decision-making approach **87**
  contributions approach **85**
  decision-making approach **86**
  product approach **87**
  social-action approach **86**
  transformational approach **85**
Multicultural infusion **87**
Multiculturalism
  Christian perspective **75**
Multiethnic education **64**
Mythemes **20**

N

Native-American family **152**
Nida, Eugene **29**

Niebuhr, Richard 14
Nisei 185–89, 191
Noninterference 139, 145
Novak, Michael 74

P

Pacific Islander 159
Paradigm 22, 24, 84–85, 238
Patriarchal family 171–73
Peoplehood 222
Perkins, John M. 240, 251
Pluralism 60, 64, 69–71, 75, 83, 161
Political correctness 54, 68, 70
Postmodernism 60
Prague Linguistic Circle 21
Pratte, Richard 74
Praxis 15, 36, 41, 47, 62–63, 72, 205, 218, 220
Prejudice 61

R

Racism 58, 61
Ramm, Bernard 51
Ravitch, Diane 56, 234
Reconciliation 41, 60, 214, 247, 250
Relational orientation 91
Resurgent ethnicity 74
Revisionism 48, 132
Ricoeur, Paul 22
Role distance 187
Rooy, Sidney 35
Ruether, Rosemary Radford 47, 50

S

Sansei 185–87, 189, 191
Schaff, Philip 52
Schlesinger, Arthur M. 40, 67, 69, 75, 204
Schreiter, Robert J. 19, 21, 26, 35
Segregation 107, 113–14
Serow 80
Situational stress patterns 92–93

Socialization 58–59, 97, 114, 116, 148, 183
Söllee, Dorothee 49
Starhawk 50
Stranger anxiety 73
Strodtbeck, F.L. 90
Structural assimilation 60
Synan, Vinson 254

T

Takaki, Ronald 40
Taoism 179, 202
Tillich, Paul 45
Time orientation 91, 139–40
Torres, Camilo 50
Trans-racial communication 60
Transcultural patterns 92
Triandis, Harry C. 74
Triple jeopardy 226
Tylor, E.B. 22

V

Value orientation 90, 92, 98, 121, 135–37, 142, 148, 169–70, 191, 207, 209
Vanhoozer, Kevin J. 24

W

Wagley, Charles 58
Walker, Wyatt 10
Wallace, Dan 244
Watney, Paul 44
Westerhoff, John 59
White, James 63
Wilson, Monica 48
Wirth, Louis 58
Woo, Wesley S. 252
World Council of Churches 41, 122
Wurzel, James S. 46

Y

Yonsei 185, 187